OFFICERS, 1914

THE
FIFTH LEICESTERSHIRE.

A record of the
1/5th Battalion the Leicestershire Regiment, T.F.,
during the War,
1914—1919.

By

CAPTAIN J. D. HILLS,

M.C., Croix de Guerre.

With an introduction by

LT.-COLONEL C. H. JONES,

C.M.G., T.D., Légion d'honneur (officier).

LOUGHBOROUGH.
PRINTED AND PUBLISHED AT THE ECHO PRESS.
1919.

THE FIFTH LEICESTERSHIRE.

XVII.
5.

To

COLONEL HIS GRACE DUKE OF RUTLAND, K.G.,

who has watched over us and lived with us
in all our losses and in all our joys,
this book is gratefully dedicated.

PREFACE.

No literary merit is claimed for this book. It is intended to be a diary of our progress as a Battalion since mobilisation until the signing of peace, and the return of the Colours to Loughborough. I have written the first chapter, the remainder, including the maps, has been done by Captain J. D. Hills.

This is scarcely the place to attempt an estimate of what the members of our County Territorial Force Association, individually and collectively, have done for the 5th Leicestershire Regiment. We would merely place this on record, that there has ever been one keen feeling of brotherhood uniting us all, from President or Chairman, to the latest joined recruit or humblest member of the regiment, whether actively engaged on the battlefield, or just as actively engaged at home. Never has the Executive Committee failed us. And to Major C. M. Serjeantson, O.B.E., we would offer a special tribute for his untiring work, wonderful powers of organisation and grasp of detail, and hearty good fellowship at all times.

To the men of the regiment we hope that the incidents which we narrate here will recall great times we spent together, and serve as a framework on which to weave other stories too numerous for the short space of one book.

C. H. JONES.

MEADHURST,
    UPPINGHAM,
Sept., 1919.

AUTHOR'S NOTE.

THE following narrative is based mainly on the Regimental War Diary. For the rest, my thanks are due to Lt.-Colonels C. H. Jones, C.M.G., T.D., and J. Ll. Griffiths, D.S.O., Major C. Bland, T.D., Captains D. B. Petch, M.C., J. R. Brooke, M.C., and A. D. Pierrepont, and R.Q.M.S. R. Gorse, M.S.M., for sending me notes and anecdotes; to Captains G. E. Banwell, M.C., and C. S. Allen, Corpl. J. Lincoln, and L/Corpl. A. B. Law, for taking me round the battle-fields and explaining the Lens fighting of 1917; to 2nd Lieut. G. H. Griffiths, for supplying me with many of the battle-field photographs; to all officers, N.C.O.'s and men of the Battalion who have always been ready to answer my questions and to give me information; to Major D. Hill, M.C., Brigade Major, for the loan of his Brigade documents; and lastly to Mr. Deakin of Loughborough, for undertaking the publication of this book and for giving to it so much time and personal care.

J. D. HILLS.

16, SOMERSET ST.,
    LONDON, W. 1.

Sept., 1919.

CONTENTS.

CHAPTER.		PAGE.
1.	ENGLAND	1
2.	EARLY EXPERIENCIES	16
3.	THE SALIENT	39
4.	HOHENZOLLERN	70
5.	FLANDERS MUD TO THE MEDITERRANEAN	90
6.	THE VIMY RIDGE	106
7.	GOMMECOURT	127
8.	MONCHY AU BOIS	145
9.	GOMMECOURT AGAIN	163
10.	LENS	179
11.	HILL 65	196
12.	ST. ELIE LEFT	206
13.	CAMBRIN RIGHT	227
14.	GORRE AND ESSARS AT PEACE	253
15.	GORRE AND ESSARS AT WAR	267
16.	PONTRUET	279
17.	CROSSING THE CANAL	298
18.	FRESNOY AND RIQUERVAL WOODS	325
19.	THE LAST FIGHT	352
20.	HOME AGAIN	372

APPENDIX.

I.	OFFICERS, FEB., 1915	376
II.	HONOURS	377
III.	THE CADRE, 1919	379

ILLUSTRATIONS.

		PAGE.
1.	OFFICERS, 1914 (Frontispiece).	
2.	R.S.M.s SMALL AND LOVETT, R.Q.M.S. GORSE	34
3.	YPRES	35
4.	HOHENZOLLERN MEMORIAL	50
5.	VERMELLES WATER TOWER	51
6.	LENS FROM THE AIR	130
7.	OFFICERS AT MARQUEFFLES	131
8.	RED MILL AND RIAUMONT HILL	146
9.	HOHENZOLLERN CRATERS, 1917	147
10.	COMPANY HEADQUARTERS, LOISNE, AND GORRE CANAL	322
11.	PONTRUET	323
12.	LIEUT. J. C. BARRETT, V.C.	338
13.	THE CADRE AT LOUGHBOROUGH	339

MAPS.

		PAGE.
1.	YPRES DISTRICT	44
2.	BETHUNE DISTRICT	82
3.	ATTACK ON GOMMECOURT, 1/7/16	130
4.	MONCHY DISTRICT	154
5.	LENS DISTRICT	190
6.	ATTACK ON PONTRUET, 24/9/18	286
7.	ADVANCE, 24/9/18 to 11/11/18	314 & 315

CHAPTER I.

ENGLAND.

4th Aug., 1914.   25th Feb., 1915.

THE Territorial Force, founded in 1908, undoubtedly attracted many men who had not devoted themselves previously to military training, nevertheless it took its character and tone from men who had seen long service in the old Volunteer Force. Hence, those who created the Territorial Force did nothing more than re-organise, and build upon what already existed. In the 5th Leicestershire Regiment there crossed with us to France men who had over 30 years' service. At the outbreak of war in 1914, R.Q.M.S. Stimson could look back on 36 years of service, and, amongst other accomplishments he spoke French fluently. Other names that occur to us are Serjt. Heafield, with 28 years, and C.S.M. Hill with 16 years, both of Ashby, and both of whom served in the Volunteer Company in South Africa. R.S.M. Lovett (27 years), of Loughborough, also wears the South African medal for service in the same Company. Then there are Pioneer-Serjt. Clay (27 years' service), C.S.M. Garratt, of Ashby, C.S.M. Wade, of Melton, R.Q.M.S. Gorse, of Loughborough, Signal-Serjeant Diggle, of Hinckley—all long service men. The senior N.C.O. in Rutland was C.S.M. Kernick, who had done 18 years' service when war was declared.

The infantry of the 46th (North Midland) Division

consisted of the Nottinghamshire and Derbyshire, the Lincolnshire and Leicestershire, and the Staffordshire Brigades. Our brigade, the 138th, was commanded at first by General A. W. Taylor, who was succeeded a few days before we left England by General W. R. Clifford. Staff officers changed frequently, and we hope we did not break the hearts of too many. Staff-Captain J. E. Viccars survived most of them, and we owe him much for the able and vigorous assistance he was always ready cheerfully to give us.

The 5th Leicestershire was a County Battalion, organised in eight companies, with headquarters respectively at Ashby-de-la-Zouch, Oakham, Melton Mowbray, Hinckley, Market Harborough, Mountsorrel, Shepshed, and one at Regimental Headquarters at Loughborough. The companies thus were much scattered, and it was only at the annual training camps that we met as a battalion.

The Territorial Force was better prepared for mobilisation than is generally supposed, and if the history of the assembly of the regiment at Loughborough in the first week, their train journey to Duffield in the second week, the purchase of horses, the collection of stores, the requisitions for food and the sharpening of bayonets, be demanded, it can be read in the orders printed many months before war even threatened. The orders were drawn up by Lt.-Colonel G. German, T.D., our former commanding officer, now D.S.O., and by his conscientious and indefatigable adjutant, Captain W. G. King Peirce, who was killed early in the war fighting with his old regiment, the Manchesters. It is due to these officers to record that every detail was studiously followed and found exactly correct. We heard of one officer who, at the time the printed book of orders was issued, was so fearful lest it should fall into the hands of some indiscreet or improper person, that he packed and sealed it, addressed it to his executors, and locked it up in a safe, so that even sudden death on his part would not force him to betray his trust.

Of all hard-worked people in the early days it is possible that upon Major R. E. Martin fell the greatest share. Not only did he see that supplies were forthcoming, and that dealers delivered the goods expected of them, but he set himself to design water-carts, and troughs-water-feet-for-the-washing-of, and cunningly to adapt stock material to the better service and greater comfort of all, many of whom were for the first time dragged from the civilities and luxuries of home life.

At Loughborough from the 5th to the 11th of August we did little more than pull ourselves together generally, and enjoy the good will of the inhabitants, led by our firm friend, the oft-repeated Mayor, Mr. Mayo, J.P.

It did not demand much wit to foretell that sooner or later we should be asked to offer ourselves for service abroad. The question was put for the first time on the 13th of August, at Duffield. A rough estimate was made that at least 70 per cent. would consent gladly and without further thought, and of the others hesitation was caused in many cases because men wondered whether in view of their positions in civil life they had the right to answer for themselves. It should be understood that a very large number were skilled men, and had joined the home army merely because they thought it a good thing to do. And because they liked it, and knew it was a good thing to do, they were content to accept humble places in a force formed for home service and home defence only. Also, at that stage it was not perfectly certain that everyone would be wanted, and when the question of war service abroad was raised, and other men were not serving at all, it is only natural that the thought passed through some men's minds that the appeal was not for them. We think that the battalion might be congratulated upon the general spirit of willingness shown, especially as in the 17th August when the question was put again more definitely, the percentage of those ready to extend the terms of service was estimated at 90.

There were other phases of this call for extension of service, too numerous to detail here; for example, on one occasion we were asked to get six companies ready at once. This for a time upset everything, for, as we have said, the original eight companies were taken from different parts of the county, and there was a strong company comradeship, as well as a battalion unity; and if six be taken out of eight it means omissions, amalgamations, grafts, and all sorts of disturbances.

We left Duffield on the 15th of August, and marched to Derby Station. Our train was timed to start at 11 p.m., and seeing that we arrived at Luton at 2 p.m. the next day, the rate of motion was about 6 miles an hour, not too fast for a train. But the truth is we did not start at 11 p.m., but spent hours standing in the cattle yard at Derby, while trucks and guns were being arranged to fit one another. As that was our first experience of such delay, the incident was impressed upon our minds, and it counts one to the number of bars we said our medal should have.

As in Loughborough, so in Luton, our billets were schools. There was one advantage about the Beech

Hill Schools of Luton, namely, that the whole battalion could assemble in the big room, sit on the floor, and listen in comfort to words of instruction and advice. But day schools were not intended for lodging purposes, and here again was displayed Major Martin's skill in the erection of cookhouses and more wash-tubs and other domestic essentials. The moment we got settled, however happened to coincide with the moment at which the education branch of the Town Council determined that the future of a nation depended upon the education of her children, and thus it came to pass that on the 28th of August we moved out of the schools, and entered billets in West Luton.

The long rows of houses were admirably suited to company billets. Occupiers dismantled the ground floor front and took in three, and generally four men at various rates. On the 2nd of October a universal rate of 9d. a day each man was fixed. That made twenty-one shillings a week towards paying off a rent which would average at the most twelve shillings. The billets delighted us, and we hope the owners were as pleased. We thank them and all we met in those billeting times for their kind forbearance.

The headquarters and billets of senior officers were at Ceylon Hall. The building was owned by the Baptists, and we found their committee most willing and obliging. On one occasion they lent us their chapel and organ for a Sunday service, and set their own service at a time to suit ours, when churches in the town could not help us.

Altogether we were in Luton just 3 months training for war. To a great extent the training was on ordinary lines. A routine was followed, and all routines become dull and wearisome. We had been asked to go abroad, we had expressed our willingness to go. This willingness grew into a desire, which at intervals expressed itself in petulant words of longing—"Are we ever going to France?" The answer was always the same: "You will go soon enough, and you will stay long enough." This increased our irritation. Suddenly, on one still and dark November day, parade was sharply cancelled, we clad ourselves in full marching order, there was just a moment to scrawl on a postcard a few last words home, tender words were exchanged with our friends in the billets, and with heavy tread and in solemn silence we marched forth along the Bedford Road. There was a pillar box beside the road. It was only the leading companies that could put the farewell card actually in the box, for it was quickly crowded out, and in the end the upper portion of the red pillar was visible standing on a conical pile of postcards.

Never had a field day passed without some reference to the 16th milestone on the Bedford Road, but on this particular day orders did not even mention the milestone. This in itself was sufficient to convince us that real war had at length begun. Long before the 16th milestone was sighted, we were diverted into a field, our kit was commented upon, and we marched back to the same old billets. For convenience of reference this incident is entered in our diary as the march to France along the Bedford Road, and no bar was awarded. The march formed a crisis in our history, for subsequent to it leave home was not sought so eagerly. Positively the last words of farewell had been said, and it was difficult to devise other forms of good-bye nearer the absolute ultimate with which to engage our home friends, who, to our credit be it said, were just as anxious as we were.

It was about this time that our attention was drawn to the anomaly of the discharge rule. A man who had served for four years could take his discharge as a time-expired soldier. At the same time men were enlisting freely. One young man of under 21 was said to have claimed his discharge on the very day that his grandfather, newly enlisted, entered upon three days' "C.B." for coming on parade with dirty boots.

It was in Luton, too, that we overcame our distrust and dislike of vaccination and inoculation against typhoid. We remember C.S.M. Lovett being inoculated in public to give a lead to others, and we smile now to think that in those days it was power of character and leadership only that accomplished things, and incidentally made the way smooth for a Government's compulsory bill.

We were inspected several times, in fact so often that the clause "We are respected by everyone," which comes in our regimental ditty—(and how could it not ! !) —was given the alternative rendering "inspected." Twice his Majesty the King honoured us with a visit, and in addition General Ian Hamilton, Lord Kitchener, and others.

Regiments differ much ; each has its peculiarities. The 5th Leicestershire a county battalion, if in nothing else, excelled individually in work across country. Though all may not have been as clever as "Pat" Collins (G.A.), who acted as guide to the commanding officer for many months—and we have the commanding officer's permission to add " counsellor and friend "— there was never any difficulty in finding the way in the day or at night. If we may anticipate our early days in France, a few months hence, we can remember being occupied all one night in extricating parties of men who had lost their way hopelessly in open country in the dark. Those were men who came from a city battalion, brought up amongst labelled thoroughfares, street lamps, and brilliantly-illuminated shop windows. We practised night work at Luton, and all was easy and natural, though we added to our experiences, as on the night when in the thrilling silence of a night attack the fair chestnut bolted with the machine gun; and having kicked two men and lost his character, reverted to the rank of officer's charger.

On a day in October the whole division had entrenched itself in the vicinity of Sharpenhoe and Sundon. To enliven the exercise night manœuvres were hastily planned. Our share was to march at about 11 p.m., after a hard day and half a tea, and to continue marching through the most intricate country until five o'clock the next morning. At that time we were within charging distance of the enemy, and day was breaking. Filing through a railway arch we wheeled into extended order and lay down till all were ready. When the advance was ordered, though we had lain down for two minutes only, the greater number were fast asleep. Despite this hitch the position was taken, and then a march home brought the exercise to an end at 8.10 a.m. For this operation we voted a second bar to our medal.

To those who knew all the details of the plan the most brilliant feature was the wonderfully accurate leading of our Brigade Major, now Brigadier-General Aldercron. He led us behind the advanced posts of the enemy and it was their second line that we attacked.

ENGLAND.

Many officers were joining us. Since war had been declared, E. G. Langdale, R. C. L. Mould, C. R. Knighton, S. R. Pullinger, C. H. Wollaston, G. W. Allen, J. D. Hills, and R. Ward-Jackson had all been added to our strength. Later came D. B. Petch, R. B. Farrer, and J. Wyndham Tomson, of whom Petch was straight from school, and he, with the last two named, served a fortnight in France before being gazetted. Their further careers can be followed in later chapters with the exception, perhaps, of Hills, who himself writes those chapters. As his service is a combination of details, many of which are typical of the young officer who fought in the early days of the war, for general information we narrate so much. John David Hills, though not 20, had already seen six years' service in his school O.T.C., including one year as a Cadet Officer. He surrendered his Oxford Scholarship and what that might have meant in order to join up at once. He passed through the battalion from end to end, occupying at various times every possible place: signalling officer, intelligence officer, platoon commander, company commander, adjutant, 2nd in command, and finished up in command of what was called "the cadre." For some time, too, he was attached to the brigade staff, and when we add that he excelled in every position separately and distinctly, and won the admiration and love of all, we may spare him further embarrassment and let the honours he has won speak for him.

Clothing was a lasting trouble. We were now wearing out our first suits, and from time to time there confronted us statements that sounded rather like weather reports, for example—" No trousers to-day;

tunics plentiful." Then the question arose as to whether a man should wear a vest, and, if so, might he have two, one on the man, the other at the wash. Patient endurance was rewarded by an answer in the affirmative to the first part of the question, but the correspondence over the second portion has only just reached the armistice stage.

And as with men, so with animals. " The waggon and horses " sounds beautifully complete as well as highly attractive, but in the army we must not forget to see that harness comes as well. And this thought, the lack of harness, carries us to another great event in our history, the end of the Luton days, the march to Ware.

Why was the march to Ware planned exactly like that? It is not in the hope of getting an answer we ask the question. Waggons and horses and no harness, and whose fault? Waggons and horses with harness, and carrying a double load to make up,—no fault, a necessity. Officers away on leave,——but let us set things down in order. Barely a fortnight after the march to France along the Bedford Road, on Saturday, the 14th of November, a proportion of officers and men went on leave as usual till Monday, and all was calm and still. At 1 a.m. on Monday, orders were received to move at 7 a.m., complete for Ware, a distance, by the route set, of 25 to 30 miles,—some say 50 to 100 miles. Official clear-the-line telegrams were poured out recalling the leave takers. Waggons were packed—(were they not packed!)—billets were cleared, and we toed the line at the correct time. For want of harness, the four cooks' carts and two water carts were left behind; for want of time, meat was issued raw; for want of orders, no long halt was given at mid-day. One short and sharp bit of hill on the way was too much for the horses, and such regimental transport as we had with us had to be man-handled. This little diversion gave regiments a choice of two systems, gaps between regiments, or gaps between sections of the same regiment, and gave spectators, who had come in considerable numbers, a subject for discussion. But the chief feature of the day was that we reached Ware that day as complete as we started. We arrived at 7-20 p.m. except for two Companies who were detached as rear guard to the Division. The tail end of the Divisional train lost touch and took the wrong turning, and for this reason the two Companies did not come in till 11-30 p.m. We understand that the third bar on our medal will be the march to Ware.

Amongst those who watched us pass near the half-way post we noticed our neighbour, General Sir A. E. Codrington, then commanding the London District, who as an experienced soldier knew the difficulties and gave us, as a regiment, kindly words of praise and encouragement.

We have often wondered what was the verdict of the authorities upon this march. As this is regimental history only, it may be permitted to give the regiment's opinion. We fancied we accomplished passing well an almost impossible task. It is true that not long afterwards we were well fitted out and sent to France. We are persuaded, too, to add here that we said we owed one thing at least to our Divisional Commander, General E. Montagu-Stuart-Wortley; we were the first complete Territorial Force Division to cross the seas and go into action as a Division against the Germans. And it may be that the whole Territorial Force owe to our General, too, that they went in Divisions, and were not sent piecemeal as some earlier battalions, and dovetailed into the Regular Army, or, perhaps, even into the New Army. We live in the assurance that the confidence the Army Council extended to us was not misplaced.

Having rested a day at Ware, we marched to Bishops Stortford, where we cannot say we were billeted neither can we use again the word rest, for the town was overcrowded, and queues were formed up to billets; queues composed of all arms of the service, and infantry did not take the front place. Let us say we were " stationed " there one week. The week was enlivened by strange rumour of German air attacks, and large patrols were kept on the watch at night.

On the 26th of November, the time of our life began when the regiment marched into billets at Sawbridgeworth. The town was built for one infantry regiment and no more. The inhabitants were delightful, and we have heard, indirectly, more than once that they were pleased with us. We soon learnt to love the town and all it contained, and we dare not say that our love has grown cold even now. The wedding bells have already rung for the regiment once at Sawbridgeworth, when Lieut. R. C. L. Mould married Miss Barrett, and we do not know that they may not ring again for a similar reason. In Sawbridgeworth, our vigorous adjutant, Captain W. T. Bromfield, was at his best. Everyone was seized and pulled up to the last notch of efficiency, pay books were ready in time, company returns were faultless, deficiency lists complete, saluting was severer than ever, and echos of heel clicks rattled from the windows in the street. Best of all were the drums. Daily at Retreat, Drum Sergt. Skinner would salute the orderly officer, the orderly officer would salute the senior officer, then all the officers would salute all the ladies, the crowd would move slowly away, and wheel traffic was permitted once more in the High Street.

The ordinary routine of military life was broken into at times by sudden and violent efforts dictated by lightning ideas of the Divisional or Brigade Staff, or by the latest news from the front. There was a time, for example, when we could think of one thing only,—the recessed trench. That gave place to the half company trench, a complete system, embracing fire trenches, supports, inspection trenches, with cook houses, wash houses, and all that a well regulated house could require; and so important was it, and its dimensions so precise, that an annotated copy was printed on handkerchiefs.

Then came a sudden desire to cross streams, however swollen, and a party rode off to Bishops Stortford to learn the very latest plans. We had just received a set of beautiful mules, well trained for hard work in the transport. As horses were scarce, and the party large, our resourceful adjutant ordered mules. Several mules returned at once, though many went with their riders to the model bridge, and in their intelligent anxiety to get a really close view, went into the water with them.

On another day we did a great march through Harlow, and saluted Sir Evelyn Wood, V.C., who stood at his gate to see us pass.

Football, boxing and concerts, not to mention dancing, filled our spare time, and there was the famous race which ended :—BOB, Major Toller, a, 1., BERLIN, Capt. Bromfield, a, 2. And we are not forgetting that it was at Sawbridgeworth that we ate our first Christmas war dinner. Never was such a feed. The eight companies had each a separate room, and the Commanding officer, Major Martin, and the adjutant made a tour of visits, drinking the health of each company in turn—eight healths, eight drinks, and which of the three stood it best? Some say the second in command shirked.

Officers had their dinner, too. After the loyal toast there was one only—" Colour Sergt. Joe Collins, and may he live for ever ! " The reply was short—" Gentlemen, I think you are all looking very well." It was his only thought, and we were well. We know how much we owe to him as our mess sergeant; he studied our individual tastes and requirements, and kept us well for many months. Good luck to him!

It was not till January, 1915, that a most important, and as a matter of fact the very simplest, change in our organisation was made. To be in keeping with the regular forces, our eight companies were reorganised as four. This system would always have suited our County battalion even in 1908, and our only wonder is that it was not introduced before.

When, on the 18th of February, the G.O.C. returned from a week's visit to France, and gave us a lecture upon the very latest things, we knew we might go at any time. Actually at noon on the 25th we got the order to entrain at Harlow at midnight, and the next morning we were on Southampton Docks.

We left behind at Sawbridgeworth Captain R. S. Goward, now Lieut. Colonel and T.D., in command of a company which afterwards developed into a battalion called the 3rd 5th Leicestershire. This battalion was a nursery and rest house for officers and men for the 1st Fifth. It existed as a separate unit until the 1st of September, 1916, and during those months successfully initiated all ranks in the ways of the regiment, and kept alive the spirit which has carried us through the Great War.

CHAPTER II.

EARLY EXPERIENCES.

26th Feb., 1915.   16th June, 1915.

AFTER spending the greater part of the day (the 26th February) lounging about the Hangars at Southampton, we at length embarked late in the afternoon—Headquarters and the right half battalion in S.S. Duchess of Argyle, left half, under Major Martin, in S.S. Atalanta. The transport, under Capt. Burnett, was due to sail later in S.S. Mazaran, since torpedoed in the Channel, but they embarked at the same time as the rest. Four other ships containing Divisional Headquarters and some of the Sherwood Foresters were to sail with us, and at 9 p.m., to the accompaniment of several syrens blowing "Farewell," we steamed out, S.S. Duchess of Argyle leading. The Captain of the ship asked us to post a signaller to read any signals, Serjt. Diggle was told to keep a look out and assist the official signaller, a sort of nondescript Swede or other neutral, like the rest of the crew. We soon sighted some war vessel, and asked if they had any orders, the reply being, according to Serjt. Diggle, "No go"—according to the Swede, "No no." The Captain preferred to believe the latter, and as there were no orders continued his course, though we could see the remainder of our little fleet turn round and sail back. The weather was appalling, the sea very rough, and long before we had reached half way we were all very ill. This was not surprising, as our transport was built for pleasure work on the Clyde, and, though fast, was never intended to face a Channel storm. Each time a wave crashed into the ship's side we imagined we had been torpedoed; in fact, it was one long night of concentrated misery.

We reached Le Havre in the early hours of the morning, and disembarked, feeling, and probably looking, very bedraggled. From the quay we crawled up a long and terribly steep hill to the rest camp—some lines of tents in a muddy field. Here, while we waited 24 hours for our left half Battalion, of whom we had no news, we were joined by our first interpreter, M. Furby. M. Furby was very anxious to please, but unfortunately failed to realise the terrible majesty of the Adjutant, a fact which caused his almost immediate relegation to the Q.M. Stores, where he always procured the best billets for Capt. Worley and himself. On the morning of the 28th we received an issue of sheepskin coats and extra socks, the latter a present from H.M. the Queen, and after dinners moved down to the Railway Station, where we found Major Martin and the left half. Their experiences in the Channel had been worse than ours. Most of them, wishing to sleep, had started to do so before the ship left Southampton on the 26th; they were almost all ill during the night, so were glad to find a harbour wall outside their port-holes the following morning, and at once went on deck " to look at France "— only to find they were back in Southampton. They stayed there all day, and eventually crossed the next night, arriving on the 28th, feeling as bad as we did, and having had all the horrors of two voyages.

We were kept waiting many hours on the platform, while the French Railway staff gradually built an enormous train, composed of those wonderful wagons labelled "HOMMES 36-40, CHEVAUX EN LONG 8," which we now saw for the first time. Hot in summer, cold in winter, always very hard and smelly, and full of refuse, they none the less answered their purpose, and a French troop train undoubtedly carries the maximum number of men in the minimum of accommodation. During this long wait we should all have starved had it not been for the kindness of an English lady, Mrs. Sidney Pitt, who, with other English ladies, served out an unlimited supply of tea and buns to all. Eventually at 5 p.m. our train was ready, and we entrained—all except two platoons, for whom there was no room. The transport was loaded on to flats which were hooked on behind our wagons, and we finally started up country at about 7 o'clock. The train moved slowly northwards all night, stopping for a few minutes at Rouen, and reaching Abbeville just as dawn broke at 7 a.m. Here, amidst a desolation of railway lines and tin sheds, we stayed for half an hour and stretched our cramped limbs, while six large cauldrons provided enough hot tea for all. From this point our progress became slower, and the waits between stations proportionally longer, until at last we reached a small village, where, according to our train orders, we should stop long enough to water horses. This we began to do, when suddenly, without any whistling or other warning, the train moved on, and Major Martin and Captain Burnett, who were with the horses, only just managed to catch the train, and had to travel the next stage on a flat with a limber. At St. Omer we were told where we should detrain, a

EARLY EXPERIENCES.

fact hitherto concealed from us, and eventually at 2-35 p.m. in a blizzard and snow storm we reached Arneke, detrained at once, and marched about five miles to the little village of Hardifort, where we arrived in the dark.

We were, of course, entirely inexperienced at this time, and in the light of subsequent events, this, our first attempt at billeting, was a most ludicrous performance. The Battalion halted on the road in fours outside the village, at the entrance to which stood a group headed by the C.O. with a note-book; behind him was the Mayor—small, intoxicated and supremely happy, the Brigade Interpreter, M. Löst, with a list of billets, and the Adjutant, angry at having caught a corporal in the act of taking a sly drink. Around them was a group of some dozen small boys who were to act as guides. The Interpreter read out a name followed by a number of officers and men; the C.O. made a note of it and called up the next platoon; the Mayor shouted the name at the top of his voice, waved his arms, staggered, smacked a small boy, and again shouted, at which from three to five small boys would step out and offer to guide the platoon, each choosing a different direction. How we ever found our homes is still a mystery, and yet by 10 p.m. we were all comfortably settled in quarters. We were joined the next morning by the two remaining platoons, 2nd Lieuts. Mould and Farrer.

The billets were slightly re-arranged as soon as daylight enabled us to see where we were, and we soon settled down and made ourselves comfortable, being told that we should remain at Hardifort until the 4th March, when we should go into trenches for a week's instruction with some Regular Division. We had nothing much to do except recover from the effects of our journey, and this, with good billets and not too bad weather, we soon did. The remainder of our Brigade had not yet arrived, so we were attached temporarily to the Sherwood Foresters, whose 8th Battalion was also absent, and with them on the 4th moved off Eastwards, having the previous day received some preliminary instructions in trench warfare from General Montagu-Stuart-Wortley, who spoke to all the officers.

Preceded by our billeting party, which left at 5 a.m., we marched from Hardifort at 9 a.m., and, passing through Terdeghen, reached the main road at St. Sylvestre Capel, and went along it to Caestre. On the way we met General Smith-Dorrien, our Army Commander, and while the Battalion halted he talked to all the officers, gave us some very valuable hints, and then watched the Battalion march past, having impressed us all with his wonderful kindness and charm of manner. At Caestre we found motor buses waiting for us, and we were glad to see them, for though no one had fallen out, we were somewhat tired after marching nine miles, carrying, in addition to full marching order, blankets, sheepskin coats and some extra warm clothing. The buses took us through Bailleul and Nieppe to Armentières, at that time a town infested with the most appalling stinks and very full of inhabitants, although the front line trenches ran through the eastern suburbs. Having "debussed," we marched to le Bizet, a little village a mile north of the town, and stayed there in billets for the night. During the evening we stood outside our billets, gazed at the continuous line of flares and listened to the rifle fire, imagining in our innocence that there must be a terrific battle with so many lights.

EARLY EXPERIENCES.

The next day our instruction started, and for four days we worked hard, trying to learn all we could about trench warfare from the 12th Brigade, to whom we were attached. While some went off to learn grenade throwing, a skilled science in those days when there was no Mills but only the "stick" grenades, others helped dig back lines of defence and learned the mysteries of revetting under the Engineers. Each platoon spent 24 hours in the line with a platoon either of the Essex Regt., King's Own or Lancashire Fusiliers, who were holding the sector from "Plugstreet" to Le Touquet Station. It was a quiet sector except for rifle fire at night, and it was very bad luck that during our first few hours in trenches we lost 2nd Lieut. G. Aked, who was killed by a stray bullet in the front line. There was some slight shelling of back areas with "Little Willies," German field gun shells, but these did no damage, and gave us in consequence a useful contempt for this kind of projectile. Trench mortars were not yet invented, and we were spared all heavy shells, so that, when on the 9th we left Armentières, we felt confident that trenches, though wet and uncomfortable, were not after all so very dreadful, and that, if at any time we should be asked to hold the line, we should acquit ourselves with credit.

Our next home was the dirty little village of Strazeele, which we reached by march route, and where we found Lieut. E. G. Langdale who rejoined us, having finished his disembarkation duties. Here we occupied five large farm houses, all very scattered and very smelly, the smelliest being Battalion Headquarters, called by Major Martin "La Ferme de L'Odeur affreuse." The Signalling officer attempted to link up the farms by telephone, but his lines, which consisted of the thin enamelled wire issued at the time, were constantly broken by the farmers' manure carts, and the signallers will always remember the place with considerable disgust. One farmer was very pleased with himself, having rolled up some 200 yards of our line under the impression that all thin wire must be German. The rest of the Brigade had now arrived, and the other three Battalions were much annoyed to find that we were already experienced soldiers—a fact which we took care to point out to them on every possible occasion. Our only other amusement was the leg-pulling of some newspaper correspondents, who, as the result of an interview, made Major Martin a "quarry official," and Lieut. Vincent a poultry farmer of considerable repute!

On the 11th March we marched to Sailly sur la Lys, better known as "Sally on the loose," where with the Canadian Division we should be in reserve, though we did not know it, for the battle of Neuve Chapelle. The little town was crowded before even our billeting party arrived, and it was only by some most brazen billet stealing, which lost us for ever the friendship of the Divisional Cyclists, that we were able to find cover for all, while many of the Lincolnshires had to bivouac in the fields. Here we remained during the battle, but though the Canadians moved up to the line, we were not used, and spent our time standing by and listening to the gun fire. A 15" Howitzer, commanded by Admiral Bacon and manned by Marine Artillery, gave us something to look at, and it was indeed a remarkable sight to watch the houses in the neighbourhood gradually falling down as each shell went off. There was also an armoured train which mounted three guns, and gave us much pleasure to watch, though whether it did any damage to the enemy we never discovered. Finally, on the 16th, having taken no part in the battle, we marched to some farms near Doulieu, and thence on the 19th to a new area near Bailleul, including the hamlets of Noote boom, Steent-je (pronounced Stench), and Blanche Maison, where we stayed until the end of the month, while the rest of the Brigade went to Armentières for their tours of instruction.

Our new area contained some excellent farm houses, and we were very comfortably billeted though somewhat scattered. The time was mostly spent in training, which consisted then of trench digging and occasionally practising a " trench to trench " attack, with the assistance of gunners and telephonists, about whose duties we had learnt almost nothing in England. General Smith Dorrien came to watch one of these practices, and, though he passed one or two criticisms, seemed very pleased with our efforts. We also carried out some extraordinarily dangerous experiments with bombs, under Captain Ellwood of the Lincolnshires and Lieut. A. G. de A. Moore, who was our first bomb officer. It was just about this time that the Staff came to the conclusion that something simpler in the way of grenades was required than the " Hales " and other long handled types, and to meet this demand someone had invented the " jam tin "—an ordinary small tin filled with a few nails and some explosive, into the top of which was wired a detonator and friction lighter. For practice purposes the explosive was left out, and the detonator wired into an empty tin. Each day lines of men could be seen about the country standing behind a hedge, over which they threw jam tins at imaginary trenches, the aim and object of all being to make the tin burst as soon as possible after hitting the ground. We were given five seconds fuses, and our orders were, "turn the handle, count four slowly, and then throw." Most soldiers wisely counted four fairly rapidly, but Pte. G. Kelly, of "D" Company, greatly distinguished himself by holding on well past "five," with the result that the infernal machine exploded within a yard of his head, fortunately doing no damage.

All this time we were about nine miles from the line, and were left in peace by the Boche, except for a single night visit from one of his aeroplanes, which dropped two bombs near Bailleul Station and woke us all up. We did not know what they were at the time, so were not as alarmed as we might otherwise have been. In fact "B" Company had a much more trying time when, a few nights later, one of the cows at their billet calved shortly after midnight. The sentry on duty woke Captain Griffiths, who in turn woke the farmer and tried to explain what had happened. All to no purpose, for the farmer was quite unable to understand, and in the end was only made to realise the gravity of the situation by the more general and less scientific explanation that "La vache est malade."

On the 1st April we received a warning order to the effect that the Division would take over shortly a sector of the line South of St. Eloi from the 28th Division, and two days later we marched through Bailleul to some huts on the Dranoutre-Locre road, where we relieved the Northumberland Fusiliers in Brigade support. The same evening the Company Commanders went with the C.O. and Adjutant to reconnoitre the sector of trenches we were to occupy. It rained hard all night, and was consequently pitch dark, so that the reconnoitring party could see very little and had a most unpleasant journey, returning to the huts at 2 o'clock the next morning (Easter Day), tired out and soaked to the skin. During the day the weather improved, and it was a fine night when at 10 p.m., the Battalion paraded and marched in fours though Dranoutre and along the road to within half a mile of Wulverghem. Here, at "Packhorse" Farm, we were met by guides of the Welch Regiment (Col. Marden) and taken into the line.

Our first sector of trenches consisted of two disconnected lengths of front line, called trenches 14 and 15, behind each of which a few shelters, which were neither organised for defence nor even splinter-proof, were known as 14 S and 15 S—the S presumably meaning Support. On the left some 150 yards from the front line a little circular sandbag keep, about 40 yards in diameter and known as S.P. 1, formed a Company Headquarters and fortified post, while a series of holes covered by sheets of iron and called E4 dug-outs provided some more accommodation—of a very inferior order, since the slightest movement by day drew fire from the snipers' posts on "Hill 76." As this hill, Spanbroek Molen on the map, which lies between Wulverghem and Wytschaete was held by the Boche, our trenches which were on its slopes were overlooked, and we had to be most careful not to expose ourselves anywhere near the front line, for to do so meant immediate death at the hands of his snipers, who were far more accurate than any others we have met since. To add to our difficulties our trench parapets, which owing to the wet were entirely above ground, were composed only of sandbags, and were in many places not bullet proof.

There were large numbers of small farm houses all over the country (surrounded by their five-months' dead live stock), and as the war had not yet been in progress many months these houses were still recognizable as such. Those actually in the line were roofless, but the others, wonderfully preserved, were inhabited by support Companies, who, thanks to the inactivity of the enemy's artillery, were able to live in peace though under direct observation. In our present sector we found six such farms; "Cookers," the most famous, stood 500 yards behind S.P. 1, and was the centre of attraction for most of the bullets at night. It contained a Company Headquarters, signal office, and the platoon on the ground floor, and one platoon in the attic! Behind this, and partly screened from view, were "Frenchman's" occupied by Battalion Headquarters, "Pond" where half the Reserve Company lived, and "Packhorse" containing the other half Reserve and Regimental Aid Post. This last was also the burying ground for the sector, and rendezvous for transport and working parties. Two other farms—"Cob" and "T"—lay on the Wulverghem Road and were not used until our second tour, when Battalion Headquarters moved into "Cob" as being pleasanter than "Frenchman's," and "Pond" also had to be evacuated, as the Lincolnshires had had heavy casualties there.

The enemy opposite to us, popularly supposed to be Bavarians, seemed content to leave everything by day to his snipers. These certainly were exceptionally good, as we learnt by bitter experience. By night there was greater activity, and rifle bullets fell thickly round Cookers Farm and the surrounding country. There were also fixed rifles at intervals along the enemy's lines aimed at our communication tracks, and these, fired frequently during the early part of the night, made life very unpleasant for the carrying parties. There were no communication trenches and no light railways, so that all stores and rations, which could be taken by limbers as far as Packhorse Farm only, had to be carried by hand to the front line. This was done by platoons of the support and reserve companies who had frequently to make two or three journeys during the night, along the slippery track past Pond Farm and Cookers Corner —the last a famous and much loathed spot. There were grids to walk on, but these more resembled greasy poles, for the slabs had been placed longitudinally on cross runners, and many of us used to slide off the end into some swampy hole. One of "B" Company's officers was a particular adept at this, and fell into some hole or other almost every night. These parties often managed to add to our general excitement by discovering some real or supposed spy along their route, and on one occasion there was quite a small stir round Cookers Farm by "something which moved, was fired at, and dropped into a trench with a splash, making its escape." A subsequent telephone conversation between "Cracker" Bass and his friend Stokes revealed the truth that the "something" was "a ———y great cat with white eyes."

Like the enemy's, our artillery was comparatively inactive. Our gunners, though from their Observation Posts, "O.P.'s," on Kemmel Hill they could see many excellent targets, were unable to fire more than a few rounds daily owing to lack of ammunition; what little they had was all of the "pip-squeak" variety, and not very formidable. Our snipers were quite incapable of dealing with the Bavarians, and except for Lieut. A. P. Marsh, who went about smashing Boche loophole plates with General Clifford's elephant gun, we did nothing in this respect.

In one sphere, however, we were masters—namely, patrolling. At Armentières we had had no practice in this art, and our first venture into No Man's Land was consequently a distinctly hazardous enterprise for those who undertook it—2nd Lieut. J. W. Tomson, Corpl. Staniforth, Ptes. Biddles, Tebbutt, and Tailby, all of "A" Company (Toller). Their second night in the line, in 15 trench, this little party crawled between the two halves of a dead cow, and, scrambling over our wire, explored No Man's Land, returning some half hour later. Others followed their lead, and during the whole of our stay in this sector, though our patrols were out almost every night, they never met a German.

We stayed in these trenches for a month, taking alternate tours of four days each with the 4th Lincolnshires (Col. Jessop). We lost about two killed and ten wounded each tour, mostly from snipers and stray bullets, for we did not come into actual conflict with the enemy at all. Amongst the wounded was C.S.M. J. Kernick, of "B" Company, whose place was taken by H. G. Lovett. This company also lost Serjt. Nadin, who was killed a few weeks later.

Although we fought no pitched battles, the month included several little excitements of a minor sort, both in trenches and when out at rest. The first of these was the appearance of a Zeppelin over Dranoutre, where we were billeted. Fortunately only one bomb dropped anywhere near us, and this did no damage; the rest were all aimed at Bailleul and its aerodromes. We all turned out of bed, and stood in the streets to look at it, while many sentries blazed away with their rifles, forgetting that it was many hundred feet beyond the range of any rifle.

By the middle of April the Staff began to expect a possible Geman attack, and we "stood to" all night the 15/16th, having been warned that it would be made on our front and that asphyxiating gases would be used—we had, of course, no respirators. Two nights later the 5th Division attacked Hill 60, and for four hours and a quarter, from 4 p.m. to 8-15 p.m., we fired our rifles, three rounds a minute, with sights at 2,500 yards and rifles set on a bearing of 59°, in order to harass the enemy's back areas behind the Hill—a task which later was always given to the machine gunners. In those days it was a rare thing to hear a machine gun at all, and ours scarcely ever fired. A week afterwards, when out at rest, we heard that the second battle of Ypres had begun, and learnt with horror and disgust of the famous first gas attack and its ghastly results. Within a few days the first primitive respirators arrived and were issued; they were nothing but a pad of wool and some gauze, and would have been little use; fortunately we did not know this, and our confidence in them was quite complete. On the 10th May, just before we left the sector, we had a little excitement in the front line. A German bombing party suddenly rushed "E 1 Left," a rotten little "grouse-butt" trench only 37 yards from the enemy, and held by the 4th Leicestershires, and succeeded in inflicting several casualties before they made off, leaving one dead behind them. This in itself was not much, but both sides opened rapid rifle fire, and the din was so terrific that supports were rushed up, reserves " stood to " to counter-attack, and it was nearly an hour before we were able to resume normal conditions. The following day we returned to the huts, where we were joined by 2nd Lieut. L. H. Pearson who was posted to " A " Company; 2nd Lieut. Aked's place had already been filled by Lieut. C. F. Shields from the Reserve Battalion. 2nd Lieut. G. W. Allen, who had been away with measles, also returned to us during April.

Our next stay in the Locre huts can hardly be called a rest. First, on the 12th May, the enemy raided the 4th Lincolnshires in G1 and G2 trenches, where, at "Peckham Corner," they hoped to be able to destroy one of our mine galleries. The raid was preceded by a strong trench mortar bombardment, during which the Lincolnshire trenches were badly smashed about, and several yards of them so completely destroyed that our " A " Company were sent up the next evening to assist in their repair. They stayed in the line for twenty-four hours, returning to the huts at 4 p.m. on the 14th, to find that the rest of the Battalion was about to move to the Ypres neighbourhood. The previous day the German attacks had increased in intensity, and the cavalry who had been sent up to fill the gap had suffered very heavily, among them being the Leicestershire Yeomanry, who had fought for many hours against overwhelming odds, losing Col. Evans-Freke and many others. There was great danger that if these attacks continued, the enemy would break through, and consequently all available troops were being sent up to dig a new trench line of resistance near Zillebeke—the line afterwards known as the " Zillebeke switch." None of us had ever been to the " Salient," but it was a well known and much dreaded name, and most of us imagined we were likely to have a bad night, and gloomily looked forward to heavy casualties.

Starting at 6-40 p.m., we went by motor bus with four hundred Sherwood Foresters through Reninghelst, Ouderdom, and Vlamertinghe to Kruisstraat, which we reached in three hours. Hence guides of the 4th Gordons led us by Bridge 16 over the Canal and along the track of the Lille Road. It was a dark night, and as we stumbled along in single file, we could see the Towers of Ypres smouldering with a dull red glow to our left, while the salient front line was lit up by bursting shells and trench mortars. Our route lay past Shrapnel Corner and along the railway line to Zillebeke Station, and was rendered particularly unpleasant by the rifle fire from "Hill 60" on our right. The railway embankment was high and we seemed to be unnecessarily exposing ourselves by walking along the top of it, but as the guides were supposed to know the best route we could not interfere. At Zillebeke Church we found Colonel Jones, who came earlier by car, waiting to show us our work which we eventually started at midnight; as we had to leave the Church again at 1 a.m., to be clear of the Salient before daylight, we had not much time for work. However, so numerous were the bullets that all digging records were broken, especially by the Signallers, whose one desire, very wisely, was to get to ground with as little delay as possible, and when we left our work, the trench was in places several feet deep. The coming of daylight and several salvoes of Boche shells dissuaded us from lingering in the Salient, and, after once more stumbling along the Railway Line, we reached our motor buses and returned to the huts, arriving at 5-30 a.m. A May night is so short, that the little digging done seemed hardly worth the casualties, but perhaps we were not in a position to judge.

Two days later we went into a new sector, trenches on the immediate left of the last Brigade sector, and previously held by the Sherwood Foresters. The front line consisting of trenches " F4, 5 and 6," " G1 and 2," was more or less continuous, though a gap between the " F's " and " G's," across which one had to run, added a distinct element of risk to a tour round the line. The worst part was Peckham Corner, where the Lincolnshires had already suffered; for it was badly sighted, badly built, and completely overlooked by the enemy's sniping redoubt on " Hill 76." In addition to this it contained a mine shaft running towards the enemy's lines, some 40 yards away, and at this the Boche constantly threw his " Sausages," small trench mortars made of lengths of stove piping stopped at the ends. It was also suspected that he was counter-mining. In this sector three Companies were in the front line, the fourth lived with Battalion Headquarters, which were now at Lindenhoek Châlet near the cross roads, a pretty little house on the lower slopes of Mont Kemmel. Though the back area was better, the trenches on the whole were not so comfortable as those we had left, and during our first tour we had reason to regret the change. First, 2nd Lieut. C. W. Selwyn, taking out a patrol in front of " F5," was shot through both thighs, and, though wonderfully cheerful when carried in, died a few days later at Bailleul. The next morning, while looking at the enemy's snipers' redoubt, Captain J. Chapman, 2nd in Command of " D " Company, was shot through the head, and though he lived for a few days, died soon

EARLY EXPERIENCES.

after reaching England. This place was taken by Lieut. J. D. A. Vincent, and at the same time Lieut. Langdale was appointed 2nd in Command of " C." There were also other changes, for Major R. E. Martin was given Command of the 4th Battalion, and was succeeded as 2nd in Command by Major W. S. N. Toller, while Captain C. Bland became skipper of " A " Company.

During this same tour, the Brigade suffered its first serious disaster, when the enemy mined and blew up trench " E1 left," held at the time by the 5th Lincolnshire Regiment. This regiment had many casualties, and the trench was of course destroyed, while several men were buried or half-buried in the debris, where they became a mark for German snipers. To rescue one of these, Lieut. Gosling, R.E., who was working in the G trenches, went across to E1, and with the utmost gallantry worked his way to the mine crater. Finding a soldier half buried, he started to dig him out, and had just completed his task when he fell to a sniper's bullet and was killed outright. As at this time the Royal Engineers' Tunnelling Companies were not sufficient to cover the whole British front, none had been allotted to this, which was generally considered a quiet sector. Gen. Clifford, therefore, decided to have his own Brigade Tunnellers, and a company was at once formed, under Lieut. A. G. Moore, to which we contributed 24 men, coalminers by profession. Lieut. Moore soon got to work and, so well did the " amateurs " perform this new task, that within a few days galleries had been started, and we were already in touch with the Boche underground. In an incredibly short space of time, thanks very largely to the personal efforts of Lieut. Moore, who spent hours every day down below within a few feet of the enemy's miners, two German mine-shafts and their occupants were blown in by a "camouflet," and both E1 left and E1 right were completely protected from further mining attacks by a defensive gallery along their front. For this Lieut. Moore was awarded a very well deserved Military Cross.

After the second tour in this sector we again made a slight change in the line, giving up the "F" trenches and taking instead "G3," "G4," "G4a," "H1," "H2" and "H5," again relieving the Sherwood Foresters, who extended their line to the left. Unfortunately, they still retained the Doctor's House in Kemmel as their Headquarters, and, as Lindenhoek Châlet was now too far South, Colonel Jones had to find a new home in the village, and chose a small shop in one of the lesser streets. We had scarcely been 24 hours in the new billet when, at mid-day, the 4th June, the Boche started to bombard the place with 5.9's, just when Colonel Jessop, of the 4th Lincolnshires, was talking to Colonel Jones in the road outside the house, while an orderly held the two horses close by. The first shell fell almost on the party, killing Colonel Jessop, the two orderlies, Bacchus and Blackham, and both horses. Colonel Jones was wounded in the hand, neck and thigh, fortunately not very seriously, though he had to be sent at once to England, having escaped death by little short of a miracle. His loss was very keenly felt by all of us, for ever since we had come to France, he had been the life and soul of the Battalion, and it was hard to imagine trenches, where we should not receive his daily cheerful visit. We had two reassuring thoughts, one that the General had promised to keep his command open for him as soon as he should

R.Q.M.S. R. Gorse, M.S.M.   R.S.M. H. G. Lovett, M.C., D.C.M.

R.S.M. R. E. Small, D.C.M.

Bomb Corner, Ypres 1915.

Bomb Corner, Ypres 1915.

Barracks, Ypres 1915.

(Photos by Capt. C. R. Knighton.)

EARLY EXPERIENCES.

return, the second that during his absence we should be commanded by Major Toller, who had been with us all the time, and was consequently well known to all of us.

Meanwhile we had considerably advanced in our own esteem by having become instructors to one of the first "New Army" Divisions to come to France, the 14th Light Infantry Division, composed of three battalions of Rifle Brigade and 60th, and a battalion of each of the British Light Infantry Regiments. They were attached to us, just as we had been attached to the 12th Brigade at Armentières, to learn the little details of Trench warfare that cannot be taught at home, and their platoons were with us during both our tours in the "G's" and "H's." They were composed almost entirely of officers and men who had volunteered in August, 1914, and their physique, drill and discipline were excellent—a fact which they took care to point out to everybody, adding generally that they had come to France "not to sit in trenches, but to capture woods, villages, etc." We listened, of course, politely to all this, smiled, and went on with our instructing. Many stories are told of the great pride and assurance of our visitors, one of the most amusing being of an incident which happened in trench "H2." Before marching to trenches the visiting Platoon Commander had, in a small speech to his platoon, told them to learn all they could from us about trenches, but that they must remember that we were not regulars, and consequently our discipline was not the same as theirs. All this and more he poured into the ears of his host in the line, until he was interrupted by the entry of his Platoon Sergeant to report the accidental wounding of Pte. X by Pte. Y, who fired a round when cleaning his rifle. There was no need for the host to rub it in, he heard no more about discipline.

Credit, however, must be given where credit is due, and the following tour our visitors distinguished themselves. On the 15th June, at 9.10 p.m., when the night was comparatively quiet, the enemy suddenly blew up a trench on our left, held by the Sherwood Foresters, at the same time opening heavy rifle fire on our back areas and shelling our front line. Captain Griffiths, who held our left flank with " B " Company, found that his flank was in the air, so very promptly set about moving some of his supports to cover this flank, and soon made all secure. Meanwhile Lieut. Rosher, machine gun officer of the visiting Durham Light Infantry, hearing the terrific din and gathering that something out of the ordinary was happening, though he did not know what, slung a maxim tripod over his shoulders, picked up a gun under each arm, and went straightaway to the centre of activity—a feat not only of wonderful physical strength, but considerable initiative and courage. We did not suffer heavy casualties, but 2nd Lieut. Mould's platoon had their parapet destroyed in one or two places, and had to re-build it under heavy fire, in which Pte. J. H. Cramp, the Battalion hairdresser, distinguished himself. Except for this one outburst on the part of the Boche we had a quiet time, though Peckham Corner was always rather a cause of anxiety, for neither R.E. nor the Brigade Tunnellers could spare a permanent party on the mine shaft. Consequently, it was left to the Company Commander to blow up the mine, and with it some of the German trench, in case of emergency, and it was left to the infantry to supply listeners down the shaft to listen for counter-mining. On one occasion when Captain Bland took over the trench with " A "

EARLY EXPERIENCES.

Company, he found the pump out of order, the water rising in the shaft, and the gallery full of foul air, all of which difficulties were overcome without the R.E.'s help, by the courage and ingenuity of Serjeant Garratt.

There was one remarkable feature of the whole of this period of the war which cannot be passed over, and that was the very decided superiority of our Flying Corps. During the whole of our three months in the Kemmel area we never once saw a German aeroplane cross our lines without being instantly attacked, and on one occasion we watched a most exciting battle between two planes, which ended in the German falling in flames into Messines, at which we cheered, and the Boche shelled us. Towards the end of the war the air was often thick with aeroplanes of all nationalities and descriptions, but in those days, before bombing flights and battle squadrons had appeared, it was seldom one saw as many as eight planes in the air at a time, and tactical formations either for reconnaissance or attack seemed to be unknown; it was all "one man" work, and each one man worked well.

On the night of the 16th June the Battalion came out of trenches and marched to the Locre huts for the last time, looking forward to a few days' rest in good weather before moving to the Salient, which we were told was shortly to be our fate. We had been very fortunate in keeping these huts as our rest billets throughout our stay in the sector, for though a wooden floor is not so comfortable as a bed in a billet, the camp was well sited and very convenient. The Stores and Transport were lodged only a few yards away at Locrehof Farm, and Captain Worley used to have everything ready for us when we came out of the line.

During the long march back from trenches, we could always look forward to hot drinks and big fires waiting for us at the huts, while there was no more inspiring sight for the officers than Mess Colour-Sergeant J. Collins' cheery smile, as he stirred a cauldron of hot rum punch. Bailleul was only two miles away, and officers and men used often to ride or walk into the town to call on "Tina," buy lace, or have hot baths (a great luxury) at the Lunatic Asylum. Dividing our time between this and cricket, for which there was plenty of room around the huts, we generally managed to pass a very pleasant four or six days' rest.

CHAPTER III.

"THE SALIENT."

22nd June, 1915.   1st Oct., 1915.

ON the 22nd June, 1915, after resting for five days in the Huts, where General Ferguson, our Corps Commander, came to say good-bye, we marched at 9.0 p.m. to Ouderdom, while our place in the line was taken by the 50th Northumbrian Territorial Division, who had been very badly hammered, and were being sent for a rest to a quiet sector. At Ouderdom, which we reached about midnight, we discovered that our billets consisted of a farm house and a large field, not very cheering to those who had expected a village, or at least huts, but better than one or two units who had fields only, without the farm. It was our first experience in bivouacs, but fortunately a fine night, so we soon all crawled under waterproof sheets, and slept until daylight allowed us to arrange something more substantial. The next day, with the aid of a few " scrounged " top poles and some string, every man made himself some sort of weatherproof hutch, while the combined tent-valises of the officers were grouped together near the farm, which was used as mess and Quartermaster's Stores. Unfortunately, we had no sooner made ourselves really comfortable than the Staffordshires claimed the field as part of their area, and we had to move to a similar billeting area a few hundred yards outside Reninghelst where we stayed until the 28th. The weather remained hot and fine, except for two very heavy showers in the middle of one day, when most of the officers could be seen making furious efforts to dig drains round their bivouacs from inside, while the other ranks stood stark naked round the field and enjoyed the pleasures of a cold shower-bath. We spent our time training and providing working parties, one of which, consisting of 400 men under Capt. Jeffries, for work at Zillebeke, proved an even greater fiasco than its predecessor in May. For on this occasion, not only was the night very short, but the guides failed to find the work, and the party eventually returned to bivouacs, having done nothing except wander about the salient for three hours. Two days before we left Reninghelst the first reinforcements arrived for us, consisting of 12 returned casualties and 80 N.C.O.'s and men from England —a very welcome addition to our strength.

The time eventually arrived for us to go into the line, and on the 29th the officers went up by day to take over from the Sherwood Foresters, while the remainder of the Battalion followed as soon as it was dark. Mud roads and broad cross-country tracks brought us over the plain to the "Indian Transport Field," near Kruisstraat White Chateau, still standing untouched because, it was said, its peace-time owner was a Boche. Leaving the Chateau on our right, and passing Brigade Headquarters Chalet on our left, we kept to the road through Kruisstraat as far as the outskirts of Ypres, where a track to the right led us to Bridge 14 over the Ypres-Comines Canal. Thence, by field tracks, we crossed the Lille road a few yards north of Shrapnel Corner, and leaving on our left the long, low, red buildings of the "Ecole de Bienfaisance," reached Zillebeke Lake close to the white house at the N.W. corner. The lake is triangular and entirely artificial, being surrounded by a broad causeway, 6 feet high, with a pathway along the top. On the western edge the ground falls away, leaving a bank some twenty feet high, in which were built the "Lake Dug-outs,"—the home of one of the support battalions. From the corner house to the trenches there were two routes, one by the south side of the Lake, past Railway Dug-outs—cut into the embankment of the Comines Railway—and Manor Farm to Square Wood; the other, which we followed, along the North side of the Lake, where a trench cut into the causeway gave us cover from observation from "Hill 60." At Zillebeke we left the trench, and crossed the main road at the double, on account of a machine gun which the Boche kept at the "Hill 60" end of it, and kept moving until past the Church—another unpleasant locality. Thence a screened track led to Maple Copse, an isolated little wood with several dug-outs in it, and on to Sanctuary Wood, which we found 400 yards further East. Here in dug-outs lived the Supports, for whom at this time was no fighting accommodation except one or two absurdly miniature keeps. At the corner of the larger wood we passed the Ration Dump, and then, leaving this on our left, turned into Armagh Wood on our right.

From the southern end of Zillebeke village two roads ran to the front line. One, almost due South, kept close to the railway and was lost in the ruins of Zwartelen village on "Hill 60"; the other, turning East along a ridge, passed between Sanctuary and Armagh

Woods, and crossed our front line between the "A" and "B" trenches, the left of our new sector. The ridge, called Observatory, on account of its numerous O.P.'s, was sacred to the Gunners, and no one was allowed to linger there, for fear of betraying these points of vantage. Beyond it was a valley, and beyond that again some high ground N.E. of the hill, afterwards known as Mountsorrel, on account of Colonel Martin's Headquarters, which were on it. The line ran over the top of this high ground, which was the meeting place of the old winter trenches (numbered 46 to 50) on the right, and, on the left the new trenches "A," "B," etc, built for our retirement during the 2nd Battle. The 5th Division held the old trenches, we relieved the Sherwood Foresters in the new "A1" to "A8," with three companies in the line and only one in support. The last was near Battalion Headquarters, called Uppingham in Colonel Jones' honour, which were in a bank about 200 yards behind the front line. Some of the dug-outs were actually in the bank, but the most extraordinary erection of all was the mess, a single sandbag thick house, built entirely above ground, and standing by itself, unprotected by any bank or fold in the ground, absolutely incapable, of course, of protecting its occupants from even an anti-aircraft "dud."

We soon discovered during our first tour the difference between the Salient and other sectors of the line, for, whereas at Kemmel we were rarely shelled more than once a day, and then only with a few small shells, now scarcely three hours went by without some part of the Battalion's front being bombarded, usually with whizz-bangs. The Ypres whizz-bang, too, was a thing one could not despise. The country round Klein Zillebeke

THE SALIENT.

was very close, and the Boche was able to keep his batteries only a few hundred yards behind his front line, with the result that the "Bang" generally arrived before the whizz. "A6" and "A7" suffered most, and on the 1st July Captain T. C. P. Beasley, commanding "C" Company, and Lieut. A. P. Marsh, of "B" Company, were both wounded, and had to be sent away to Hospital some hours later. The same night we gave up these undesirable trenches, together with "A5" and "A8" to the 4th Battalion, and took instead "49," "50" and the Support "51" from the Cheshires of the 5th Division. These trenches were about 200 yards from the enemy except at the junction of "49" and "50," where a small salient in his line brought him to within 80 yards. The sniping here was as deadly as at Kemmel, though round the corner in "A1" we could have danced on the parapet and attracted no attention. On the other hand "49" and "50" were comfortably built, whereas "A1" was shallow and narrow and half filled with tunnellers' sandbags, for it contained three long mine shafts, two of which were already under the German lines. "A2," "3" and "4" were the most peaceful of our sector, and the only disturbance here during the tour was when one of a small burst of crumps blew up our bomb store and blocked the trench for a time. This was on the 5th, and after it we were left in peace, until, relieved by the Staffordshires, we marched back to Ouderdom, feeling that we had escaped from our first tour in the ill-famed salient fairly cheaply. Even so, we had lost two officers and 24 O. Ranks wounded, and seven killed, a rate which, if kept up, would soon very seriously deplete our ranks.

On reaching Ouderdom, we found that some huts on

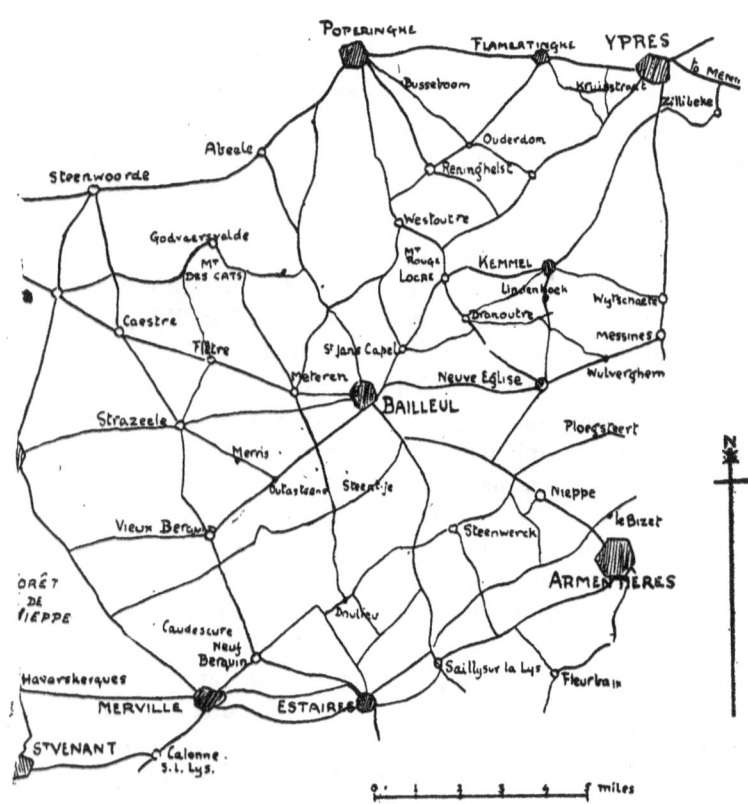

GENERAL MAP of FLANDERS
to illustrate Chap' II & III.

the Vlamertinghe road had now been allotted us instead of our bivouac field, and as on the following day it rained hard, we were not sorry. Our satisfaction, however, was short-lived, for the hut roofs were of wood only, and leaked in so many places that many were absolutely uninhabitable and had to be abandoned. At the same time some short lengths of shelter trench which we had dug in case of shelling were completely filled with water, so that anyone desiring shelter must needs have a bath as well. This wet weather, coupled with a previous shortage of water in the trenches, and the generally unhealthy state of the salient, brought a considerable amount of sickness and slight dysentery, and although we did not send many to Hospital, the health of the Battalion on the whole was bad, and we seemed to have lost for the time our energy. Probably a fortnight in good surroundings would have cured us completely, and even after eight days at rest we were in a better state, but on the 13th we were once more ordered into the line and the good work was undone, for the sickness returned with increased vigour.

Between the Railway Cutting at "Hill 60" and the Comines Canal further south, the lines at this time were very close together, and at one point, called Bomb Corner, less than 50 yards separated our parapet from the Boche's. This sector, containing trenches "35" at Bomb Corner, "36" and "37" up to the Railway, was held by the 1st Norfolks of the 5th Division, who were finding their own reliefs, and, with one company resting at a time, had been more than two months in this same front line. On the 11th July the Boche blew a mine under trench "37" doing considerable damage to the parapet, and on the following night "36" was similarly treated, and a length of the trench blotted out. The night after this we came in to relieve the Norfolks, who not unnaturally were expecting "35" to share the same fate, and had consequently evacuated their front line for the night, while they sat in the second line and waited for it to go up in the air. Captain Jefferies with "D" Company took over "35," while the two damaged trenches were held by "B" Company (Capt. J. L. Griffiths). "A" and "C" held a keep near Verbranden Molen—an old mill about three hundred yards behind our front line—and Battalion Headquarters lived in some dug-outs in the woods behind "35." Behind this again, the solitary Blaupoort Farm provided R.A.P. and ration dump with a certain amount of cover, though the number of dud shells in the courtyard made it necessary to walk with extreme caution on a dark night. In spite of the numerous reports of listening posts, who heard "rapping underground," we were not blown up during our four days in residence, and our chief worry was not mines, but again whizz-bangs. One battery was particularly offensive, and three times on the 15th Capt. Griffiths had his parapet blown away by salvoes of these very disagreeable little shells. One's parapet in this area was one's trench, for digging was impossible, and we lived behind a sort of glorified sandbag grouse butt, six feet thick at the base and two to three feet at the top, sometimes, but not always, bullet-proof.

One or two amusing stories are told about the infantry opposite "35," who were Saxons, and inclined to be friendly with the English. On one occasion the following message, tied to a stone, was thrown into our trench: "We are going to send a 40lb. bomb. We have got to do it, but don't want to. I will come this evening, and we will whistle first to warn you." All of this happened. A few days later they apparently mistrusted the German official news, for they sent a further message saying, "Send us an English newspaper that we may learn the verity."

The weather throughout the tour was bad, but on the night of 17th/18th, when we were relieved at midnight by the Sherwood Foresters, it became appalling. We were not yet due for a rest, having been only four days in the line, and our orders were to spend the night in bivouacs at Kruisstraat and return to trenches the following evening, taking over our old sector "50" to "A7." Weakened with sickness and soaked to the skin, we stumbled through black darkness along the track to Kruisstraat—three miles of slippery mud and water-logged shell holes—only to find that our bivouac field was flooded, and we must march back to Ouderdom and spend the night in the huts, five miles further west. We reached home as dawn was breaking, tired out and wet through, and lay down at once to snatch what sleep we could before moving off again at 6-30 p.m. But for many it was too much, and 150 men reported sick and were in such a weak condition that they were left behind at the huts, where later they were joined by some 40 more who had tried hard to reach trenches but had had to give up and fall out on the way. The rest of us, marching slowly and by short stages, did eventually relieve the Sherwood Foresters, but so tired as to be absolutely unfit for trenches. Fortunately for two days the weather was good and the Boche very quiet, there was time for all to get a thorough rest, and by the 20th we had very largely recovered our vigour—which was just as well, for it proved an exciting tour.

The excitement started about a mile away on our left, when, on the evening of the 19th, the next Division blew up an enormous mine at Hooge, and, with the aid of an intense artillery bombardment, attacked and captured part of the village, including the chateau stables. The enemy counter-attacked the following night, and, though he made no headway and was driven out with heavy loss, he none the less bombarded our new ground continuously and caused us many casualties. Accordingly, to make a counter attraction, the Tunnelling Company working with us was asked to blow up part of the enemy's lines as soon as possible; the blow would be accompanied by an artillery "strafe" by us. There was at this time such a network of mine galleries in front of "A1," that Lieut. Tulloch, R.E., was afraid that the Boche would hear him loading one of the galleries, so, to take no risks, blew a preliminary camouflêt on the evening of the 21st, destroying the enemy's nearest sap. This was successful, and the work of loading and tamping the mines started at once. 1500lbs. of ammonal were packed at the end of a gallery underneath the German redoubt opposite "A1," while at the end of another short gallery a smaller mine was laid, in order to destroy as much as possible of his mine workings. The date chosen was the 23rd, the time 7 p.m.

At 6-55 p.m., having vacated "A1" for the time, we blew the smaller of the two mines—in order, it was said, to attract as many of the enemy as possible into his redoubt. To judge by the volume of rifle fire which came from his lines, this part of the programme was successful, but we did not have long to think about it, for at 7 p.m. the 1500lbs. went off, and Boche redoubt, sandbags, and occupants went into the air, together with some tons of the salient, much of which fell into our trenches. A minute later our Artillery opened their bombardment, and for the next half hour the enemy must have had a thoroughly bad time in every way. His retaliation was insignificant, and consisted of a very few little shells fired more or less at random—a disquieting feature to those of us who knew the Germans' love of an instant and heavy reply to our slightest offensive action. "Stand to," the usual time for the evening "hate," passed off very quietly, and, as we sat down to our evening meal, we began to wonder whether we were to have any reply at all. Meanwhile, three new officers arrived—2nd. Lieut. R. C. Lawton, of "A" Company, who had been prevented by sickness from coming abroad with us, and 2nd Lieuts. E. E. Wynne and N. C. Marriott, both of whom were sent to "B" Company, where they joined Capt. Griffiths at dinner. They were half way through their meal when, without the slightest warning, the ground heaved, pieces of the roof fell on the table, and they heard the ominous whirr of falling clods, which betokens a mine at close quarters.

Before the débris had stopped falling, Capt. Griffiths was out of his dug-out and scrambling along his half-filled trench, to find out what had happened. Reaching the right end of "50," he found his front line had been completely destroyed, and where his listening post had been, was now a large crater, into which the Boche was firing trench mortars, while heavy rifle fire came from his front line. Except for a few wounded men, he could see nothing of Serjt. Bunn and the garrison of the trench, most of whom he soon realized must have been buried, where the tip of the crater had engulfed what had been the front line. For about 80 yards no front line existed, nor had he sufficient men in the left of his trench to bring across to help the right, so, sending down a report of his condition, he started, with any orderlies and batmen he could collect, to rescue those of his Company who had been only partially buried. Meanwhile, help was coming from two quarters. On the right, Colonel Martin, of the 4th Battalion, also disturbed at dinner, was soon up in "49" trench, where he found that his left flank had also suffered from the explosion, but not so badly. His first thought was to form some continuous line of defence across the gap, if possible linking up with the crater at the same time, and, with this object in view he personally reconnoitred the ground and discovered a small disused trench running in front of "49" towards the crater. Quickly organizing parties of men, he sent them along this cut, first to continue it up to the crater, then with sandbags for the defence of the "lip." He himself superintended the work inside the crater, where he had a miraculous escape from a trench mortar, which wounded all standing round him. At the same time, R.S.M. Small, finding a dazed man of "B" Company wandering near Battalion Headquarters, heard what had happened, and without waiting for further orders sent off every available man he could find with shovels and sandbags to assist Capt. Griffiths. Half an hour later, Capt. Bland also arrived with two platoons of "C" Company, sent across from the left of our line, and by dawn with their help a trench had been cut through from "50" to "49." This, though not organized for defence, yet

Hohenzollern Memorial.

The Water Tower and Railway Track, Vermelles.

enabled one to pass through the damaged area. At the same time the miners started to make a small tunnel into the bottom of the crater, so that it would no longer be necessary to climb over the lip to reach the bomb post which was built inside.

During the next day we were fortunately not much harassed by the enemy, and were consequently able to continue the repair work on "50." "B" Company had had 42 casualties from the mine itself, of whom eight were killed and seven, including Sergt. Bunn, were missing, while in the rest of the Battalion about 30 men were wounded, mostly by trench mortars or rifle fire when digging out "50" trench. At the time of the explosion the enemy had thrown several bombs at "A2," and it was thought for a time that he intended making an attack here, but rapid fire was opened by the garrison, and nothing followed. On the evening of the 24th we were due for relief, but, as "50" was still only partially cleared, and we had not yet traced all our missing, we stayed in for another 24 hours, during which time we thoroughly reorganized the sector, and were able to hand over a properly traversed fire trench to the Lincolnshires when they came in. Before we left we found Sergt. Bunn's body; he had been buried at his post, and was still holding in his hand the flare pistol which he was going to fire when the mine exploded. The men of the listening post were not found until some time later, for they had been thrown several hundred yards by the explosion.

On relief, we marched back to Ouderdom, taking with us the officers and men of the 17th Division, who had been attached for instruction during the last tour, and reached a bivouac field near the windmill at 4-30 a.m. Here we stayed 24 hours, and then moved into the " E " huts—an excellent camp, further E. along the Vlamertinghe road than that which we had previously occupied. We were due to remain here for six days, and accordingly started our usual training in bomb and bayonet fighting. Meanwhile, Lieut. Moore and the Battalion Tunnellers were once more hard at work helping the R.E. in " 50 " and " A1," and on the 30th July two of them, Serjt. J. Emmerson and Pte. H. G. Starbuck, working underground, came upon a German gallery. Without a moment's hesitation, Starbuck broke in and found that the charge was already laid, and wires could be seen leading back to the enemy's lines. If the Germans had heard him at work there was no doubt that they would blow their mine at once, but heedless of this danger, he stayed in the gallery until he had cut the leads, and so made it possible for the Engineers to remove the half ton of " Westphalite " which they found already in position, immediately under " 49." For their daring work, the two miners were awarded the D.C.M., Starbuck getting his at once, Serjt. Emmerson in the next honours list. Two nights later the enemy suddenly opened rapid rifle fire opposite "49," which equally suddenly died away, and we like to think that some Boche officer had at the same time pressed the starting button to explode his " Westphalite," only to find that nothing happened.

Towards the end of June, there appeared in the German official communiqué a statement that the French had been using liquid fire in the Champagne fighting, and those who had studied the Boche methods recognized this as a warning that he intended to make use

THE SALIENT.

of it himself at an early date. The prophets were right, and at dawn on the 30th July the enemy, anxious to recapture Hooge, attacked the 14th Division who were holding the village, preceding the attack wtih streams of liquid fire, under which the garrison either succumbed or were driven out. At the same time an intense bombardment was opened, and we, whose rest was not due to end until the following day, were ordered to stand by ready to move at 30 minutes' notice. As we waited we wondered whether the 3rd Battle of Ypres had begun, there certainly seemed to be enough noise. By mid-day, however, we had not been used, and as no news of the battle reached us we were preparing to settle down again for another day of peace, when at 2-30 p.m. orders came for us to go to Kruisstraat at once. We marched by Companies, and on arrival bivouacked in a field close to the Indian Transport Lines, where we met several Battalions of the 3rd Division on their way up to Hooge, though they were unable to tell us anything definite about what had happened. The wildest rumours were heard everywhere, that the Germans had used burning oil, vitriol, and almost every other acid ever invented, that the salient was broken, that our Division had been surrounded. One thing was certain—that at 4 p.m. the gunfire had almost ceased, and there was no sign of any German near Ypres.

As soon as it was dark we left Kruisstraat and marched by Bridge 14 and Zillebeke to Maple Copse, where we were told to bivouac for the night, still being ready to move at very short notice if required. Here we found a Battalion of the Sherwood Foresters, from whom we were at last able to learn the truth of the morning's battle. It appeared that at dawn the enemy, carrying flame projectors, had crept close up to the front line trenches in Hooge, and suddenly lighting these machines had sent a spray of burning vaporised oil over the trench. The garrison, 14th Division, were surprised, many of them burnt, and all thrown into confusion, during which the Boche atacked in considerable force, drove them out and broke in as far as Zouave Wood. The left of the Sherwood Foresters had been attacked, but stood firm, even though the Germans in Zouave Wood were almost behind them, until General Shipley ordered the flank to be dropped back to conform with the new line. A counter-attack was delivered during the day by two Battalions of the Rifle Brigade, who, relieved the night before, had marched eight miles out to rest and eight miles back again at once, and were hopelessly tired before they started. In spite of this, they made a gallant effort, and were wiped out almost to a man in Zouave Wood. At the time of the morning attack the Germans could if they liked have walked on into Ypres, for they had broken into the salient, and there was no other organized line of defence between them and the town. Fortunately they did not realise this, or, as is more probable, they never imagined that their flame attack would prove so successful. Still, they might make a further effort at any moment, and it was to meet this that we had been moved into Maple Copse.

All through the night and the following day there were continual short artillery bombardments by both sides, and on four occasions the Copse was shelled with salvoes of shrapnel in rapid succession. As not more than half of us had any sort of dug-outs, and the remainder had to rely mainly on tree trunks for protection, our casualties were fairly heavy, and in a short time we had lost 23 wounded, including H. West, the mess cook, L.-Corpl. J. H. Cramp, and several other notabilities. We might, during the day, have built ourselves some sort of cover, but every available man had to be sent carrying bombs, ammunition, and trench mortars for the Sherwod Foresters, whose left flank was constantly in touch with the enemy. One of these carrying parties found by " D " Company had the misfortune to be led by a guide, who lost his way, into the corner of Zouave Wood, and in a few minutes six of them were wounded by a machine gun which opened fire on them at twenty yards' range; they were carried out by the rest of the party, who escaped under cover of the brushwood, but one, Carroll, died a few days later. By the evening of the 31st the situation was more satisfactory, and a new front line trench had been organized west of the wood, linking up with the Sherwood Foresters, who now no longer required carrying parties. Meanwhile, it was discovered that from his newly captured position, the Boche completely overlooked the track from Zillebeke to Maple Copse, and accordingly we were ordered to start at once to dig a communication trench alongside the track. All that night, the next day, Bank Holiday, and the following night, we worked till we could hardly hold our shovels, and by the time we stopped, at dawn on the 3rd, there was a trench the whole way—not very deep in places and not perhaps very scientifically dug, but still enough to give cover. As soon as work was over we returned to the copse and slept, for at dusk that night we were to go once more to the line and relieve the Lincolnshires in " 50 " to " A7." Maple Copse had cost us altogether 35 killed and wounded.

We found the trenches very much as we had left them except that "A1" had been battered into an almost unrecognizable condition by the enemy's latest trench weapon, the heavy Minenwerfer. Unlike the "Rum Jar" or "Cannister," which was a home-made article consisting of any old tin filled with explosive, this new bomb was shaped like a shell, fitted with a copper driving band and fired from a rifled mortar. It weighed over 200lbs., was either two feet two inches or three feet six inches long and nine inches in diameter, and produced on exploding a crater as big as a small mine. It could fortunately be seen in the air, and the position of the mortar was roughly known, so we posted a sentry whose duty was to listen for the report of discharge, sight the bomb, and cry at the top of his voice "Sausage left" or "Sausage right." Our Artillery had tried hard to destroy the mortar, but it apparently had a small railway to itself, and moved away as soon as we opened fire. For retaliation we had nothing except rifle grenades, which were like flea-bites to an elephant, or the Howitzers, who had to be called on the telephone, all of which took time.

The rest of the line was fairly quiet except for a few small "sausages" on trench "50," and our chief concern was now the shortage of men. In those days a trench was not considered adequately garrisoned unless there were at least three men in every fire bay, so that although we had many more men to the yard than we have many times had since, we imagined, when we found it necessary to have one or two empty fire bays, that we were impossibly weak. So much was this the case, that, on the night of the 4th August, C.Q.M. Serjeants Gorse and Gilding were ordered to bring all available men from the stores at Poperinghe to help hold the line—a most unpleasant journey because the Boche, always fond of celebrating anniversaries, commemorated the declaration of war with a " strafe " of special magnitude. As most of this came between Ypres and Zillebeke, the two Quarter-master Serjeants had a harassing time, and did not reach their bivouacs in Poperinghe until 5-15 the following morning. All through the tour the pounding of " A1 " continued, while our only effort at retaliation was a 60lb. mortar which the Royal Garrison Artillery placed in rear of " 50 " trench. This one day fired six rounds, the last of which fell in the German front line, and for nearly twenty-four hours we were left in peace, while a " switch " line was built across the back of " A1 " salient. All hope of ever recovering the old " A1 " was given up.

Meanwhile, the Division on our left was not being idle. For the past week our Artillery in the salient had fired a half-hour bombardment every morning at 2-45, and on the 9th this was repeated as usual. The Boche had become used to it, and retired to his dug-outs, where he was found a few minutes later by the 6th Division, who had relieved the 14th, and were now trying to recapture all the lost ground. The surprise was perfect, and the enemy, never for a moment expecting an attack at that hour, were killed in large numbers before they could even " stand-to." During the battle 200 of the 4th Lincolnshires occupied our support trenches, in case of any trouble on our front, and in the evening the rest of the Battalion arrived and took over the line, while we replaced them in Brigade Support—Battalion Headquarters, " B " and " C " Companies in the " Lake " dug-outs, " A " and " D " Companies in the Barracks of Ypres.

During the next six days we were worked harder than we had been worked before, digging, carrying, and trench revetting. Fortunately both halves of the Battalion had fairly comfortable quarters to which to return after work was over, though those in Ypres lived a somewhat noisy life. The barracks were close to the centre of the town, and each day the Boche fired his 17in. Howitzer from dawn to dusk, mostly at the Cathedral and Cloth Hall, with occasional pauses to shoot at the Ecole de Bienfaisance, just outside the Menin gate. The shell, arriving with great regularity every 15 minutes, was generally known as the "Ypres express," for it arrived with the most terrifying roar, buried itself deep in the ground before exploding, and then made an enormous crater. As it burst, not only did every house shake, but the whole street seemed to lift a few feet in the air and settle down again. In the barracks we had bricks and falling débris from the Cloth Hall, but nothing more, and these slight disadvantages were easily outweighed by the comfort in which we lived. Every man had a bed, and, as the barracks' water supply was still in working order, we all had baths. A piano was borrowed from the Artillery, and provided us with an excellent concert, which was held in one of the larger rooms, and helped us to forget the war for a time, in spite of a 40-foot crater in the Barrack Square, and the ever-present possibility that another would arrive. Incidentally, the piano became later a cause of much trouble to us, for the police refused to allow us to move it through the streets without a permit from the Town Major; the Town Major would have nothing to do with the matter, having only just arrived in place of his predecessor, who had given us permission to have the piano, and had then been wounded (Town Majors never lasted long in Ypres); and the Gendarmerie would not accept responsibility, so in the end we had to leave it in the barracks. The other two companies, though not so comfortably housed, none the less had an enjoyable time by the lake side, chasing the wild fowl, and watching the shelling of Ypres.

Just at this time several changes took place in the personnel of the Brigade and the Battalion. First, Brig.-Gen. G. C. Kemp, R.E., late C.R.E., 6th Division, was appointed our Brigade Commander in place of General Clifford, who left us to take up an appointment in England, having been exactly six months in command. Capt. Bromfield, our Adjutant, whose health had been bad for the past month, was finally compelled to go to Hospital, whence he was shortly afterwards transferred to England. As his assistant, Lieut. Vincent was also away sick, Lieut. Langdale was appointed Adjutant, while 2nd Lieut. C. H. F. Wollaston took the place of Lieut. A. T. Sharpe as machine gun officer, the latter having left sick to Hospital at the end of July. Lieut. Moore sprained his ankle, and 2nd Lieut. R. C. L. Mould went down with fever, both being sent home, and with them went 2nd Lieut. L. H. Pearson, who had severe concussion, as the result of being knocked down by a Minenwerfer bomb. Capt. Bland became 2nd in command with the rank of Major, and Captain R. Hastings and Lieut. R. D. Farmer were now commanding "A" and "C" Companies. Capt. M. Barton, our original medical officer, had come out in June and relieved Lieut. Manfield, who had been temporarily taking his place. We had also one reinforcement—2nd Lieut. G. B. Williams, posted to "D" Company, who the following tour lost 2nd Lieut. C. R. Knighton who sprained his knee. At the same time Serjt. A. Garratt, of "A" Company, became C.S.M. of "D" in place of C.S.M. J. Cooper, who was sent home with fever.

On the 16th August we went once more to the line for a six-day tour, which proved to be the first in which our artillery began to show a distinct superiority to the enemy's, not only in accuracy but in weight of shell. Several 8″ and 9.2″ Howitzers appeared in the Salient and, on the evening of the 18th, we carried out an organized bombardment of the lines opposite "50" trench, paying special attention to the neighbourhood of the Minenwerfer. The accuracy of these large Howitzers was surprising, and they obtained several direct hits on the Boche front line, the resulting display of flying sandbags and trench timbers being watched with the utmost pleasure by almost every man in the Battalion. The enemy retaliated with salvoes of whizz-bangs on "50," and a few on "A6" and "A7," but did not carry out any extensive bombardment, though, when relieved by the Lincolnshires on the 22nd, we had had upwards of 45 casualties. Among the killed was L/Cpl. Biddles of "A" Company, who had risked death many times on patrol, only to be hit when sitting quietly in a trench eating his breakfast. This N.C.O., old enough to have his son serving in the company with him, was never happier than when wandering about in No Man's Land, either by day or night, and from the first to the last day of every tour he spent his time either patrolling, or preparing for his next patrol. Early in the morning of the 23rd we reached once more the huts at Ouderdom, having at last had the sense to have the limbers to meet us at Kruisstraat to carry packs, which at this time we always took into the line with us. We had been away from even hut civilisation for twenty-four days—quite long enough when those days have to be spent in the mud, noise and discomfort of the Salient.

Our rest, while fortunately comparatively free of working parties, contained two features of interest, an inspection by our new Brigadier, and an officers' cricket match against the 16th Lancers. For the first we were able, with the aid of a recently-arrived draft of 100 men, to parade moderately strong, and Gen. Kemp was well satisfied with our "turn-out." It was, however, to be regretted that the only soldier to whom he spoke happened to be a blacksmith, for which trade we had the previous day sent to Brigade Headquarters a "nil" return. The cricket match was a great success, and thanks to some excellent batting by Lieut. Langdale, we came away victorious. The light training which we carried out each day now included a very considerable amount of bomb throwing, and it seemed as though the bomb was to be made the chief weapon of the infantry soldier, instead of the rifle and bayonet, which always has been, and always will be, a far better weapon than any bomb. However, the new act had to be learnt, and a Battalion bomb squad was soon formed under 2nd Lieut. R. Ward Jackson, whose chief assistants were L/Cpl. R. H. Goodman, Ptes. W. H. Hallam, P. Bowler, E. M. Hewson, A. Archer, F. Whitbread, J. W. Percival and others, many of whom afterwards became N.C.O.'s. Every officer and man had to throw a live grenade, and, as there were eight or nine different kinds, he also had to have some mechanical knowledge, while the instructor had to know considerably more about explosives than a sapper.

The excitement of our next tour started before we reached Kruisstraat. All day long (the 28th August) a single 9.2″ Howitzer had been firing behind a farm house on the track to the Indian Transport Field, and, as we marched past the position by platoons, all of us interested in watching the loading process, it suddenly blew up, sending breach-block, sheets of cast iron and enormous fragments of base plate and carriage several hundred yards through the air. We ran at once to the nearest cover, but three men were hit by falling fragments, and we were lucky not to lose more, for several of us, including 2nd Lieut. J. W. Tomson, had narrow escapes. We eventually reached the line, and relieved the Lincolnshires in Trenches " 49 " to " A3." The 3rd Division had now taken " A4 " to " A7." Three days later 2nd Lieuts. H. Moss, N. C. Stoneham and C. B. Clay joined us, and were posted to "A," "D" and "B" Companies respectively. At the same time 2nd Lieut. J. D. Hills was appointed Brigade Intelligence Officer, a new post just introduced by General Kemp.

We suffered the usual scattered shelling and trench mortaring during the first half of the tour, to which our Artillery could only reply lightly because they were saving ammunition for an organised bombardment further North. However, no serious damage was done, so this did not matter. The bombardment took place at dawn on the 1st September, and in reply the Germans, instead of shelling the left as was expected, concentrated all their efforts on the " 50," " A1 " corner, starting with salvoes of whizz-bangs, and finishing with a heavy shoot, 8″, 5.9″ and shrapnel, from 10.45 to mid-day. Our Artillery replied at once, but nothing would stop the Boche, who had the most extraordinary good fortune in hitting our dug-outs, causing many casualties. 2nd Lieut. Clay, not yet 24 hours in trenches, was among the first to be wounded, and soon afterwards Serjt. B. Smith, of "B" Company, received a bad wound, to which he succumbed a few hours later. In "A" Company, except for C.S.M. Gorse's and the Signallers', every dug-out was hit, and C. E. Scott and F. W. Pringle, the two officers' batmen, were killed, while A. H. Cassell was badly wounded. The officers themselves had two miraculous escapes. First, 2nd Lieuts. Tomson and Moss were sitting in their dug-out, when a 5.9″ dud passed straight through the roof and on into the ground almost grazing 2nd Lieut. Tomson's side. These two then went round to wake Capt. Hastings, who was resting in another dug-out, and the three had only just left, when this too was blown in, burying Capt. Hastings' Sam Browne belt and all his papers. Many brave deeds were done during the shelling, two of which stand out. T. Whitbread, of "A" Company, hearing of the burying of the two officers' servants, rushed to the spot, and, regardless of the shells which were falling all round, started to dig them out, scraping the earth away with his hands, until joined by Sergeants Gore and Baxter, who came up with shovels. The other, whose work cannot be passed over, was our M.O., Captain Barton. Always calm and collected, yet always first on the spot if any were wounded, he seemed to be in his element during a bombardment, and this day was no exception. He was everywhere, tying up wounds, helping the Stretcher Bearers, encouraging everyone he met, and many a soldier owed his life to the ever-present "Doc."

On the 2nd September we were relieved by the Lincolnshires again, and once more became Brigade reserve for six days—six of the most unpleasant days we spent in the Salient. First the Railway dug-outs, to which Battalion Headquarters and half the Battalion should have gone, had been so badly shelled while the Lincolnshires were there that only one company was allowed to go, while the remainder were sent to bivouac at Kruisstraat. The fine weather came to an end the same day, and it rained hard all the time, which would have been bad enough in bivouacs, and was worse for us who had to spend most of our day on some working party, either dug-outs, or trying to drain some hopelessly waterlogged communication trench, such as the one from Manor Farm to Square Wood. Altogether we had a poor time, and were quite glad on the 8th to return to trenches, where we were joined two days later by Lieut.-Col. C. H. Jones, who had returned from England and took over command. He had had the greatest difficulty in returning to France, and it was only when he had applied to the War Office for command of a Brigade in Gallipoli that the authorities at last took notice of him and sent him back to us. On his arrival Major Toller resumed his duties of 2nd in command; Major Bland was at the time in England sick.

The arrival of an officer reinforcement was always the signal for a Boche strafe, and the return of the Colonel they celebrated with a two days' "hate" instead of one. "A1" and "50" and their supports suffered most, and much damage to trenches was done by heavy Minenwerfer, 8″ and 5.9″ shells. Towards evening the situation became quieter, but just before 10 o'clock the Boche exploded a camouflet against one of our "A1" mine galleries, and killed three Tunnellers, whose bodies we could not rescue owing to the gasses in the mine, which remained there for more than twenty-four hours. The next day the bombardment of "50" and "50S" continued, and amongst other casualties, which were heavy, Capt. J. L. Griffiths and 2nd Lieut. R. B. Farrer of "B" Company were both hit and had to be evacuated, the one with 13, the other 35 small fragments of shell in him. The enemy had now become so persistent that we asked for help from our heavy artillery, and the following day—our last in the line—we carried out several organized bombardments of important enemy centres, such as "Hill 60," to which he replied with a few more large "crumps" on "50" support and was then silent. In the evening the Lincolnshires took our place, and, having lost 11 killed and 39 wounded in 6 days, we marched back to rest at Dickebusch huts.

For some considerable time there had been many rumours about a coming autumn offensive on our part, and on the 22nd September, having returned to trenches two days previously, we received our first orders about it. We were told nothing very definite except that the 3rd and 14th Divisions would attack at Hooge, while we made a vigorous demonstration to draw retaliation from their front to ourselves, and that there would also be attacks on other parts of the British front. We were to make a feint gas attack by throwing smoke-bombs and lighting straw in front of our parapet, to frighten the Boche into expecting an attack along the "Hill 60" —Sanctuary Wood front. Capt. Burnett and his transport were, therefore, ordered to bring up wagon-loads of straw, much to their annoyance, for they already had a bad journey every night with the rations, and extra horses meant extra anxiety. It was seldom that the transport reached Armagh Wood without being shelled on an ordinary night, and whenever there was fighting in any part of the Salient, the area round Maple Copse became so hot that they had to watch for an opportunity and gallop through. In spite of this they never failed us, and rations always arrived, even in the worst of times.

On the 23rd there were two preliminary bombardments, one short but very heavy at Hooge, the other lasting most of the morning on "Hill 60"—a bluff. During the night it rained and the arrival of our straw was consequently postponed until the following night, which proved to be little better. The wagons were late and there was not much time to complete our task; however, all worked their utmost, and by 1.0 a.m. on the 25th a line of damp straw had been spread along our wire in front of "50." Unfortunately, the Battalion on our right were unable to put their straw in position in time, but as the Brigade beyond them had theirs, we thought this would not make any difference to the operation. Just before daylight a general order from G.H.Q. arrived, starting with the words, "At Dawn, on the 25th September, the British Armies will take the offensive on the Western Front." We felt that the time had now come when the war was going to be won and the Boche driven out of France, and some of us were a little sorry that our part was to consist of nothing more than setting fire to some damp straw.

At 3.50 a.m. Hooge battle started with an intense artillery bombardment from every gun in the salient, and it was an inspiring sight to stand on the ridge behind "50" trench and watch, through the half-light, the line of flashes to the west, an occasional glare showing us the towers of Ypres over the trees. The Germans replied at once on "A1" trench, but finding that we remained quiet, their batteries soon ceased fire and opened instead on Sanctuary Wood and Hooge. This was expected, for it was not in the initial attack, but during the consolidation that the 3rd Division wanted to draw the enemy's fire. At a few minutes before six our time had come, smoke bombs were thrown, and, though the wind was against us, Col. Jones, feeling that we must make the biggest possible display, ordered the straw to be lit. This promptly drew fire, and in five minutes there was not one single gun on our side of the Salient still firing at Hooge, they had all turned on us. At first sight of the smoke several machine guns had opened fire opposite "50" and "49," but these died away almost at once as the Boche, thoroughly frightened at the prospect of gas, evacuated his trenches. Half-an-hour later he actually bombarded his own lines on the Northern slopes of "Hill 60" with 11″ shells, presumably imagining that we had occupied them. The bluff was complete.

But such a success cannot be purchased without loss, and our losses had been heavy. The Staffordshires had not lit their straw because of the wind, so that the enemy's retaliation, which should have been spread along the whole front from "A1" to "Hill 60" was concentrated entirely on our three trenches "49," "50" and "A1." "C" Company (Lt. R. D. Farmer) in "50" suffered most. Choked and blinded by the smoke from the straw, which blew back and filled the trench, their parapet blown away by salvo after salvo of small shells, their supports battered with 8″ and heavy mortars, with no cover against the unceasing rain of shells from front and left, they had to bear it all in silence, unable to hit back. Serjts. J. G. Burnham and J. Birkin were killed, and with them 10 others of the battalion, while 30 more were wounded. Once more the "Doc." and his stretcher-bearers were everywhere, and many who might otherwise have bled to death, owed their lives to this marvellous man, who wandered round and dressed their wounds wherever the shelling was hottest. At the first opening of the battle our telephone lines to the Artillery were broken, and for some time we could get no support, but the Derby Howitzers and one of the Lincolnshire batteries fired a number of rounds for us, and later, thanks to the efforts of Lieut. C. Morgan, R.F.A., the F.O.O., we were able to call on Major Meynell's Staffordshire battery as well. By 7.15 a.m. all was once more quiet, and we spent the rest of the day evacuating our casualties, and trying to clear away some of the litter of straw from our trenches.

The following day passed quietly, and in the evening, relieved by the Lincolnshires, we marched out of trenches. Ten minutes later the enemy blew up trench "47" and opened heavy rifle fire on all sides of the salient. The Battalion was marching by companies, and "A" and "D" had just reached Manor Farm when the noise began, and bullets fell all round them. Capt. Jefferies, who was leading, was hit almost at once and fell mortally wounded, never again recovering consciousness, and several others became casualties before the party could reach cover on the far side of the Farm. "B" and "C" were still in Armagh Wood, so Colonel Jones at once decided to man the new breastwork between it and Square Wood, and there they remained until the situation became once more quiet. Finally, at midnight, we moved into our Brigade Support positions, Headquarters and "B" Company in Railway Dug-outs, "C" Company in Deeping Dug-outs near the Lake, and the others in Kruisstraat bivouacs. Even now we were not allowed to live in peace, for the following morning, at 11.0 a.m., the enemy bombarded Railway Dug-outs for two hours, firing 90 8″ shells, and (so says the War Diary) "plenty of shrapnel." No one was hit, though Col. Jones' dug-out and the Orderly Room were destroyed, and the bomb store, which was hit and set on fire, was only saved from destruction by the efforts of C.S.M. Lovett, who with Pte. Love and one or two others, fetched water from the pond and put out the fire. From 6.30 to 7.30 p.m. the dug-outs were again bombarded and a few more destroyed, so that we were not sorry when, on the 1st October the Wiltshire Regiment came to relieve us, and we marched back to bivouacs at Ouderdom.

On the 2nd, after a farewell address to the officers by the Corps Commander, the Battalion marched during the morning to Abeele, where at 3.30 p.m. we entrained for the South and said good-bye to the "Salient" for ever. We were not sorry to go, even though there were rumours of a coming battle, and our future destination was unknown.

CHAPTER IV.

"HOHENZOLLERN."

1st Oct., 1915.   15th Oct., 1915.

WE journeyed southwards in three parts. Battalion Headquarters and the four Companies went first, reached Fouquereuil Station near Béthune after a six hours' run, and marched at once to Bellerive near Gonnehem. Here, at noon the following day—the 3rd October—they were joined by Lieut. Wollaston with the machine guns and ammunition limbers which had entrained at Godewaersvelde and travelled all night, and at 4.30 p.m., by Capt. John Burnett with the rest of the Transport. The latter had come by road, spending one night in bivouacs at Vieux Berquin on the way. This move brought us into the First Army under Sir Douglas Haig, who took an early opportunity of being introduced to all Commanding Officers and Adjutants in the Division, coming to Brigade Headquarters at Gonnehem on the afternoon of the 3rd, where Col. Jones and Lieut. G. W. Allen went to a conference. Lieut. Allen had become Adjutant when Capt. Griffiths was wounded, and Capt. Langdale was wanted for command of "B" Company. Our other Company Commanders remained unchanged except that Major Bland returned from England and took charge of "D."

The billets at Bellerive, consisting of large, clean

farm-houses, were very comfortable, but we were not destined to stay there long, and on the 6th marched through Chocques to Hesdigneul, where there was less accommodation. The following day there was a conference at Brigade Headquarters, and we learnt our fate. On the 25th September, the opening day of the Loos battle, the left of the British attack had been directed against " Fosse 8 "—a coal mine with its machine buildings, miners' cottages and large low slag dump—protected by a system of trenches known as the "Hohenzollern Redoubt," standing on a small rise 1,000 yards west of the mine. This had all been captured by the 9th Division, but owing to counter-attacks from Auchy and Haisnes, had had to be abandoned, and the enemy had once more occupied the Redoubt. A second attempt, made a few days later by the 28th Division, had been disastrous, for we had had heavy casualties, and gained practically no ground, and except on the right, where we had occupied part of " Big Willie " trench, the Redoubt was still intact. Another attempt was now to be made at an early date, and, while 12th and 1st Divisions attacked to the South, the North Midland was to sweep over the Redoubt and capture Fosse 8, consolidating a new line on the East side of it.

Apart from the Fosse itself, where the fortifications and their strength were practically unknown, the Redoubt alone was a very strong point. It formed a salient in the enemy's line and both the Northern area, " Little Willie," and the southern " Big Willie," were deep, well-fortified trenches, with several machine gun positions. Behind these, ran from N.E. and S.E. into the 2nd line of the Redoubt, two more deep trenches, " N. Face " and " S. Face," thought to be used for communication purposes only, and leading back to "Fosse" and "Dump" trenches nearer the slag-heap. The last two were said to be shallow and unoccupied. In addition to these defences, the redoubt and its approach from our line were well covered by machine gun posts, for, on the North, "Mad Point" overlooked our present front line and No Man's Land, while "Madagascar" Cottages and the Slag-heap commanded all the rest of the country. The scheme for the battle was that the Staffordshires on the right and our Brigade with the Monmouthshires on the left would make the assault, the Sherwood Foresters remain in reserve. Before the attack there would be an intense artillery bombardment, which would effectually deal with "Mad Point" and other strongholds. In our Brigade, General Kemp decided to attack with two Battalions side by side in front, 4th Leicestershires and 5th Lincolnshires, followed by 4th Lincolnshires and Monmouthshires, each extended along the whole Brigade frontage, while, except for one or two carrying parties, he would keep us as his own reserve. The date for the battle had not been fixed, but it would probably be the 10th.

Reconnaissances started at once, and on the 8th Col. Jones and all Company Commanders and 2nds in Command went by motor 'bus to Vermelles, and reconnoitred our trenches, held at the time by the Guards Division. Our first three lines, where the assembly would take place the night before the battle, were all carefully reconnoitred as well as the "Up" and "Down" communication trenches—Barts Alley, Central, Water and Left Boyaus. These were simply cut into the chalk and had not been boarded, so, with the slightest rain, became hopelessly slippery, while to make walking worse a drain generally ran down the centre of the trench, too narrow to walk in and too broad to allow one to walk with one foot each side. From the front line we were able to see the edge of the Redoubt, Mad Point, and the mine with its buildings and Slag-heap. The last dominated everything, and could be seen from everywhere. It was not very encouraging to see the numbers of our dead from the previous two attacks, still lying out in No Man's Land, whence it had not yet been possible to carry them in. The party reached home soon after 5 p.m., and a few minutes later a heavy bombardment in the direction of Vermelles was followed by an order to "stand to," which we did until midnight, when all was quiet again, and we were allowed to go to bed.

The following day the remainder of the officers and a party of selected N.C.O.'s went again to the line to reconnoitre. While they were away we heard the meaning of the previous night's noise. The Boche had attacked our posts in "Big Willie" held by a Battalion of the Coldstream Guards, and after a long fight had been driven back with heavy losses, leaving many dead behind them. Both sides had used no other weapon than the bomb, and our success was attributed to our new Mills grenade, which could be thrown further and was easier to handle than the German stick bomb, and the Coldstreams were said to have thrown more than 5,000 of these during the fight. This little encounter had two results. First, it definitely postponed our attack to the 13th; secondly, it brought the Mills grenade into so much prominence that we were ordered to practise with that and that only, and to ensure that during the next three days every man threw them frequently. At the same time we were definitely promised that no other grenade would be issued during our coming battle.

As it was not intended that we should go into trenches until the night before the assault, only very few of the N.C.O.'s and none of the men would have any opportunity of previously studying the ground. In order, therefore, that all might be made familiar with the general appearance and proportionate distances of the various objectives, a small scale model of the Redoubt and Fosse 8 was built opposite Divisional Headquarters at Gosnay, and Sunday afternoon was spent in studying this and explaining full details to all concerned. In the evening the Corps Commander, General Haking, spoke to all officers of the Division in the Chateau courtyard, and told us some further details of the attack. We were to be supported by the largest artillery concentration ever made by the British during the war up to that time, and there would be 400 guns covering the Divisional front. Under their fire we need have no fear that any machine guns could possibly be left in "Mad Point," "Madagascar," or any of the other points due for bombardment. At the same time he told us that if the wind were in the right direction we should be further assisted by the " auxiliary." In this case there would be an hour's bombardment, followed by an hour's " auxiliary," during which time the guns would have to be silent because High Explosive was apt to disperse chlorine gas. At the end of the second hour we should advance and find the occupants all dead. Attacks at dawn and dusk had become very common lately and seemed to be expected by the Boche; we would therefore attack at 2 p.m.

During the next two days we spent most of our time throwing Mills grenades, and certainly found them a very handy weapon, which could be thrown much further than our previous patterns. We also had to make several eleventh hour changes in personnel, Major Bland and Lieut. Allen were both compelled by sickness to go to Hospital—the former to England. It was exceptionally bad luck for both, to endure the routine of six months' trenches and training and then have to leave their unit on the eve of its first great fight, in which both these officers were so keen to take part. In their places Lieut. Hills was appointed to " D " Company, but as he was taken by General Kemp for Intelligence Work, 2nd Lieut. G. B. Williams took command. No one was appointed Adjutant, and Colonel Jones decided that as officers were scarce he and Major Toller would between them share the work at Battalion Headquarters. Two new officers also arrived and were posted, 2nd Lieut. G. T. Shipston to " C " and 2nd Lieut. L. Trevor Jones to " D " Company.

On the 12th, after some last words of advice from Colonel Jones, who addressed the Battalion, we set off to march to trenches, wearing what afterwards became known as " Fighting Order," with great coats rolled and strapped to our backs. The Brigade band accompanied us through Verquin, and a Staffordshire band played us into Sailly Labourse, where General Montagu-Stuart-Wortley watched us turn on to the main road. There was an hour's halt for teas between here and Noyelles, and finally at 10-5 p.m. we marched into Vermelles. The next eight hours were bad, for it took eight hours to reach our assembly position, the third line—eight hours standing in hopelessly congested communication trenches, waiting to move forward. For men heavily laden—each carried six sandbags and every third man a shovel—this delay was very tiring, for it meant continuous standing with no room to rest, and resulted in our arriving in the line tired out, to find that it was already time to have breakfasts. The Reserve Line was full of troops, but it was found possible to give all a hot breakfast, and many managed to snatch a couple of hours' sleep before the bombardment opened at 12 noon.

Compared with the bombardments of the Somme and the later battles, our bombardment was small, but it seemed to us at the time terrific, and it was very encouraging to see direct hits on the mine workings and the various trenches. The enemy retaliated mostly on communication trenches, using some very heavy shells, but not doing a great deal of damage. At 1 p.m. chlorine gas was discharged from cylinders packed in our front line, and at the same time a quantity of smoke bombs and mortar shells were fired towards the Redoubt by parties of our Divisional Artillery who were not covering us in the battle. The enemy at once altered his retaliation targets, and opened a heavy fire on our front line, trying to burst the gas cylinders, and succeeding in filling the trench with gas in three places by so doing. At 1-50 p.m. the gas and smoke was gradually diminished and allowed to disperse, and, ten minutes later, wearing gas helmets rolled on their heads, the leading waves moved out to the assault.

The start was disastrous. Colonel Martin and his Adjutant were both wounded, Colonel Sandall was wounded and his Adjutant killed in the first few minutes, and the machine gun fire along the whole of our front was terrific. Still, the nature of the ground afforded them some protection and they pushed forward, losing heavily at every step, until they had crossed the first line of the Redoubt. The 4th Lincolnshires and Monmouthshires followed, and we moved up towards the front line so as to be ready if required, and at the same time a party of our Signallers went forward to lay a line to the newly captured position. L.-Corpl. Fisher himself took the cable and, regardless of the machine gun fire, calmly reeled out his line across No Man's Land, passed through the enemy's wire and reached the Redoubt. Communication was established, and we were able to learn that all waves had crossed the first German line and were going forward against considerable opposition. Meanwhile, on the right the Staffordshires had fared far worse even than our Brigade. Starting from their second line, they were more exposed to machine gun fire from all sides, and very few reached even their own front line, whilst row upon row were wiped out in their gallant effort to advance.

In case of failure and the consequent necessity of holding our original front line against strong counter attacks, it had been arranged that our machine guns should take up permanent positions in this line. This was done, and Lieut. Wollaston was supervising the work of his teams and improving their positions when he saw that a considerable number of men were coming back from the Redoubt. Their officers and N.C.O.'s killed, they themselves, worn out by the exertions of the past 24 hours, half gassed by the chlorine which still hung about the shell holes, shot at by machine guns from every quarter, had been broken by bombing attacks from every trench they attacked and now, having thrown all their bombs, were coming back. The situation was critical, and Lieut. Wollaston, deciding to leave his guns now that they were in good positions, made his way along the trench and tried to rally the stragglers. Many were too badly shaken to go forward again, but some answered his call and collecting some more grenades the little party started back towards the Redoubt. Lieut. Wollaston was knocked down and wounded in the back by a shell, but still went forward, and, reaching the first German line, turned left towards "Little Willie," which the Boche was still holding in force. At the same time General Kemp ordered two of our Companies to be sent up to assist, and Colonel Jones sent word to "B" and "A" to move up. One message from the Redoubt which reached Colonel Jones at this time said "Please send bombs and officers."

Captain Langdale decided to advance in line, and leaving their trenches the four platoons started off in that formation. The platoon commanders became casualties in the first few yards, 2nd Lieut. Marriott being wounded and the two others gassed, and by the time they reached our front line the Company Commander was leading them himself. Walking along with his pipe in his mouth, Captain Langdale might have been at a Field Day, as he calmly signalled his right platoon to keep up in line, with "keep it up, Oakham," as they crossed our trench. The line was kept, and so perfectly that many of the stragglers who had come back turned and went forward again with them. But once more as they were reaching the German front line came that deadly machine gun fire, and their gallant Commander was one of the first to fall, killed with a bullet in the head. C.S.M. Lovett was badly wounded at the same time, Serjt. Franks killed, and the Company, now leaderless, was broken into isolated parties fighting with bombs in the various trenches.

"A" Company followed. Keeping his platoons more together and on a smaller frontage, Captain Hastings decided to attempt a bayonet attack against the German opposition on the left of the Redoubt, and himself led his men up to the attack. Again Platoon Commanders were the first to fall, and as they climbed out of our trenches, 2nd Lieut. Lawton was mortally wounded in the stomach and 2nd Lieut. Petch badly shot through the arm. However, this did not delay the attack, and the Company, crossing the German front line, quickened their pace and made for the junctions of "Little Willie" and "N. Face." Once more bombs and machine guns were too hot for them, and first Capt. Hastings, then 2nd Lieut. Moss were killed near the German second line, leaving the Company in the hands of 2nd Lieut. Tomson and C.S.M. Gorse, who at once organized the platoons for the defence of the second line, realizing that it was useless to try to advance further. 2nd Lieut. Petch, in spite of his wound, remained several hours with his platoon, but eventually had to leave them. The ground was covered with the dead and wounded of the other Battalions, Fosse and Dump trenches were filled with Germans and machine guns, "S. Face" and both "Willies" were full of bombers, and worst of all the machine guns of Mad Point, Madagascar and the Slag-heap had apparently escaped untouched. There was only one thing left to do, and that to hold what we had got against these bombing attacks, and consolidate our new position without delay.

Meanwhile, in addition to our two Companies, there were several other parties and units fighting in various parts of the Redoubt, and of these Colonel Evill, of the Monmouthshires, himself on the spot, took command, sending down for more men and more bombs. Of these little parties the most successful was that under Lieut. Wollaston, who, although wounded, led a bombing attack into "Little Willie," and pushed on so resolutely that he gained some eighty yards of trench before being compelled to withdraw owing to lack of bombs and ammunition. Unfortunately there was no other party near to help him, or "Little Willie" would probably have been ours. On the right, Lieut. Madge, of the Lincolnshires, held on for an incredibly long time with only a few machine gunners far in advance of anyone else, only coming back after 5 p.m., when he found that part of the captured ground had been evacuated by us. Here, too, Lieut. Morgan, of the Staffordshire Brigade R.F.A., was killed leading his gunners forward to help the infantry who were in difficulties. Some of "D" Company were also in action at this time. Thirteen and Fourteen Platoons set off, as originally ordered, under Royal Engineer officers, to put out barbed wire in front of the Redoubt, but as they reached our front line were heavily shelled and lost touch with the Engineers, many of whom were killed. 2nd Lieut. Stoneham had already been badly wounded, and Lieut. Williams, with a blood-stained bandage tying up a wounded ear, was with his other half Company, so the two platoons were left without officers. Serjt W. G. Phipps, who was leading, knew nothing about the wiring orders, having been told simply to follow the R.E., so he ordered his platoon to collect all the bombs they could find and make for the Redoubt. Serjt. G. Billings with 14 followed, and the half Company entered the fight soon after "A" Company. Their fate was the same. Serjt. Billings, with Corporals A. Freeman and T. W. Squires, were all killed trying to use their bayonets against "N. Face," and the rest were scattered and joined the various bomb parties. F. Whitbread and A. B. Law found themselves in "Little Willie," and helped rush the enemy along it, only to be forced back each time through lack of bombs. Whitbread was particularly brave later, when he went alone over the top to find out the situation on their flank. One other officer was conspicuous, in the Redoubt, in our trenches, everywhere in fact where he could be of use—Captain Ellwood, in charge of machine guns and forward bomb stores, was absolutely indefatigable, and quiet and fearless performed miracles of energy and endurance.

At 5 p.m., the German bombing attacks increased in vigour, and this time a large part of our garrison of the German second line trench gave way and came back to the original front line of the Redoubt—some even to our front line. Who gave the order for this withdrawal was never discovered, but there was undoubtedly an order "Retire" passed along the line, possibly started by the Boche himself. Such a message coming to tired and leaderless men was sure to have a disastrous effect, and in a few minutes we had given up all except Point 60, a trench junction at the N. end of "Big Willie," and the front line of the Redoubt. In this last there were still plenty of men, and these, led by a few resolute officers and N.C.O.'s such as 2nd Lieut. Tomson, C.S.M. Gorse, and others, were

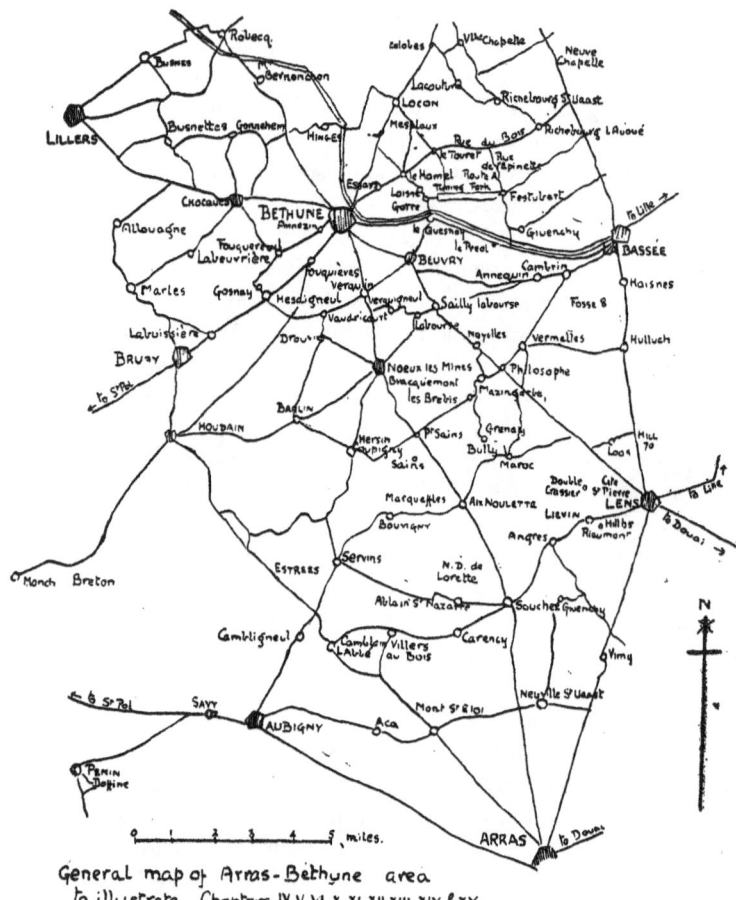

General map of Arras-Béthune area to illustrate Chapters IV, V, VI, X, XI, XII, XIII, XIV & XV.

prepared to hold it against all attacks. The original parados was cut into fire steps, bomb blocks were built in " Little Willie " and " North Face," and the garrison generally reorganized. Messages were sent for more bombs, and these were carried up in bags and boxes from Brewery Keep, Vermelles to the old front line, and thence across No Man's Land by parties of " C " and " D " Company.

While this took place in the Redoubt, Colonel Jones occupied the old front line with " C " Company (Lieuts. Farmer and Shields), and elements of " D " Company occupying the bays which were free from gas. The trench had been badly battered by shells at mid-day, and there were many killed and wounded still in it, amongst the latter being Colonel Martin, of the 4th Battalion, who garrisoned about 100 yards by himself. Shot through the knee and in great pain, he refused to go down, but sat at the top of " Barts Alley " receiving reports, sending information to Brigade, and directing as far as possible the remnants of his Battalion. For twenty-one hours he remained, calm and collected as ever, and only consented to be carried out when sure that all his Battalion had left the Redoubt. Meanwhile further to the left along the same trench, Colonel Jones made it his business to keep the Redoubt supplied with bombs. He was here, there, and everywhere, directing parties, finding bomb stores, helping, encouraging, and giving a new lease of life to all he met. Many brave deeds were done by N.C.O.'s and men and never heard of, but one stands out remembered by all who were there. L.-Corpl. Clayson, of " D " Company, during the time that his platoon was in this trench, spent all his time out in the old No Man's Land, under heavy machine gun fire, carrying in the wounded, many of whom would have perished but for his bravery.

With darkness came orders that the Sherwood Foresters would take over the line from us, but long before they could arrive our Companies in the Redoubt were being very hard pressed, and scarcely held their own. The German bombers never for a moment ceased their attack, and for some time our bombers held them with difficulty. Then came the cruellest blow of fortune, for many of the bags and boxes of bombs sent up during the afternoon were found to contain bombs without detonators, many others were filled with types of grenades we had never seen. In spite of this there was one officer who always managed to find the wherewithal to reply to the German attacks. Escaping death by a miracle, for his great height made him very conspicuous, 2nd Lieut. Tomson stood for hours at one of the bombing blocks, smoking cigarettes and throwing bombs. With him was Pte. P. Bowler, who proved absolutely tireless, while in another part of the line Pte. W. H. Hallam and one or two others carried out a successful bombing exploit on their own, driving back the enemy far enough to allow a substantial block to be built in a vital place. To add to the horrors of the situation, the garrison had ever in their ears the cries of the many wounded, who lay around calling for Stretcher Bearers or for water, and to whom they could give no help. The Bearers had worked all day magnificently, but there is a limit to human endurance, and they could carry no more. Even so, when no one else was strong enough, Captain Barton was out in front of the Redoubt, regardless of bombs, and thinking only of the wounded, many of whom he helped to our lines, while to others, too badly hit to move, he gave water or morphia. Hour after hour he worked on alone, and no one will ever know how many lives he saved that night.

Soon after 6 p.m., the Sherwood Foresters started to arrive and gradually worked their way up towards the Redoubt, a long slow business, for the communication trenches were all choked and no one was very certain of the route. One large party arriving at midnight happened to meet Colonel Jones, who advised them to try going over the top, and actually gave them their direction by the stars. So accurate were his instructions that the party arrived exactly at the Redoubt—incidentally at a moment when the Germans were launching a counter attack over the open. Such an attack might well have been disastrous, but the Boche, seeing the Sherwood Foresters and over-estimating their strength, retired hurriedly. By dawn the Sherwood Foresters had taken over the whole Redoubt, though many of our "A" and "B" Companies were not relieved and stayed there until the following night. Our task now was the defence of the original British front line, for which Colonel Jones was made responsible, and which we garrisoned with "C" (Farmer) right, "D" (Williams) centre, and "A" and "B" (Tomson) left. Major Toller, several times knocked down by shells and suffering from concussion, Lieut. Wollaston wounded, and 2nd Lieut. Wynne gassed, had all been sent down, and 2nd Lieut. Williams followed some hours later. Our only other officer, Lieut. R. Ward Jackson, was in charge of the Grenadiers, and spent his time in the Redoubt organizing bomb attacks and posts and trench blocks, himself throwing many bombs, and in a very quiet way doing a very great deal.

Twice during the night General Kemp visited the line, and went round the Redoubt before it was handed over to the Sherwood Foresters. He wanted very much to do more for the wounded, but the Stretcher Bearers were worked out, and though volunteers worked hard and rescued many, there were still numbers who had to be left until the following night. Rations were brought by the Company Q.M. Serjeants under Capt. Worley to the Quarry—a few hundred yards behind the left of our old front line—and waited there until parties could be sent for them, a matter of several hours. However, they were distributed at dawn, when they were very welcome, for many had been nearly twenty-four hours without food. 2nd Lieut. Tomson was one of of these, remarking, as C.S.M. Gorse gave him some rum, that he had had nothing since the attack but " two biscuits and over 300 cigarettes ! "

Throughout the following day we remained in our old front line, listening to the continuous bombing attacks in the Redoubt, and giving what assistance we could with carrying parties. The morning was very misty, and in expectation of a counter attack we were ordered to keep double sentries, so that the trench was more than usually full of men, when the enemy suddenly bombarded it with heavy shells. There were several direct hits, and the trench was blown in in many places, while one shell fell into the middle of a machine gun team. Serjt. W. Hall, of " D " Company, L/Corpl. A. F. Brodribb, and Pte. Bartlam were all killed, and the rest of the team were badly shaken, until C.S.M. Gorse and Corpl. B. Staniforth came along and helped to reorganize the post with a few new men. The trench contained no real cover, and the bombardment lasted for about half an hour; a severe ordeal for men who had already had a stiff fight followed by a night of bombing. Many of the telephone lines were broken, and L.-Corpl. Fisher, who had done such gallant work the pervious day, was killed entering our trench just after he had re-opened communication. In the afternoon we were again bombarded, this time with lachrymatory as well as H.E. shells, but our casualties were not so heavy, though the trench was again demolished in several places. Finally at 11-30 p.m. the Sherwood Foresters started to relieve us. They arrived in small parties, and some did not appear until dawn the following day, so that relief was not complete until 8 a.m. We then went back to Lancashire trench between the Railway and Vermelles, where we slept for several hours.

At 2 p.m., motor 'buses arrived to take the Brigade back to Hesdigneul, and made several journeys, but had not room for all the Battalion, so 70 set off to march under Major Toller, who had returned to us in Lancashire trench. It proved to be a dark night, and the party lost their way slightly in Verquigneul, but finally arrived singing (led by C.S.M. Gorse) at Hesdigneul, and reached their billets about midnight.

In so far that Fosse 8 still remained in the hands of the enemy, the battle was a failure, but in capturing the Redoubt the Brigade had prevented it being a complete failure. Though we only held the German front line and one small point in advance of it, we made it impossible for the enemy to hold any of the Redoubt himself, and so robbed him of his commanding position on the high ground. Our casualties had been heavy, and the two attacking Battalions had only one officer left between them, while we in reserve had lost four officers and 22 men killed, six officers and 132 men wounded and 13 men missing. Two officers and 22 men had been gassed, but presently returned to us. The causes of our failure were mainly two. First, the failure of the Artillery to wipe out "Mad Point" and Madagascar and their machine guns; secondly, the gas. This last was undoubtedly a mistake. It caused us several casualties; it made it necessary for the attackers to wear rolled up gas masks which impeded them, it stopped our H.E. bombardment an hour before the assault and so enabled German machine gunners to come back to their guns, and above all it had a bad effect on us, for we knew its deadly effects, and many a man swallowing a mouthful or smelling it became frightened of the consequences and was useless for further fighting. There was also the mistake of leaving Fosse and Dump trenches untouched by the bombardment, because they were reported weeks before to be shallow and unoccupied; as it happened we found them full of men. Finally, there were the bombs. We had been promised Mills only, and yet found many other types during the battle. Possibly a shortage of Mills might account for this, but there can be no possible excuse for sending grenades into a fight without detonators, and no punishment could be too harsh for the officer who was responsible for this.

Honours and Rewards were not given in those days as they were later, and many a brave deed went unrecognized. There were only nine D.C.M.'s in the Division, and of these the Brigade won seven, to which we contributed one, Hallam, the grenadier. Of the officers, Capt. Barton, Lieut. Wollaston, and 2nd Lieut. Williams received the Military Cross, and the Colonel's name appeared in the next list for a C.M.G. It was not until long afterwards that those who had been with him began to talk of the splendid deeds of 2nd Lieut. Tomson throughout the day and night of the 13th, and he was never one to talk about himself. Had anyone in authority known at the time he, too, would have had some decoration.

CHAPTER V.

FLANDERS MUD TO THE MEDITERRANEAN.

15th Oct., 1915.   28th Jan., 1916.

The whole Brigade was left very weak after the battle, and there was a serious shortage of officers. As in this respect we, as a Battalion, had suffered least, we had to supply the needs of other units, and Major Toller went to command the 4th Battalion, taking with him 2nd Lieut. Trevor Jones, as they had no subaltern officers. At the same time 2nd Lieut. H. E. Chapman was sent to help the 5th Lincolnshires, and Capt. Burnett and Lieut. Ward Jackson went to Brigade Headquarters to look after Transport and Bombs, while their duties in the Battalion were performed by Serjt. Brodribb and Serjt. Goodman. We could not afford a machine gun officer, so Serjt. Jacques was made responsible for the guns until an officer reinforcement should arrive. " A," " B " and " D " Companies were commanded by Lieuts. Tomson, Wynne, and Shields, and, as Lieut. Allen was still in hospital, Lieut. Hills acted as Adjutant. The officers all messed together at first, and tried to maintain the old cheerful spirit of the Battalion mess—a little difficult after losing in one day more than three-quarters of the mess.

On Sunday, General Montagu-Stuart-Wortley came

to talk to the Battalion after Church parade, and congratulated us on the fighting, saying that, considering the odds against us, he thought we had done very well indeed. He then went round the ranks talking to some of the men who had taken part in the battle, and was very amused by some of the answers he received to his questions. One soldier, asked what he had done in the fight, replied that he had "blown half a Boche officer's leg off with a bomb." The General thought this excellent, but wanted to know why he had chosen half an officer only, and not a whole one.

We stayed ten days at Hesdigneul, and then moved to Drouvin and Vaudricourt, where the billets were better, and we were able to have a Battalion officers' mess. During this time, many reinforcement officers arrived and two large drafts of other ranks. Two of our original officers returned—Capt. Beasley, who now took command of "B" Company, and Lieut. Knighton, who returned to "D" as 2nd in Command. The remainder were new to us, and were posted as follows: "A" Company—2nd Lieuts. M. A. Hepworth, C. H. Pickworth, and G. Russell; "B" Company—2nd Lieuts. J. W. Brittain and, when they returned, the two officers lent to other Battalions; "C" Company—Capt. S. J. Fowler, 2nd Lieuts. A. M. Barrowcliffe and A. L. Macbeth; "D" Company—2nd Lieuts. A. H. Dawes, H. W. Oliver, and J. R. Brooke. 2nd Lieut. C. L. Saunders became Machine Gun Officer. With these additions we were able to start training again, and devoted our time to route marching, bayonet fighting, and, most of all, bomb throwing. At no time during the war was more reliance placed on bombs, and scheme after scheme was invented for "bombing attacks up a trench," to such an extent that the platoon organisation was now re-modelled with the one idea of forming bomb parties. The rifle seemed to be temporarily forgotten.

On the 28th October, as many Units as possible of the 1st Army were inspected by H.M. The King. Our Brigade formed a composite Battalion commanded by Col. Jones, and, with the rest of the Division, and representatives of other Divisions, was drawn up along the Hesdigneul-Labuissière Road. His Majesty rode past us from Labuissière and, after taking the salute, came down the hill again in his car with the Prince of Wales. He acknowledged our cheers with a smile, and it was not until afterwards that we learnt of his accident soon after passing us, and knew the pain he was suffering during his drive back, pain which he had so admirably concealed.

After the inspection we sent a large party, six officers and 230 N.C.O.'s and men, to Sailly Labourse, to carry gas cylinders and other material to trenches, but except for this we were spared all fatigues during our period of rest. A week later we marched through Béthune and Robecq to Calonne sur la Lys, a little village outside Merville, where we remained another week before going to the line. Lieut. Allen rejoined us and became Adjutant; Lieut. Hills, after a few days with "A" Company, went to Brigade Headquarters as a Staff Learner. At the same time, Major Toller returned to the Battalion as 2nd in Command. After commanding the 4th Battalion until a new Colonel arrived for them, he had been posted to the 5th Lincolnshires, and for a time it looked as though he would be permanently given command. However, bad luck pursued him, and, as two new Colonels arrived for that Battalion the same day, he again lost his Command. Considering that he had commanded us for three months during the summer with great success, and was easily senior Major in the Brigade, it was exceptionally bad luck that he had to wait another eight months before finally getting his Battalion.

On the 10th November, we were told that we should once more take over a part of the line, and the following morning we marched to Lacouture and went into billets for one night. "B" Co. (Beasley) went on at once and spent the night in support positions near the Rue du Bois between Festubert and Neuve Chapelle. The rest of us moved up the next day and took over our new line from the Sherwood Foresters the same night. Battalion Headquarters lived in a little cottage, "No. 1" Albert Road, two Companies occupied a large farm house in the same neighbourhood fitted up as a rest house, one Company lived in a series of curiously named keeps—"Haystack," "Z Orchard," "Path," and "Dead Cow," and one Company only was in the front line.

The Brigade now held the line from "Kinkroo," a corruption of La Quinque Rue, crossing to the "Boar's Head," and of this we held the stretch opposite the two farms in No Man's Land, Fme du Bois and Fme Cour d' Avoué. The latter, surrounded by a moat, had an evil reputation, and was said to have been the death-trap of many patrols, which had gone there and never been seen since. The trenches had been dug in the summer when the country was dry, with no regard to the fact that in winter the water level rises to within two inches of the surface of the ground. In consequence, the trenches were full of mud and water, and most of the bivouacs and shelters were afloat. The mud was the worst, for although only two feet deep, yet it was of the clinging variety, and made walking impossible, so much so, that many a man has found it impossible to withdraw his foot, has had to leave his gum-boot behind, go on in his socks, and come back later with a shovel to rescue his boot. The water was deeper and often came over one's gum-boots and up to one's waist, but at least it was possible to walk slowly through it without fear of getting stuck. To add to the discomfort of the garrison, the weather was bitterly cold and often very wet, and though no Company remained more than 24 hours in the front line, yet that was long enough for many to become chilled and so start the terrible "trench foot."

"Trench foot," as it was called, was one of the most terrible afflictions of winter trenches. After standing for a long period in water or mud, or with wet rubber boots, the feet became gradually numbed and the circulation ceased, while as the numbed area increased a dull aching pain spread over the whole foot. Exercise to restore the circulation would have prevented this, but for men who were compelled to spend the entire day in one fire bay, exercise was impossible, and by evening the numbness had almost always started. As soon, therefore, as a Company came from the front line, it marched to the rest house. Here, every man was given a hot drink, his wet boots and socks were taken away, his feet rubbed by the Stretcher Bearers until the circulation was restored, and then with dry socks and dry boots he remained for the next 24 hours in the warmer atmosphere of the rest house.

Should action not be taken in time, and a man be left for 48 hours with wet boots and socks, the rest house treatment was insufficient, and he had to be sent to Hospital, where, if gangrene had not set in, he could still be cured. Many in the early days did not realize its dangers, for once gangrene starts, the foot has to be amputated.

The enemy's trenches were probably as bad as our own, and he only manned his front line at night, leaving a few snipers to hold it by day. These were active for the first hour or two after morning "stand to," but then had breakfast and apparently slept for the rest of the day, at all events they troubled us no more. This was a distinct advantage, for it enabled communication to be kept between posts and from front to rear, without the orderly having either to swim up a communication trench or run a serious risk of being sniped. One, Kelly, a famous "D" Company character, tried to walk too soon one morning to fetch his rum ration and was hit in the knee, much to his annoyance; but on the whole there were very few casualties. By night, too, there was not much firing, probably because both sides were hard at work taking up rations, relieving front line posts, or trying to get dry with the aid of a walk "on top." In our case, with 24 hour reliefs, there were no ration parties, because each Company as it went to the line took its rations and fuel with it.

Our only communication trench was "Cadbury's," which started near "Chocolat Menier," corner of the Rue du Bois, so called after an advertisement for this chocolate fastened to the side of a house. It was even more water logged than the front line, and consequently, except when the ice was thick enough to walk on, was seldom used. With a little care it was possible to reach the front line even by day without the help of a trench at all, and Lieut. Saunders always used to visit his machine guns in this way, making the journey both ways over the top every day that we held the sector, and never once being shot at.

The Rue du Bois we used as little as possible, for every other house was an O.P., and the gunners preferred us at a distance. The "Ritz," "Carlton," "Trocadero," and "Princes" all gave one an excellent view of the enemy's front line, and, knowing this, the Boche concentrated most of the little artillery he used on this neighbourhood. There was seldom any heavy shelling, mostly field artillery only, and this of a poor order, for not only were there many "duds" in every shoot, but also the gunners seemed to lack imagination. So regular were they in their choice of targets, times of shooting, and number of rounds fired, that, after being in the line one or two days, Col. Jones had discovered their system, and knew to a minute where the next shell would fall. His calculations were very accurate, and he was able to take what seemed to uninitiated Staff Officers big risks, knowing that the shelling would stop before he reached the place being shelled.

Amongst the new subaltern officers was one unlike any we had seen before—2nd Lieut. J. R. Brooke. He loved patrolling for its own sake, and during his first few days in the line explored everything he could find including the German wire and trenches. From this time onwards he spent more of his days crawling about on his stomach than sitting like a respectable soldier in a trench, and even when years later he became a

Company Commander it was found impossible to break him of the habit. Captains were forbidden to go on patrol, but this did not matter to him, he would take a subaltern with him and make the latter write the report, calling it 2nd Lieut. ——— and one other Rank. One would expect such a man to be large, strong, and of a fierce countenance; 2nd Lieut. Brooke was small, of delicate health, and looked as though his proper vacation in life was to hand cups of tea to fair ladies at a village tea fight.

It seemed probable that we should have to remain in this sector for the whole winter, and our first thought was, therefore, how to make the trenches somewhat more habitable. It was obvious that digging was out of the question, and that nothing less than a large breastwork, built entirely above ground, would be of any use. General Kemp visited the lines several times before finally deciding on his plan, and then sighted two works, the front a few yards behind our present front line, the second just behind what was called the "old British Line," now used for our supports. It was a gigantic task, and the work was very slow, even though every available man worked all night. The inside of the breastwork was to be revetted with frames of woodwork and expanded metal, and, in order that the parapet might be really bullet proof, the soil for it had to be dug from a "borrow pit" several yards in front. The soil was sticky and would not leave the shovel, which added terribly to the work; for each man had literally to dig a shovel full, walk five or six yards and deposit it against the revetting frames. Fortunately for us the Boche did not seem to object to our work, in any case he left us in peace each night.

While this was in progress, an effort was also made to try and drain the area. In many places water was lying, held up by sandbag walls and old trenches, actually above the ground level, and it was hoped that by cleaning ditches and arranging a general drainage scheme for the whole area, this surplus water might be drained off, and, in time, the whole water level lowered. Lieut. A. G. Moore, M.C., who returned from England at this time, was made "O.C. Drainage," and set to work at once with what men he could collect, but so big were the parties working on the breastworks each night, that only a very few could be spared for this other work, and not very much could be done.

Soon after Lieut. Moore, 2nd. Lieut. G. B. Williams also returned to us, and became Battalion Intelligence Officer, a post now started for the first time. At the same time four new officers arrived—2nd Lieuts. G. Selwyn and W. Ashwell to "A" Company, 2nd Lieut. A. N. Bloor to "B," and 2nd Lieut. V. J. Jones to "D." C.S.M. Gilding and Serjt. Brodribb both left us to be trained as officers, and their places were taken by C.Q.M.S. Johnson who became C.S.M. of "C" Company, and Corpl. Roberts who took charge of the Transport. The latter was still under the special care of Capt. Burnett, although he had all the Transport of the Brigade to look after.

Our first tour ended on the 25th, when, after 12 days' mud and frost, we were relieved by the 4th Lincolnshires, and came back to billets in the Rue des Chavattes, not far from Lacouture, where Stores and Transport remained throughout this time. Our casualties had not been very heavy, and we lost more through the weather conditions than at the hands of the enemy, for Capt. Fowler and several N.C.O.'s and men, unable to stand the exposure, had to be sent to Hospital. Our billeting area included several keeps or strong points—L'Epinette, le Touret, and others—for which we found caretakers, little thinking, as we stocked them with reserve rations, that the Boche would eventually eat our "Bully," and it would fall to our lot in three years time to drive him from these very positions. The day after relief, the Brigadier went on leave, and Col. Jones took his place at Brigade Headquarters—"Cense du Raux" Farm—somewhat to the annoyance of one or two of the other Commanding Officers, who, though junior to the Colonel, were all "Regular Time-serving Soldiers."

Up to this time our covering Artillery had belonged to another (New Army) Division, but now our own Gunners took over the line, making it more than ever certain that we were to spend the whole winter in these abominable trenches. We were very glad to see our own Artillery again, for, though their predecessors had done quite well, we always preferred our own, even in the days of 15 pounders and 5 inch howitzers. Not only were they more accurate than other people, but they were also more helpful, and were obviously intent on serving us Infantry, not, as some others, on carrying on a small war of their own. Besides, we knew the F.O.O.'s so well and looked forward to seeing them in the Mess, where, between occasional squabbles about real or imaginary short shooting, they were the most cheerful companions. Lieuts. Wright, Morris-Eyton, Watson of the 1st Staffs., Morgan, Anson of the 4th, and Lyttelton, Morris, and Dixie of the 2nd Lincolnshires, were the most frequent visitors for the "pip squeaks," while Lieuts. Newton, Cattle, and F. Joyce performed the same duties for the Derby Howitzers. They always took care to maintain their superiority over the mere foot soldier by a judicious use of long technical words which they produced one at a time. At Kemmel they were always "registering"; at Ypres, as we, too, had learnt the meaning of "register" and even dared to use the word ourselves, they introduced "bracketing," and as this became too common, "calibrating" and so on; the more famous of recent years being "datum point" and M.P.I. (mean point of impact). Occasionally our officers used to visit the Batteries, in order to learn how a gun was fired—an opportunity for any F.O.O. to wreak vengeance on some innocent Infantry Subaltern, who had dared to suggest that he had been shooting short. The Infantryman would be led down to the gun pit, and told to stand with one leg on each side of the trail, "so that he could watch the shell leave the gun"; some Gunner would then pull a string and the poor spectator, besides being nearly deaf, would see some hideous recoiling portion shoot straight at his stomach, stop within an eighth of an inch of his belt buckle, and slide slowly back—a ghastly ordeal.

On the night of the 2nd December, we went once more to the line and relieved the 4th Lincolnshires in our old sector, which we found very much as we had left it, perhaps a little wetter, as it had been raining. For this tour we slightly altered our dispositions, and instead of each of the four Companies taking a tour in the front line, two Companies only would do so for this tour, the other two doing the same the following tour.

It was hoped that in this way the garrison would take more interest in improving their surroundings if they knew they would return to the same place every other day. Under the old system, no one took much interest in a trench which he only occupied for 24 hours, and would not see again for four days. We did not, however, have a chance of testing this new arrangement, for at 3-45 the following morning, orders came that the Division would be relieved the following night, and was under orders to go to the East. As soon as it was dark, the 19th Division took our place in the line, and we marched back for the night to the Rue des Chavattes, whence, after ridding ourselves of gumboots, sheepskin coats, and extra blankets, we marched the following day by Locon, Lestrem and Merville to Caudescure, a little village on the edge of Nieppe Forest.

We found fairly good billets here, though they were too scattered to allow of a Battalion Mess, and we spent a very enjoyable fortnight training, playing football, and listening to rumours about our destination. The most persistent of the last was Egypt, based in the first instance on a telephone conversation between a Corps and Divisional Signaller, overhead by a telephonist at Brigade, in which the Corps Signaller told his friend that he had seen a paper in one of the offices which said that we were to go to Egypt. On the other hand, Lieut. X of the Lincolnshires had a brother in the Flying Corps, who had ridden on a lorry with an A.S.C. Serjeant from G.H.Q., and had been told that all the Territorial Divisions in India were being relieved by Divisions from France. Against this was Captain Z's batman, who had a friend in the Staffordshires who was batman to an officer who had a cousin in the War Office, and he said we were going to the Dardenelles. On the top of all these came General Montagu-Stuart-Wortley to inspect us, and, incidentally, to tell us that he himself had not the slightest idea where we were going.

On the 19th we moved to the little hamlet of Tannay, still on the edge of the woods, between Haverskerque and Thiennes. As we paraded in the morning there were many who said they could smell gas, but as the wind was N.E. and the line very far away, we thought they must be mistaken. However, the next day the official communiqué told us of a big gas attack at Ypres on the 9th and 49th Divisions, and though Ypres was 18 miles away, it must have been this that could be smelt. In these new billets we spent Christmas—the first Christmas in France for us, and managed with the aid of plum puddings and other luxuries sent out to us by the good people at home, to enjoy ourselves immensely. Not only were many good things to eat sent us, but we also received some very welcome gifts of tobacco, cigarettes, books and stationery from the "Leicester Daily Post and Mercury" funds. Both these papers have been most faithful throughout the war, never failing to send us "themselves," and often adding boxes of comforts for all. Our celebrations included a Brigade Football Cup competition, for which we entered a hot side, including many of our old players—"Banger" Neal, "Mush" Taylor, Toon, Archer, Skelly, Fish, Serjt. Allan, Kirchin and others. We met the 5th Lincolnshires in the semi-finals and beat them 2—1, and then turned our attention to their 4th Battalion, who after beating our 4th Battalion, our old rivals, met us in the final and went down 1—0. The final was a keen, hard game, played well to the finish, and we deserved our win. The trophy—a clock, mounted into a French "75" shell—was taken back to Leicestershire by Capt. Farmer when he next went on leave.

On the 27th we again moved, this time to some farms round Widdebroucq, just west of Aire, to be nearer our entraining station Berguette, which with Lillers had already been reconnoitred. As Captains Hills and Ward Jackson had already gone forward with an advance party to Marseilles, it began to look as though we really should go East before the end of the war—a fact which some of us were beginning to doubt. Training still continued each day, special attention being paid to open warfare tactics, which fortunately included more musketry and less bombing, and we also carried out a number of route marches and field days. Scouts, having become obsolete, were resurrected, and Field Service Regulations rescued from the dim recesses of valises. It was a pleasant change after the previous nine months' trench work.

At last, on the 6th January, we marched to Berguette station and boarded a long train of cattle trucks, leaving at 4.40 p.m. The first part of the journey was uninteresting, but after passing Paris, the train seemed happier, went quite fast at times, and did not stop so long between stations. The weather on the 8th was lovely, and the third day's travelling under a hot sun was delicious; doors were pushed back, and those for whom there was no room on the foot-boards, sat on the carriage roofs. Finally, at 1.0 a.m. on the 9th, the train reached Marseilles, and we marched out to a camp on the west side of the town, in a suburb called Santi, where there were tents for all, and a large room for an officers' mess. Here we remained 14 days in the most excellent surroundings, and with heavenly weather.

The Staffordshires and Lincolnshires had already sailed for Egypt when we arrived, and a few days later another ship carried some Padres and other officers of the Division to the same destination. For the rest of us there were for the moment no transports, so we had to wait—not a very terrible task, when our most strenuous exercise was sea-bathing or playing water polo, and our recreation consisted of walking into the town, to which an almost unlimited number of passes were given. Here, it must be admitted, there was often too much to eat and far too much to drink, and the attractions were so great that everybody waited for the last possible tram back to camp, with the result that this vehicle arrived with human forms clinging to every corner of the sides, ends and roof—a most extraordinary sight. On one occasion two well-known soldiers who had dined too well and not too wisely, stood solemnly at the side of the road holding up their hands to a tram to stop, when a party of lively French scavengers turned the hosepipe on to them, and they had to be rescued from the gutter, where they lay with the water running in at their collars and out at their ankles. The officers, too, had many popular resorts, such as Therese's Bar and the Bodega for cocktails, the Novelty for dinner, and a host of entertainments to follow, ranging from the opera, which was first-class, for the serious, through the "Alcazar" and "Palais de Crystal" for the frivolous, to the picture palaces for the utterly depraved.

On the 20th we learnt that our Transport was now ready for us, and the following morning we marched to the docks and embarked in H.M.T. "Andania," late Cunard, which can only be described as a floating palace, fitted with every modern luxury. We were all rather glad to be leaving Marseilles, for it was an expensive place, and many of the officers were beginning to be a little apprehensive about the lengths to which Mr. Cox would let them go. However, all would now be right, because once in the desert we should draw extra pay and find no Bodegas. We were to sail on the morning of the 22nd, and soon after dawn orders arrived—to disembark! Sadly we left our palace and walked back to Santi Camp—now hateful to look upon, as we realised that within a few days we should be back once more in the mud, rain, cold and snow of Flanders. The reason for the sudden change, for taking half the Division to Egypt for a fortnight only, was never told us, but probably it was owing to the successful evacuation of the Dardanelles. Had this been a failure, had we been compelled to surrender large numbers to save the rest, the Turks would have been free to attack Egypt, which had at that time a small garrison only. As it was the Division from Gallipoli went to Egypt, and we were not wanted.

On the 27th Pte. Gregory, who died as the result of a tram accident, was given a full military funeral, and the following day at 4.30 a.m. we left Marseilles for the North.

CHAPTER VI.

THE VIMY RIDGE.

6th Feb., 1916.   9th May, 1916.

OUR return train journey was uneventful until we reached Paris, where a German air raid started just as we arrived, and the train was compelled to stop. We had a beautiful view, and, as the French depended more on their own planes than on anti-aircraft guns, it was well worth watching. The French machines all carried small searchlights, and, in addition to these, the sky was light up with the larger searchlights from below, while the efforts of the Boche to avoid the lights, and the French to catch their opponents, produced some wonderful air-manœuvering, which ended in the retirement of the Boche. As soon as they had gone, our train went on, and we reached Pont Remy station outside Abbeville at 8-30 a.m. on the 30th—back once more in rain, snow, and mud.

We marched at once to Yaucourt Bussus, a small village with comfortable billets, which we occupied for nearly a fortnight, spending our time training and playing football. Meanwhile, as the Brigadier and the two Lincolnshire Battalions had not yet returned from Egypt, Col. Jones, taking with him 2nd Lieut. Williams as Staff Officer, went to command the half Brigade and lived with Captain Burnett at Ailly le haut Clocher, another small village, to which the Brigadier came on his return on the 11th. While the Colonel was away, Major Toller took command and Major T. C. P. Beasley acted as 2nd in Command. For the time no one seemed to have the slightest idea what was going to happen to the Division next.

On the 10th we marched to Gorenflos, and the following day were taken by lorries to billets in Candas, where, with an East wind, we could occasionally hear the distant sounds of gunfire for the first time for two months. Our new area we found was full of preparation for something; what the exact nature of this something might be we did not know. Several large railways and dumps were being built, new roads made, and here and there with great secrecy big concrete gun platforms were laid. Each day we sent large numbers to work, mostly on the railways, and once more we heard the words "Big Push." We were always living on the verge of the Big Push, and many times in 1915 had thought that it had started—at Neuve Chapelle, Givenchy, Loos—only to give up hope when these battles stagnated after a day or two. Now there were preparations going forward again, this time apparently on a much larger scale than we had ever seen before, so we felt justified once more in hoping for the great event. Curiously enough the possibilities of a Boche big push were never considered, and everyone of us was firmly convinced that, except perhaps for a blow at Ypres, offensive action on the part of the enemy was out of the question. This spirit animated all our work, which was consequently very different from our opponents.' Our trenches always had a we-shall-not-stay-here-long air about them, his were built to resist to the last man. It was the same in training and in billets, we unconsciously considered ourselves an advancing army, and thereby, though we may not have realized it, we ourselves supplied the finest possible stimulant to our moral.

The IIIrd. Army (Gen. Allenby), to which we now belonged, introduced at this time the Army School—an important innovation, shortly taken up by all the other Armies. This School, first commanded by Col. Kentish—afterwards Commandant of the Senior Aldershot School—aimed at training junior officers to be Company Commanders, who owing to casualties were now hard to find. The course, which lasted five weeks, consisted of drill, tactical exercises, physical training, musketry, bayonet fighting and bombing, lectures on esprit de corps—in fact everything that a Company Commander should know, but many things that in trench warfare had been forgotten. The Instructors were always up-to-date, and the best use was at once made of any of the latest inventions, while the school also kept a very efficient "Liaison" between all parts of the Army. Students from one Division would exchange latest schemes, ruses, and devices with others from another part of the line, and so no valuable lessons were lost or known to a few only. Our first students to this school were Capt. Ward Jackson, who was in charge of "A" Company, and Capt. G. W. Allen, the latter for a special Adjutant's refresher course. After these, all the Company Commanders went in turn, first to Flixecourt, and later to Auxi le Chateau, whither the school moved in the early summer. There were similar courses for senior N.C.O.'s, which were of the utmost value.

Another important innovation at this time was the introduction of the Lewis light machine gun. The Maxim, and even the Vickers machine gun had been found for many reasons unsuitable for infantry work, being too heavy and cumbersome for rapid movement, too conspicuous for easy concealment. It was therefore decided to form Brigade Machine Gun Companies, who would be armed with Vickers guns, while Battalions would have Lewis guns only, on a scale of two per Company, for they were to be considered a company rather than a Battalion weapon. This light gun had no tripod, was air-cooled, and fired a pan instead of a belt of ammunition. It was as easy to carry as to conceal, and was in every way an enormous improvement on the " Vickers " from the infantry point of view. Training in the new weapon started at once, and as 2nd Lieut. Saunders and Serjt. Jacques were required for the Brigade Machine Gun Company, 2nd Lieut. Shipston was made Lewis Gun Officer, with Corporal Swift to help him, and these two trained as many men as possible with the two guns issued to us, so that when more arrived the teams would be ready for them. Captain Ellwood commanded the Brigade Machine Gunners, and in addition to our chief instructors, we also sent 2nd Lieut. Stentiford and 30 N.C.O.'s and men to start the Company. 2nd Lieut. Stentiford was a new subaltern officer who, with 2nd Lieuts. T. P. Creed and C. J. Morris, had arrived while the battalion was at Marseilles.

On the 16th February orders came that at an early date we should take over the line North of the River Ancre, opposite Beaumont Hamel, and the following day several lorry loads of officers reconnoitred the country round Forceville, Englebelmer and Mailly Maillet, where there were some rear defence lines. Maps of the front were issued, and we were about to arrange trench reconnaissances, when the orders were cancelled and we moved instead, on the 20th, to Bernaville, and joined the rest of the Brigade. The other Battalions and Brigade Headquarters were in the neighbouring villages. At this time the people of Leicestershire were once more very good to us, and our War Diary contains a note that "This day the C.O. acknowledges with thanks the gifts of 30,000 cigarettes from our 2/5th Battalion, also a hand ambulance from Messrs. Symington and Co., Market Harborough." The last survived the rough usages of war for a very long time, and many a wounded man has been thankful for its springs and rubber tyres.

The rest of the month was spent in doing a little training and a deal of road-clearing. It snowed very hard once or twice, and many of the roads became impossible for traffic, so each Battalion was allotted a road to keep clean, ours being the main road to Fienvillers, along which we spread ourselves armed with picks and shovels, while the village boys threw snowballs at us. The 5th Division were moving North at the time, and a whole day was spent by some of the Battalions dragging their transport up a steep hill, a task beyond the strength of the horses. Fortunately we were spared this, probably because we took care not to clear the road to Brigade Headquarters, and so were left untouched. During this very bad weather we lost 2nd Lieut. Brooke, who had to go to Hospital with nephritis.

On the 29th we moved to Doullens, where we spent

an enjoyable week, and were introduced to yet another innovation. In August, 1915, the French had introduced a steel helmet for their machine gunners, finally extending the issue to all ranks. This had been found of the greatest value, and there had been at once a marked decrease in the percentage of head wounds. The British helmet now appeared, and was generally voted, as it first seemed, a hideous flat object, though some humorists admitted that it might have distinct possibilities as a washing basin. A few soldiers of the vainer sort thought they looked more "becoming" with a "tin-hat" over one eye, but the vast majority hated them, and it was with the greatest difficulty that those to whom they were issued, could be persuaded not to throw them away. This aversion, however, soon passed, and within a few months the infantryman standing under an aeroplane battle without his "tin-hat" felt distinctly naked.

It was now definitely decided that we were to relieve the French in the Neuville St. Vaast-Souchez Sector, both places where the French had had terrific fighting the previous year, and consequently a sector with a bad reputation. The roads were still in bad condition, and a char-a-banc, full of officers, who tried to reconnoitre reached no further than the French Brigade Headquarters and had to return. On the 6th March we marched to Magnicourt and two days later to Villers-au-bois, about three miles behind the line, going up to trenches on the 9th.

Early in 1915 the French line North of Arras had run through la Targette, Carency and over the East end of the Lorette heights to Aix Noulette. In May our allies made their first attack here and, driving the

Boche from the heights, gained possession, after terrific fighting, of Ablain St. Nazaire, Souchez and Neuville St. Vaast. Later, in conjunction with our September attack at Loos, they had again advanced, and finally a brilliant assault by the Zouaves carried the line to the Vimy ridge and on to these heights, beyond which the roads to Lens and Douai lay open. The fighting for the summit had been severe, and in the end each side retained its grip on the hill top, the opposing trenches running 30 yards apart along the ridge. Active mining operations had started soon afterwards, and shortly before our arrival the French had been compelled to give up a considerable portion of their line, and so lose their hold on the summit. With it they lost also their view Eastwards, while the Boche, occupying their evacuated trenches, regained his view of the next ridge to the West.

This second ridge was more in the nature of a large plateau, stretching back to Villers-au-bois, and separated from the Vimy ridge by a narrow steep-sided valley—the "Talus des Zouaves," where the support Battalion lived in dug-outs. Crossing the plateau from North to South was the main Béthune, Souchez, Arras road, on which stood the remains of an old inn, the Cabaret Rouge, where some excellent deep dug-outs provided accommodation for the French Poste de Colonel and an Advanced Dressing Station. The plateau was two miles wide, and over the first half (up to "Point G") ran a long and very tiring duck-board track; beyond "Point G" were two communication trenches to the line. One, "Boyau 1, 2, 3," was seldom used, being in bad condition; the other, "Boyau d'Ersatz," was boarded and well cared

THE VIMY RIDGE.

for, and used by all. It ran via the Cabaret Rouge into the Talus des Zouaves, most of the way revetted with a wonderful "wedding arch" revetment, and thence to the front line, passing the left Poste de Commandant. The forward part of "Boyau 1, 2, 3," East of the "Talus," was called "Boyau Internationale," leading to "Boyau Vincent" and so to the front line past the right Poste de Commandant. Carency, Ablain and Souchez were houseless, Villers au bois was little better, and our rest billets were huts at Camblain L'Abbé, about four miles behind the line.

The Brigade took over the left sector of the Divisional front and we were allotted the left sub-sector, our right and left boundaries being the two Boyaus "Internationale" and "Ersatz." The whole relief was to be kept as secret as possible, and all reconnoitering and advance parties were given French helmets to wear in the line, so that the Boche might have no idea what was going to happen. It was a little disconcerting, therefore, when a French listening post, two days before the relief, reported that a Boche had suddenly looked into their post, and after saying "Les Anglais n'sont pas encore donc arrivés," equally suddenly disappeared. In spite of this we were not disturbed during the relief and by 10-30 p.m. on the 9th had taken the place of the 68th Regiment, who marched out at one end of the trench as we appeared at the other, having told us that we had come to a very quiet sector. The trenches were in fair condition, though very dirty, and we had a quiet night so began to hope that the sector might not be too terrible after all. The next day the French left the area, leaving behind them two companies of Engineers to carry on the mining operations on the Divisional front. In handing over their posts the French had said nothing about their countrymen whom they were leaving in the mines, and during the first night several of them, coming up from below and talking a strange language, narrowly escaped being killed for Boche.

The enemy opposite us were very quiet, and obviously knowing of the relief, were waiting to see what we should do. With the French there is no doubt that they had had a tacit understanding not to wage a vigorous war, though, while seeming inactive, they had all the time been undermining the French trenches. With us they were uncertain what to do, so for 24 hours did nothing except fire a few rifle shots, one of which came through the parapet and killed C.S.M. E. Thompson, of "B" Company. On the evening of the second day they went one step further, and threw a single grenade, received two in return, and remained quiet for the night. The next morning, the 11th, they threw six more, all short, and we replied with 10, five of which fell in their trench and apparently convinced them that we intended war; at any rate they made no more tentative efforts, but in the afternoon started more or less in earnest. At 4.45 p.m. they blew up a small mine opposite "A" Company, demolished a sap-head, and half buried the solitary occupant, who escaped with bruises only; after this they bombed, or tried to bomb us, until 8-0 p.m., while we replied at the rate of two to one. Unfortunately, the explosions caused a collapse in our parapet, about 10 yards of which fell down suddenly, and had to be re-built during the night.

The following night proved to be still more exciting.

Soon after midnight a French sapper, narrowly escaping several sentries who thought he was a Boche, came running along the line excitedly waving his arms, and saying: "Mine, mine, faire sauter, demi-heure." No one knew what he meant, though we gathered a mine would probably go up somewhere in half-an-hour, whether ours or theirs we had not the least idea. Eventually he was led to Battalion Headquarters, where he explained that the French were going to blow a camouflêt in half-an-hour. It was already nearly an hour since he first said this, and nothing had yet happened, so we hurriedly cleared a small portion of our front line and waited, while we sent for the Tunnelling Officer. He arrived, and the "blow" was arranged for 5-0 a.m., at which hour there was a terrific explosion, a forty-foot crater was formed, and another ten yards of our parapet fell down. Such an explosion must have been caused by a much bigger charge than we had laid, so we probably included in our "blow" a Boche mine laid ready for us. We easily bombed off a party of his which tried to rush the crater, and spent the day re-building our fallen parapet.

Rations, ammunition and R.E. material in this sector were brought to the "Talus des Zouaves" on mule-drawn trucks along a narrow-gauge Railway from Mont St. Eloi. Here, at a big Corps R.E. Dump, the trucks were loaded every evening, the mule teams hooked in, and the party set off, much harassed at times by bullets and shells, and seldom reaching home without losing one, and often two animals. The Dump in the "Talus" also got shelled; but the steep banks made the danger light and not much damage was done in this way, though the Boche kept up a prolonged bombardment at it with 5.9's on the evening of the 14th. Except for this, the rest of the tour passed quietly, and on the following night the 4th Lincolnshires relieved us, and we went back to rest in Camblain L'Abbé huts, where we stayed for six days.

Our second tour started on the 21st, and from this day onwards until we finally left the sector, we had a bad time. Our first trouble was the weather. Alternate frosts and thaws, rain and snow, soon filled our trenches with mud and slush, into which parapets and parados either crumbled gradually or collapsed wholesale. No sooner could we repair one length, than another would give way, and through it all many posts had to live with water over their ankles and no proper drying accommodation. There had to be three companies in the line, so 24-hour reliefs were impossible, and to increase our troubles our stay in a warm climate had made us less capable of standing the exposure to cold and wet, and there were many cases of trench fever, trench foot, and some pneumonia, while the health of all was considerably impaired. One of the most pitiful sights of the war was to see 20 of our men crawling on hands and knees to the Aid Post—their feet so bad that they could not walk.

Meanwhile the underground war was not as satisfactory as we should have liked, and the Boche undoubtedly had the upper hand in the mining. Our galleries were few and short, and in consequence useless for either offence or defence, while his were known to be near our trenches in several places. In one place between the right and centre companies the Lincolnshires had expected a " blow " at any moment, and evacuating their front line, had dug a new trench ten yards in rear of it. This seemed to have been sighted in such a haphazard sort of way that it was at once named the "Harry Tate" trench by some humorist, who pictured a Company Commander coming out and saying "What shall we do next? Let's dig a trench." And so they dug this one—quite useless, for it was bound to be engulfed by any mine which exploded under the front line. The Boche, however, thought more of the new trench than we did, and the day after it was built, bombarded it with heavy minenwerfer shells until it was unrecognisable.

In this state we found it when we came in for our second tour, "C" Company (Farmer) on the right and "A" Company (Ward Jackson) in the centre. Our first morning the Boche started just before midday, and for four hours rained heavy minenwerfer shells on these two Companies, and particularly on the new trench. Fortunately there was no one in this, and equally fortunately most of the shells fell between our front line and supports; there was a thick mist at the time, and it was almost impossible to judge their flight. Through it all Capt. Farmer walked calmly from post to post, cheering the garrison, and just before the end of the bombardment at 4-0 p.m., made his way down the small communication trench towards his support platoon. Thence he went to call on "B" Company, but was caught on the way back by a mortar, which he probably could not see coming in the mist (for no one was more accurate at judging their flight than he), and was killed instantly, being blown out of the trench and lost for several hours. Captain Farmer was perhaps the quietest, certainly the bravest, officer of his time, for he feared nothing, and nothing could shake his calm, while it was said of him that he was never angry and never despondent. When he was killed, "C" Company lost their leader, and every man his best friend, while the mess lost one who was the most cheerful comrade of every officer.

This bombardment left our front line in a terrible condition, and General Kemp decided to build a new main line of resistance 50 yards in rear, holding the front with odd posts only. Meanwhile the front parapet must be repaired, and the night was spent in doing this as far as we could—a hopeless task, for the following afternoon we were again hammered. This time "A" Company suffered most, and Corporal Williamson and one man were killed, Serjt. Staniforth and one other wounded, while the trench was blown in for several yards and a dug-out demolished. Dug-outs were few, and consisted only of little hutches formed by putting a sheet of iron over some slot. Even Company Headquarters of the centre Company had little more than this, though Battalion Headquarters and the other companies had a half-deep dug-out.

The bombardments now became daily, and all our efforts at retaliation either with artillery or trench mortars proved entirely ineffectual. There was nothing we could do except clear as many men as possible away from the danger area, and come back at dusk to rebuild our parapet. Towards the end of the tour the Boche started firing rifle grenades before each mortar, so that we should stoop to avoid the former and so miss seeing the flight of the latter. The tour ended with a four-inch fall of snow on the 26th, which melted almost at once and filled the trenches with water, which no amount of pumping would remedy. After relief we went to the " Talus des Zouaves " in Brigade support, except for " C " Company (Moore), which went to the Cabaret Rouge—now used as Brigade advanced Headquarters.

The East side of the valley, where the Support Battalion's dug-outs had been built, was immune from German shells owing to the steepness of the hill side, and here for six days we had comparative rest, except at nights, when we most of us went digging on the new line. The Battalion Grenadiers under Serjeant Goodman particularly enjoyed themselves, and their dug-out in the valley became a regular anarchists' arsenal. Fiendish missiles were made out of empty bottles stuffed with ammonal and other explosives, which they managed to obtain in large quantities from the French miners, while the strength of various poisons and gases was tested against the rats, against whose habitations they carried on an endless war. A catapult was erected for practice purposes, and our bombers became adepts in its use, knowing exactly how much fuse to attach to a T.N.T.-filled glass beer bottle to make it burst two seconds after landing in the Boche trench. The valley was a little dangerous during practice hours, but nobody minded this so long as the enemy suffered in the end.

At the same time another innovation was introduced in the shape of the Stokes light trench mortar—a stove-pipe-like gun firing a cylindrical shell some 400 yards at the rate of 8 in the air at once. It was simply necessary to drop the shell into the gun, at the bottom of which was a striker, and the rest was automatic and almost noiseless, the shock of discharge being rather like a polite cough. Brigade Trench Mortar Companies were formed, in our case 2nd Lieuts. A. N. Bloor and W. R. Ashwell, with several other ranks, went to join the first company.

On the 2nd March, having received a draft of three N.C.O.'s and 106 men, we went once more to the line and took over from the 4th Lincolnshires. This time we were able to have two Companies in front, one in Boisselet trench, part of the new work, and one in reserve, a far more satisfactory distribution. The trenches were still in a very bad state, and it was found in many places quite impossible to dig new lines, because the ground had been so shaken by continuous bombardment for more than a year, that the soil would no longer bind, and the sides of any new trench collapsed almost as soon as they were dug. The tour was fairly quiet, though Boche snipers and artillery were more active than before, and we reached Camblain L'Abbé at the end of it without having suffered any repetition of the trench mortar bombardments.

Our six days' rest included two big working parties, two inspections, and one demonstration, to say nothing of such minor details as church parades, conferences, baths, and the usual overhauling of boots and clothing. The work consisted of clearing dug-outs in the Bois des Alleux, and only lasted two days, after which we polished ourselves for General Kemp, who inspected us in a field near Camblain, and said that he was much pleased indeed with our turnout. General Montagu-Stuart-Wortley was equally complimentary at the second inspection, and congratulated all ranks on their appearance and smartness, which, considering the state of the trenches, was very creditable. The demonstration was particularly interesting, and proved the futility of the famous German flame projector. As many men as possible were placed in a trench, while the demonstrator, standing at 30 feet away with the machine, turned on the flame. The wind was behind him, and the flame, with a tremendous roar, leapt out about 30 yards. But the noise was the worst part, for the burning liquid, vapourising as it left the machine, became lighter than air, and in spite of all the efforts of the Demonstrator, could not be made to sink into the trench, whose occupants were untouched. The men were all rather amused at the whole performance and suggested that we should bring the machine into the line to warm them up on cold days.

On the 12th we marched once more to the line and relieved the 4th Lincolnshires, this time for a four-day tour. We found on arrival that the Boche a few hours previously had blown a large mine in the left sector, to be occupied by " D " Company (Shields), so that in addition to the work on the new trench, we had to supply many men for repairing this new damage—no light task, for many yards of our front trench had disappeared. To make work more difficult the Boche was continually throwing bombs and rifle grenades to try and catch our working parties, and it was only after two days' vigorous retaliation that we taught him that it was wiser to keep quiet. The leading spirit in this retaliation was Captain Shields himself, who would sit in his dug-out listening for a German bomb. If he heard one he would rush out, coat off and sleeves rolled up, and throw back as many Mills' bombs as he could lay hands on, a formidable attack, for he could throw a tremendous distance. 2nd Lieut. A. E.

Brodribb was also a keen bomber who would stand at a post and send back bomb for bomb until he had the Boche beaten. Meanwhile the Battalion anarchists, though they had bad luck with the "West" spring gun, which got buried in the bombardment, were very successful in other ways. Serjeant Goodman, with his catapult, flinging home-made infernal machines, first from one post, then from another, must have been very annoying to the German sentries, while Cpl. Archer, firing salvoes of rifle grenades, eight at a time, always had a quietening effect on any Boche bomber who ventured to try his luck in this way. So far as bombs were concerned we had the upper hand, but the Boche could always start heavy shelling or mortaring, and against this we seemed to have no effective retaliation. He did particularly heavy damage with these one morning in this tour, a few hours after we had been visited by General Byng, the Corps Commander, who went round the front line. On this occasion we had two killed and six wounded by a direct hit on the trench, while the F.O.O., who was observing at the time, was also badly wounded.

Towards the end of the tour the situation became quieter and we went once more into the Talus to wait for relief by the 25th Division, whose advance parties had already visited the line, and who were expected in a few days. The Boyau d'Ersatz, re-named Ersatz Alley for the sake of simplicity, had lately been heavily shelled, and it was therefore decided to open up Boyau 1, 2, 3, as an alternative route to trenches, calling it "Wortley Avenue," in honour of the Major General. Parties from all companies worked day and night at this, soon making it passable, though it would always be dangerously exposed to view. Unfortunately "A" Company were shelled one day while at work, and we lost 2nd Lieut. Pickworth, who had to be sent to Hospital, and eventually to England, with a bad wound in the lungs.

Meanwhile offensive mining operations were being undertaken by both sides with increased activity. The British Tunnellers, who had relieved the French mining companies, found that in several places, unless they themselves blew big mines at once, the Boche would blow them instead, so blew big craters without delay. To this the Boche retaliated, and for the past week there had been an average of two mines a night on the Divisional front, most of them in the sector on our right. But on the night of the 20th our Brigade was also involved, and the 4th Lincolnshires lost most of their centre company in an explosion which demolished nearly 100 yards of their front line. The shock was terrific, and could be felt so violently even in our valley behind, that Captain Barton went to see what had happened. Some half-hour later, when the Lincolnshire C.O. went to the scene of the disaster, he found the "Doc" there by himself, digging out an injured man in the middle of the gap. No British troops had yet arrived, and his nearest neighbours were the Boche lobbing bombs from the other side of the new crater.

This latest blow shattered our front line so badly that it was quite unfit to hand over to a new Division, taking over this part of the line for the first time, and, as the Lincolnshires had not enough men to repair it themselves, we had to help them. On the 21st, therefore, when the rest of the Battalion was relieved by the Lancashire Fusiliers and went back for the night to

Camblain L'Abbé, "D" Company stayed behind in the Talus till dusk and then went up to work, spending the night under R.E. supervision, digging in the gap. A screen of bombers lay out on the crater lip, while the rest worked, through mud, water and pouring rain to try and produce some kind of fighting trench. As fast as they dug, their new work collapsed, but at last a cut was made, and by morning there was at least communication across the gap, though the trench was terribly shallow and gave no real protection. The following day, "D" Company on lorries, the rest of the Battalion by march route, we moved through Cambligneul and Aubigny to Penin-Doffine, where we were to billet for a rest. "B" and "C" Companies were with Brigade Headquarters and the Lincolnshires in Penin. The Headquarters and "D" Company had a large farm, and "A" Company billets in the hamlet of Doffine.

Here we stayed for a week. A Staff ride under the Brigadier formed the chief incident in our training, while our recreation was enlivened by an excellent Battalion Sports Meeting. Great keenness was shown in every event, and there were consequently some well-contested races :—"A" and "C" Companies divided the prizes between them. "A" Company won the long-distance bomb-throwing, tug-of-war, relay and stretcher-bearer races, "C" the accurate bomb-throwing, ¼-mile, sack and three-legged races. Brigade Headquarters came to watch, bringing their band with them, and the General gave away the prizes at the end of the day. The weather was good and we all spent a very pleasant afternoon.

The 27th April brought us orders to return again to

the line, this time to work with the Tunnellers, French and English, in the neighbourhood of Neuville St. Vaast. The following day the C.O. and most of the Company Officers went to Mont St. Eloi to reconnoitre, returning in the evening. While getting into a car in St. Eloi Colonel Jones was slightly wounded in the left hand by a six-inch shell, which burst alongside the car. He was sent to Hospital, but returned to us ten days later. On the 29th we moved into Neuville St. Vaast, living in tunnels and dug-outs, and provided large working parties in the mines. Tactically we were at the disposal of the 25th Division, to whom we lent one or two Lewis Gun teams. The work consisted almost entirely of clearing sandbags from the mine-shafts and distributing them along our trenches, as far as possible out of sight. It was hard and dangerous work, as was proved by an accident which happened on the 7th May, the night before we were relieved. The enemy blew a counter-mine close to one of the saps where " D " Company were working, burying the French miners, and completely destroying the whole sap. Two of the four men at work were never seen again; the other two, bruised and shaken, managed to crawl half-naked out of the wreckage.

On the 9th May, after spending a night in tents at Mont St. Eloi, we went by motor-'bus through Avesnes-le-comte, Liencourt, Grand Rullecourt, to Lucheux, where we went into billets. We left at Vimy a party of 25 men under Lieut. A. M. Barrowcliffe, working with the R.E. (Tunnellers). Most of them gradually became sappers, and we saw very few of them ever again. During these two last months there had been only one important change in the personnel. R.Q.M.S.

Stimson, who had been at the Stores since the beginning of the war, and whose knowledge of French had been as invaluable to Captain Worley as his energy and skill with "mobilisation store stables," returned to England. C.S.M. Gorse became R.Q.M.S., and in his place J. Hill became C.S.M. of "A" Company.

CHAPTER VII.

GOMMECOURT.

10th May, 1916.   3rd July, 1916.

The next ten days, spent in Lucheux, were as pleasant as any in the war. After the mud, cold and damp of Vimy, we could well appreciate the spring weather, the good billets and the excellent country in which we now found ourselves. Lucheux, a very old French village with its castle and gateway, stands on the edge of a still older forest a few miles North of Doullens, and the majority of the inhabitants, under the guidance of a very energetic Mayor, did all they could to make us comfortable. Work was not too hard, and our chief labour was making wattle revetments in the forest—a good task for a hot day—and practising musketry on a home-made rifle range outside the village. The mounted officers were particularly fortunate, for the forest was full of tracks and rides, and each morning soon after dawn the more energetic could be seen cantering under the dripping trees in the early morning May mists—bare headed and in shirt sleeves.

Meanwhile the arrival of some new officers filled the gaps in the Mess caused by Vimy. First Colonel Jones returned, with the piece of shrapnel still in his hand, but otherwise very fit. Soon afterwards two new officers, 2nd Lieutenants H. A. Lowe and G. E. Banwell, joined us, and at the same time Capt. R. C.

L. Mould and Lieut. D. B. Petch returned from England. Several large drafts of N.C.O.'s and men arrived, many of them old hands, who had been wounded, some of them more than once, although as we know well there were many soldiers in England who had never yet seen a day's fighting.

Just at this time another important change was made in our training. For many months now we had been taught the bomb to the exclusion of almost every other weapon, now at last the bayonet was returning to its former position of importance. The great exponent of the art of bayonet fighting was a Major Campbell, of the Army Gymnastic Staff, whose lectures were already well known at the Army Schools, and who was now sent round the country to talk to all Battalions. He had devised an entirely new scheme of bayonet instruction on very simple yet practical lines, doing away with many of the old drill-book "points and parries," and training arm and rifle to act with the eye, not on a word of command. His powers as a lecturer were as great as his keenness for his subject, and for two hours he held the attention of a hall full of all ranks, speaking so vividly that not one of us but came away feeling that we were good enough to fight six Boche, given a bayonet. He was particularly insistent on not driving the bayonet home too far, and we shall always remember his "throat two inches is enough, kidneys only four inches, just in and out." His system has now been adopted throughout the British Army, and all 1917 recruits were trained in it, but to us it came none too soon, for we were fast forgetting that we ever had such a weapon as a bayonet.

On the 20th May our work in the forest came to an

end and, as the Brigade was wanted for fatigues nearer the line, we moved by Pommera and Pas to Souastre, a village about three miles from the front trenches. The Sherwood Foresters were at present holding the Divisional front, and our chief task in the new area was digging cable trenches from back Headquarter positions to forward batteries and observation posts, building and stocking ammunition and bomb stores, and assisting in the construction of numerous gun pits. In fact, we were once more preparing as fast as possible for a "big push," though at the moment it was not quite certain who was going to do the pushing; rumour allotted this task to the 46th Division. The work was very hard, for digging a deep narrow trench, or loading flints at Warlincourt quarries are no light tasks, and the weather made conditions even more difficult than they might otherwise have been. One day it was so hot as to make continuous work for more than a few hours impossible, while the next, there would be three or four torrential rain storms, filling all the trenches, and turning the cross-country tracks to avenues of mud.

However, in spite of our work, we managed to have some football, and the Divisional Commander once more presented a cup. We started well, beating the 5th Lincolnshires in the second round, but then found ourselves opposed to our old rivals, the 4th Battalion, for the Brigade finals. The game caused the keenest excitement, and with the score at two goals all, the enthusiasm through the second half was immense. Unfortunately, there is a fate against our defeating the 4th Battalion, and, just before the end, our opponents managed to score the winning goal.

On the 24th May the heavy rain had made the

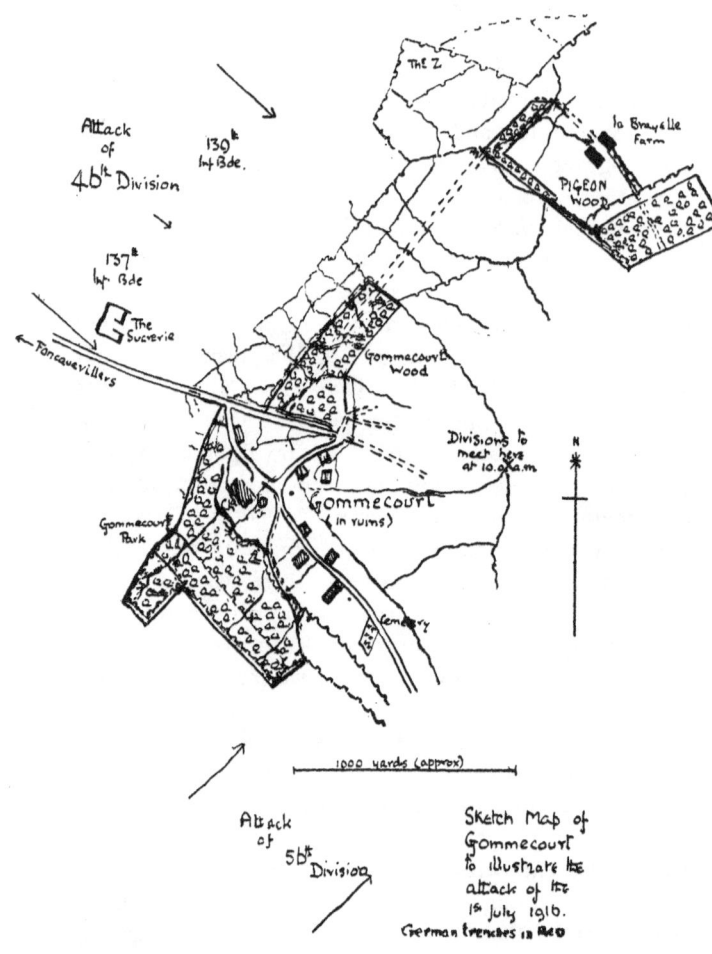

Lens from the Air
(showing Fosse III. and Bois de Riaumont).

Lt.-Col. J. B. O. Trimble, D.S.O., M.C., and the Officers, Marqueffles Farm, June, 1917.

trenches so wet that the garrison was unable to keep them clear, and in consequence we had to send a large working party up the line to help the Sherwood Foresters. The line, which we now saw for the first time, ran from about half a mile North of Hébuterne, just East of Foncquevillers, and northwards towards Monchy-au-bois, held by the enemy. Foncquevillers was the centre of the position, and opposite it lay Gommecourt, a small village and Chateau, with a wood on one flank and the Chateau park on the other—a strong position strongly held. Further North, Pigeon Wood and a little salient of trenches called the "Z" were opposite the left of our Divisional front, while in the middle of No Man's Land, which averaged about 400 yards wide, stood the ruins of Gommecourt Sucrerie, twenty yards from the main Foncquevillers-Gommecourt Road.

Our trenches were in a somewhat curious condition. During the winter the Division occupying this sector had found that they were too weak to hold the whole trench, so had selected certain positions which they had strongly fortified and wired, and then filled the remainder of the trench with loose wire. The bad weather soon caused the disused sections of the trench to collapse, fixing the loose wire very firmly on either side. From a purely defensive point of view there was no harm in this, but any attacking force would need the whole trench for assembly purposes and to "jump off," and the work of clearing the long wired-up sections was very hard indeed. The posts themselves were well dug and well sighted, there were one or two good communication trenches, and Foncquevillers, still well preserved in spite of its proximity to the Boche, provided excellent homes for Battalion Headquarters, support Companies, and even baths and canteen. The enemy, except for some "rum jars" and heavy trench mortars from Gommecourt, was fairly quiet on the whole front, and, except when trousers had to be discarded to allow of wading in the front line, the trenches were by no means uncomfortable.

For the rest of May we stayed at Souastre, occasionally visiting the line with working parties, or on tours of inspection, but for the most part working in the Foncquevillers plain, where battery positions without number were being built. By the end of the month we learnt the meaning of all these preparations. Gommecourt was to be attacked in the near future in conjunction with other greater attacks further South. The Staffords and the Sherwood Foresters were going to do the attack with their right on the Sucrerie, their left on the "Z," while the 56th Division on our right would attack the village from the S.E. The Park, most of the village, and the Chateau would thus not be directly attacked, but it was hoped that the two Divisions would meet on the East side, and so cut off large numbers of Germans in the isolated area. Our Brigade was to be in reserve. Meanwhile, a large full-sized model of the German lines was dug near Lucheux forest, where the attacking Brigades started practising at once. Incidentally the model took many acres of arable land, and, though it was very well paid for, the French grumbled loudly, and the 46th Division was known in Lucheux as "les autres Boches."

On the evening of the 4th June we moved up through Foncquevillers, and relieved the 5th Sherwood Foresters in the right sector, opposite Gommecourt

Park. A road and bank, running parallel with the front line, and about 300 yards behind it, provided Battalion Headquarters. Behind this again, the "Bluff," a steep bank, gave the support Company a good home. Here we remained until the 21st, with a two-days' holiday at Humbercamps in the middle, a holiday spent in digging cable trenches and carrying trench mortars and ammunition. It was a long time to remain in the line, but one Company lived always in a large house in Foncquevillers, where they were very comfortable, and could get baths and other luxuries.

The enemy was not very active, and our most important task was now to prevent him from guessing our intentions. This soon became impossible, for, in addition to the ever increasing Artillery, the new cable trenches, and the Lucheux model, we started to dig a new line of trenches some 100 yards in front of our front line, along the attack sector. We, being opposite the Park, did not have to do this, but the Division on our right and the rest of our Brigade on the left were both out digging every night. After the first night it became exceedingly dangerous, for the Boche, knowing exactly where we were working, kept up a steady bombardment on the right with trench mortars, and, on the left, swept the ground continuously with accurate machine gun fire. We were ordered to keep all hostile patrols out of No Man's Land, and consequently our parties were out most of the night. The Boche, however, showed no inclination to do the same, and, even though we fixed up an insulting notice board in front of his wire, never put in an appearance. Incidentally the back of the board was covered with luminous paint, and a Lewis gun was trained on it, so that any interference would have been promptly dealt with.

Before we left the sector we were reinforced by a draft of eight subaltern officers—2nd Lieuts. A. Emmerson, F. W. A. Salmon, W. H. Reynolds, A. S. Heffill, A. W. C. Zelley, M. J. S. Dyson, W. K. Callard, and S. G. H. Street, while at the same time we lost 2nd Lieut. Brittain, who went to Hospital and thence to England.

After practising their attack several times, the Staffordshires found that they had more tasks to fulfill than they could accomplish. Accordingly they asked for help, and were allotted one Battalion from our Brigade, for which duty we, having suffered least at Hohenzollern, were chosen. We were to advance as a ninth wave behind the attackers, carrying stores and ammunition; while one Company was to dig a trench joining the Sucrerie to the German front line—a communication trench for use after the fight. As soon as we left trenches and reached a hut camp at Warlincourt we, too, started practising for the battle, which, we were told, would take place at dawn on the 29th June.

Any account of our doings during this month would be incomplete without a reference to our one relaxation. The Divisional Concert Party, started in 1915, had more or less ceased to exist, but in Souastre in a large barn, the 56th Divisional troupe, the " Bow Bells," performed nightly to crowded houses. Many of us found time to go more than once, and will always remember with pleasure the songs, dances, and sketches, the drummer-ballet-dancer, and the catching melodies of " O Roger Rum " and other nonsense.

Meanwhile, feverish preparations were being made for the coming battle, while the weather was as bad as possible. There never was a wetter June, and the new assembly trenches, the recently cleared or newly dug communication trenches, Derby Dyke, Nottingham, Stafford, Lincoln and Leicester Lanes, Roberts Avenue and "Crawl Boys Lane," and the cable trenches were always full of water. Work on the gun pits was seriously delayed, and many batteries had to move in before their pits were complete. Fortunately the enemy's artillery was not too active, and Foncquevillers was almost left alone, though he did one day bombard the Church. No damage was done, except that afterwards the one remaining face of the clock stated the time as 2-15 instead of 11-45, as for the past many months. The village was full of stores and explosives, and almost every cellar held a bomb or ammunition reserve, while the Church crypt was filled with Mills and Stokes mortars under the care of Serjeant Goodman.

On the 24th June our Artillery registration started, and, with early morning bombardments and sudden harassing shoots at night, we made a considerable noise—"the sullen puffs of high explosives bursting in battalions," as Beach Thomas wrote in the "Daily Mail"—and clearly showed the Boche that we meant business. This apparently was the intention of the Staff, for, as the main attack was to be South of us, it was the object of the IIIrd. Army to attract as many enemy as possible on this the extreme flank of the attack. So successful were we, that we did actually frighten the enemy into reinforcing the Gommecourt area with an extra Division—unfortunate for us who were to attack the place, but doubtless of value to the 4th Army, who would thus have one Division less against them. Gommecourt was naturally strong, and this addition to the garrison made it doubly so, while the Artillery found it very difficult to destroy the wire which was thick along the whole front. The trees in the wood were all wired, and there were strong belts in front of every trench, so that our field guns and trench mortars were kept hard at work almost all day every day in their efforts to cut sufficient gaps for us. The enemy's guns replied by registering our communication trenches, and then remained silent.

The camp at Warlincourt was uncomfortable, and had no officers' mess, a luxury which we much needed. However, Colour-Serjeant Collins displayed his usual skill, and, while Major Toller fixed up a home-made marquee of wagon sheets and odd tarpaulins, he managed to carry on the cooking almost in the open. In spite of the rain which came through the roof and under the sides we had some excellent evenings, and managed to enjoy ourselves. Our work was mostly training, which now included rapid wiring. In this we held a competition, finally won by " B " Company, who put out a " double apron " French wire fence 20 yards long in just over four minutes—a good performance, though the other Companies declared that this fence would not have stopped a rabbit, to say nothing of a Boche. Meanwhile, Major Toller suddenly received orders to report to the 51st Division to command a battalion of the Argyle and Sutherland Highlanders, and, much to his disgust, had to leave us just before the fight. In any case he would have been out of the fight, for the authorities had at last realized the madness of sending a whole Battalion into action, and to avoid a repetition of the post-Hohenzollern difficulties, every Battalion was ordered to leave behind, at Souastre, the 2nd in Command and a proportion of officers, N.C.O.'s and specialists. These, known as the "Battle Details," were subsequently increased in number, and later a G.H.Q. publication fixed exactly who would and who would not accompany a battalion into battle. As Major Beasley had left us at Vimy and not returned, Capt. Shields became 2nd in Command and had to stay behind, a cruel blow to him, for he was essentially a fighting man. His Company, "D," was taken by Lieut. J. W. Tomson of "A" Company. Capt. Ward Jackson had "A," Capt. Knighton "B," and Capt. Moore "C." R.S.M. R. E. Small was accidentally wounded during revolver practice, and during the few weeks that he was away his place was taken by C.S.M. J. Weir.

During the last two days before the battle the weather became worse, and the rain fell in torrents. Ours was a comparatively dry sector of the line, and yet our trenches were full of water, so that the country in the neighbourhood of the Somme valley became impossible. So bad was it that at the last moment the whole offensive was postponed until 48 hours later—the 1st July. The attacking Brigades had already occupied their front line and assembly positions before the new cancelling order arrived, and the Staff had now to decide whether to leave them for 48 hours in these hopelessly wet trenches, or take them back to rest—the latter course would necessitate two marches, in and out, in two days. The matter was settled by the Corps Commander, who wished to see another practice attack over the Lucheux trenches, so the 4th Leicestershires and 4th Lincolnshires held the line while Staffords and

Sherwood Foresters marched back. It was a long way, nearly eleven miles, from Foncquevillers to Lucheux, and by the time they returned to trenches on the 30th they were all very tired. However, every man knew exactly what to do, where to go and when; the most minute details had been worked out, and even individuals as well as sections and platoons had been given definite tasks, so there was every prospect of a successful fight the next day. It was true the wire was in several places uncut, but still there were plenty of gaps, and this should be no obstacle.

Soon after midnight 30th June/1st July all the attacking troops were in position, and we moved up to Midland Trench, an assembly trench running North and South about 700 yards West of Foncquevillers Church. "A" Company (Ward Jackson) and "D" Company (Tomson) were in cellars and dug-outs in the village, since they would be wanted first. There were many communication trenches along the front, up which we should advance, for at the last moment all were made "up" trenches until after the attack; originally some were "up" and some "down." This eleventh hour alteration caused considerable confusion later. Meanwhile, throughout the night our gunners fired continuously on the Boche trenches, villages, and particularly roads and railways, for we wished, if possible, to stop all rations and ammunition from the Gommecourt garrison.

Dawn came at last—a fine day. At 6-24 our barrage started, far more intense than anything we had used during the previous days, so that the Boche may have guessed what was going to happen. Smoke shells were mixed with the H.E., and at 7-30 a smoke trench mortar screen was put down, and the Infantry advanced. Four waves crossed No Man's Land, and then the smoke blew away and the whole of our attack was revealed. On the right the Staffords, passing the Sucrerie, found the German wire still strong, and had to struggle through where they could, only to find many enemy with their machine guns undamaged by our bombardment. On the left the 5th and 7th Sherwood Foresters entered the Wood and pressed on, leaving the first enemy lines to the rear waves. But the smoke had gone and these rear waves had no protection. As the fifth line left our trenches it was met with machine gun fire from the North, from the " Z " and from the front line, over which the Sherwood Foresters had passed. None the less the wave struggled on, until artillery was added to machine guns, field guns from Monchy enfiladed No Man's Land, every German battery sent its shells into the carrying parties, and the attack was stopped. The two leading Staffordshire Battalions, except for a few who reached the enemy's lines, were held up on his wire or near the Sucrerie, where many fell. The two leading Sherwood Foresters had crossed No Man's Land almost unscathed, had entered the German lines complete, and were never seen again. Commanding Officers, Battalion Headquarters and their Companies were lost. The other four Battalions, after losing their leading wave, remained in our front trenches and sent back messages for more smoke, while here and there gallant efforts were made by platoons and sections to take help into the wood.

Meanwhile, Capt. Ward Jackson with his Company Serjeant Major—J. R. Hill—and two platoons (Hepworth and Salmon) went forward with the leading parties to dig their trench from the Sucrerie. In spite of the heavy fire, and the losses of the attacking Brigades, they started work and actually marked out their trench. But their task was impossible. Capt. Ward Jackson, hit in the back and shoulder and very badly wounded, was only saved by Serjt. Major Hill, who pluckily carried him out of the fight; and, seeing that the attack had failed, 2nd Lieut. Hepworth ordered the party back to our lines, where they found the rest of the Battalion in the support line and communication trenches, waiting for the Staffordshires to move forward.

The situation was now critical. So far as we knew, the attack of the 56th Division on our right had been successful, yet, if we did not meet them by 2 p.m. on the far side of Gommecourt, not only would the operation be a failure, but there was every probability of their being cut off by the Germans in Gommecourt Park. An attempt was therefore made to re-organize at once for another attack, but this was found impossible. Our lines, hopelessly sticky from the bad weather, were now congested with dead and wounded; the communication trenches were jammed with stretcher cases and parties coming in, the "up" and "down" rules were not observed, and, above all, the enemy's artillery enfiladed the front line from the North, the communications from the East. The Division on our left did nothing by way of counter battery work, and we were left to face their opposing artillery as well as our own. There was also another serious difficulty to re-organization. The men were too well trained in their particular duties. A private soldier who has been told every day for a month that his one duty will be to carry a box of bombs to point Q, cannot readily forget that, and take an efficient part in an ordinary unrehearsed attack. This, the Staff soon discovered, and, to give time for all arrangements to be made, a new attack was ordered for 3-30 p.m. with artillery and, if possible, a smoke screen.

Meanwhile, the enemy's artillery was still active, and we suffered. 2nd Lieut. Callard, a most promising junior officer, was killed, and with him C.S.M. F. Johnson of " C " Company. 2nd Lieuts. Russell and Creed were both wounded, and six men killed and several wounded at the same time, nearly all by shells in the communication trenches.

At 3-30 p.m. our Artillery opened once more and our Companies started forward, only to find that the Staffordshires made no move. It was not surprising. Many of them had not yet heard the time for the new attack, many were too tired to be much use, no one was really ready though some few tried to leave our lines. Such an assault was bound to fail, and fortunately Col. Jones, who was on the spot and just about to start with Capt. Allen, received the order to cancel the attack. It would have been a useless waste of lives, for no good could have come of such a half-hearted effort. Half-an-hour later the Staffordshires were ordered to withdraw and the 5th Leicestershires to take over the front line, while the 5th Lincolnshires came in on our left and relieved the Sherwood Foresters.

All hope of trying to help the Division on our right had to be abandoned. They had reached the enemy's third line and captured several prisoners in the morning; some of them actually reached the meeting place, but they, too, had to face two sectors of opposing artillery, for the attack on Serre on their right had failed, and their carrying parties and all supports for the leading units were hopelessly enfiladed from the South. Their losses were very heavy, and in the evening, when it became obvious that we could never help them, they left the enemy's lines and returned to their own trenches. But there was still hope of saving some of the missing Sherwood Foresters. They were known to have reached the wood, for their lights had been seen by our contact patrol aeroplane. Unfortunately at mid-day this aeroplane ran into the cable of the kite balloon, and both were out of action for some hours—a most unlucky accident. In case some of these Sherwood Foresters might be still alive, the 5th Lincolnshires made another advance at midnight—only a few minutes after arriving in the line—but found the enemy present in strength, and lost heavily before they could regain our lines.

The rest of the night and all the following day were spent in collecting the wounded and dead from our lines, from the newly dug and now water-logged assembly trench in front, and from No Man's Land. Once more Capt. Barton displayed the most wonderful courage, rescuing three men from a shell hole, in broad daylight, less than 200 yards from the German lines, and spending the whole day wandering about from one part to another, quite regardless of the danger so long as he could find a wounded man to help. The next day was spent in the same way, and by the evening the trenches had been considerably tidied up, when, at 9 p.m. we were relieved by the London Regt. (Rangers), and marched back to Bienvillers au Bois, leaving some guides behind to help the newcomers. These last two days cost us several casualties, amongst them Serjt. R. E. Foster, who was badly wounded by a shell.

After the battle, General Snow, the Corps Commander, sent round the following message:—"The Corps Commander wishes to congratulate the troops of the 46th Division for the manner in which they fought and endured during the fighting on the 1st July. Many gallant acts, both by units and individuals, are to hand. Although Gommecourt has not fallen into our hands, the purpose of the attack, which was mainly to contain and kill Germans, was accomplished." To this was added: "The Major General Commanding wishes all ranks to understand thoroughly that our recent attack on the Gommecourt salient in concert with the 56th Division embraced two purposes: (a) The capture of the position; (b) The retaining of considerable numbers of German troops in our immediate front in order to prevent them taking part in resisting the advance of our troops in the South. Although the first purpose was not achieved, the second was fulfilled, and there is no doubt that our action on the first materially assisted our troops in the 4th Army and contributed to their success. The above to be read to all troops on parade."

In spite of this somewhat comforting message, our action on the 1st was a failure. This cannot be denied. The retaining enemy's troops on our front was done by our Artillery and other preparation, and the extra German Division was lured into the line opposite us at least three days before the battle. Our assault made not the slightest difference to this. Our object on the 1st was to capture Gommecourt, and this we failed to do. It is comparatively easy to criticise after the event and find mistakes, but there were one or two obvious reasons for the failure which were apparent to all. The rapid dispersal of the smoke barrage, the terrible enfilade bombardment from the left consequent on the inactivity of the Division on our left, the failure of our Artillery to smash up German posts, and in some cases German wire, and, perhaps the fact that our preparations were so obvious that the Boche was waiting for us. But in the face of all this, fresh troops in ideal conditions might have succeeded. Ours were tired after their journey to Lucheux and back, had had to live several nights in hopelessly foul and waterlogged trenches, and, so far from fresh, were almost worn before they started to attack.

CHAPTER VIII.

MONCHY AU BOIS.

3rd July, 1916.   29th Oct., 1916.

NORTH of Gommecourt the enemy's line, after passing Pigeon wood, ran a few yards West of Essarts village along the high ground to within a short distance of Monchy au Bois, then, turning West, made a small salient round this village, which lay in a cup-like hollow. Between Essarts and Monchy, and on higher ground still, stood Le Quesnoy Farm, which, with some long tall hedges in the neighbourhood, provided the Boche with excellent and well concealed observation posts and battery positions. Behind Monchy itself, and again on high ground, was Adinfer wood, and near it Douchy village, both full of well concealed batteries, while the trees in Monchy itself gave the enemy plenty of cover for machine guns and trench mortars. Opposite this our line was almost entirely in the open. From Foncquevillers it ran due North to the Hannescamps-Monchy road, more than 1,000 yards from the enemy opposite Essarts and Le Quesnoy; then, crossing the ridge, dropped steeply to the Monchy cup, where, at the Bienvillers road, the lines were only 200 yards apart. The only buildings near the line were the two Monchy mills, North and South, both about 80 yards from the front line and both little more than a heap of bricks with an O.P. concealed in the middle. Just South of the Bienvillers road a small salient, some 180 yards across ran out towards the enemy's lines, overlooked from two sides, and always being battered out of recognition by trench mortars and bombs .

The rest of our front line system was more or less ordinary—deep trenches with, at intervals, a " ruined " dug-out for Company Headquarters. Owing to the appalling weather all trenches were very wet, including the communication trenches, of which there were several—Chiswick Avenue opposite Essarts, Lulu Lane alongside the Hannescamps road, with Collingbourne Avenue branching off it, and, on the Monchy side, Shell Street in the middle, and Stoneygate Street alongside the Bienvillers road. The last had been so named by the Leicestershire " New Army " Brigade, who had originally built the trench. Hannescamps, a minute village, lay 1,000 yards from the line, partly hidden by a hollow, and, with an excellent bank full of dug-outs, was a home for Battalion Headquarters and one Company. Another Headquarters was in Shell Street, and the Support Battalion, with many batteries and others, lived in Bienvillers au Bois, about 1½ behind the line. Pommier, la Cauchie, and occasionally Humbercamps were rest billets still further back. Beyond them a large farm, la Bazéque, was the home of all the Brigade transport and Q.M. Stores. Such was the sector into which the Division went after Gommecourt to rest and gradually recuperate. Our Brigade had the Monchy front and the stretch with the wide No Man's Land opposite Essarts; we, as a Battalion, were sometimes North, sometimes South of the Hannescamps Road, the other Brigades were further North, in the

Red Mill, Lens, 1917.

Bois de Riaumont from the top of the Slag Heap.

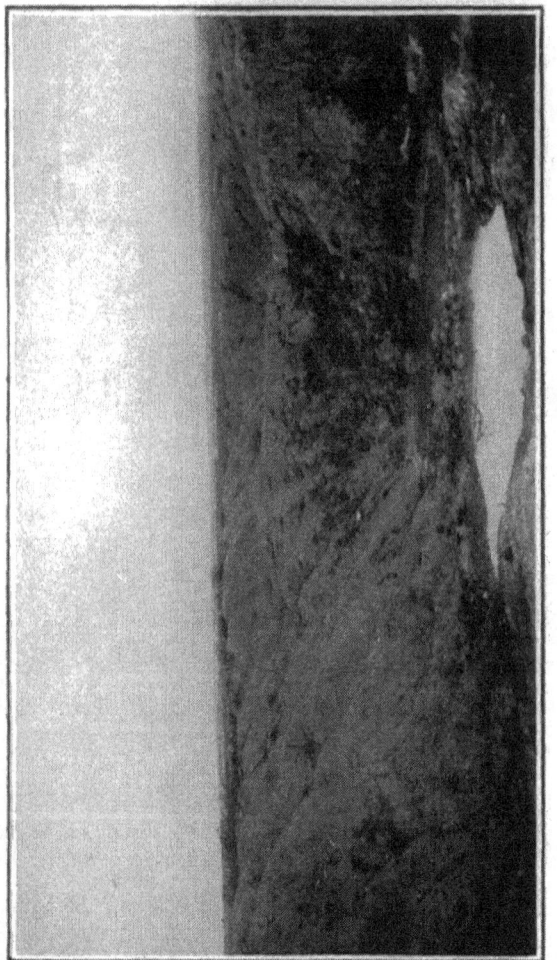

Hohenzollern Craters, 1917-1918.

MONCHY AU BOIS.

Ransart, Bailleulval and Berles area. Here we stayed, with one rest later on, for eight months.

Soon after our arrival in Bienvillers, we were much surprised to see Colonel Toller again return to us. We thought that he really had got a permanent Command when he went to the Highlanders, but apparently a former Colonel returned a few days after he arrived there, and he was consequently sent back. However, there were now many vacancies in our Division, and Col. Toller was at once sent to command the 7th Sherwood Foresters, the Robin Hoods—an appointment which poved to be permanent, and which he held for the next two years. At the same time, Lieut. N. C. Marriott, wounded at Hohenzollern, returned to us, and soon afterwards 2nd Lieut. J. C. Barrett joined us from England, while we lost 2nd Lieut. G. E. Banwell, who was slightly wounded at Gommecourt, and, after several efforts to remain with his unit, had to go to Hospital with a badly poisoned foot. We also lost our Divisional Commander, Major General the Hon. E. J. Montagu-Stuart-Wortley, C. B., C. M. G., D. S. O., M. V. O., who went to England. Before he went, the following notice appeared in orders :—" On relinquishing the Command of the Division, General Stuart-Wortley wishes to thank all ranks, especially those who have been with the Division since mobilization, for their loyalty to him and unfailing spirit of devotion to duty. He trusts the friendship formed may be lasting, and wishes the Division good luck and God speed." To quote the Battalion War Diary—" The Major General has commanded the Division since 1914; universal regret is openly expressed at his departure."

The new Divisional Commander, Major General W.

Thwaites, R.A., arrived soon afterwards, and soon made himself known to all units, introducing himself with a ceremonial inspection. Ours was at Bailleulmont, where we were billeted for a few days, and on the afternoon of the 13th we formed up 650 strong to receive him. After inspecting each man very carefully, the General addressed the Battalion, calling Col. Jones "Col. Holland," and us the 5th Leices*ters*, two mistakes which were never forgotten, though soon forgiven. He congratulated us on our appearance, and said that he read determination in our faces, promising to know us better by seeing us in the trenches. We then marched past him and went home.

Our first few tours in this new sector might well be described as a nightmare of H_2O and H_2S. It rained very hard, and all the trenches at once became full of water—in some places so full that the garrison, as the weather was warm, discarded trousers and walked about with shirts tucked into sandbag bathing drawers. Some of the communication trenches were in a particularly bad condition, and worst of all was the very deep Berlin Trench running alongside the road from Bienvillers to Hannescamps. A sort of "Southend-pier" gridded walk had been built into one side of this about four feet from the floor of the trench, and in some places even this was covered, so that the water in the trench itself was nearly six feet deep. Pumps proved almost useless, and it was obvious that something drastic would have to be done if we were to remain in this part of the world for the winter.

The H_2S was in cylinders. For some unknown reason the Special Brigade R.E., or "gas merchants" as they were more popularly called, considered the

Monchy hollow a particularly suitable place for their poison attacks. The result was that we spent all our rest periods carrying very heavy cylinders into the line or out again, terribly clumsy, awkward and dangerous things to carry, while our trenches, already ruined by the weather, were still further damaged, under-cut and generally turned upside down to make room for these cylinders. Then again, the actual gas projection caused a most appalling amount of trouble. The wind had to be exactly West, for a touch of North or South would carry the poison over our miserable little salient, but at times the wind was due East, and on one occasion it remained obstinately in the wrong quarter for three weeks, while we lived in daily terror of some chance Boche shell hitting one of the cylinders. On several occasions we had to assist with smoke candles and smoke bombs, and this, too, caused us much worry. Perhaps at dusk the wind would be favourable, and orders would arrive that gas would be discharged at 11-34. At 11-34 we, having heard nothing to the contrary, would light our smoke machines, and find no gas turned on. At 12-55 we should get another message by some orderly to say "discharge postponed until 12-55" —then, of course, no time to warn anybody, and no smoke left.

The reason for this delay in the communication of orders was that our telephones were in a state of transition. We had discovered that the Boche with his listening sets could overhear all conversations carried on by the ordinary field telephone, and consequently it was absolutely forbidden to use this instrument, except in emergency, within 2,000 yards of the front line. A new instrument, the "Fullerphone," was being introduced which could not be overheard, but one could not use it for talking; all messages had to be "buzzed." Incidentally the "buzzing" process produced a continuous whining noise, and this, in a small Company Headquarter dug-out, was almost enough to drive the unhappy Company Commander off his head. The Fullerphone, too, was very scarce at first, so that almost all messages had to be sent by orderly, or runner as he now began to be called. This caused so much trouble that the next stage was the introduction of codes and code names. At first these were very simple, we were "John" after Col. Jones, the 5th Lincolnshires "Sand," from Sandall, etc., while "gas" became the innocent "Gertie," and to attack was "to tickle." One very famous message was sent when an expected gas attack had to be suddenly postponed—"John can sleep quiet to-night, Gertie will not tickle." Later we became "Sceptre," when all units in the Division were called after race-horses, and still later, when Brigade Headquarters became "Girl," we each had a lady's name; we were "Gertrude." It sounded somewhat curious to hear a Staff Captain who had lost his Brigadier ringing up a Battalion Headquarters to ask "have you seen a 'Girl' about anywhere?" The "Bab" code was also introduced, a three-figure code with innumerable permutations and combinations. The whole thing was very secret, and added much to the worries of the Company Commander, who not only had to be careful not to lose the code book, but had to remember, without writing it down, the Corps code letter and number for the week.

In the same way the Artillery had all manner of codes for every conceivable occasion. Various mes-

MONCHY AU BOIS.

sages were devised and entered in the Defence Scheme for retaliation, S.O.S., raid purposes, etc., and woe betide the luckless F.O.O. or Infantryman who sent the wrong message. There were "concentrates" and "Test concentrates," and "attacks" and "Test attacks," and "S.O.S." and many others. If anything serious really happened, the lines were always broken at once, and there remained only the rockets and coloured lights. The S.O.S. signal was almost sacred, not to be used for a hostile raid, or when retaliation was needed, but only in the event of the enemy massing for a general attack. However, it was once used—in a rather curious little battle fought on the 4th August, 1916.

Our trench strength at the time was very weak, because two days later we were to raid the enemy's lines opposite Monchy salient, and the raiding party had been left out of the line at Pommier to practice. At 3-30 a.m. on the 4th the Boche, either annoyed at our wire-cutting, or to celebrate his favourite anniversary, the declaration of war, opened a heavy fire with guns, mortars, rifle grenades, coloured lights and everything else imaginable. The noise was terrific, and the C.O. and Adjutant rushed to the Defence Scheme to find what was the correct message to send; most of the noise was at trench 86. They decided to tell the Gunners "assist L," but, between F.O.O. and signals, this reached the Artillery as "assist 86," which was meaningless, so they did nothing. Meanwhile, our Lewis Guns could be heard, so Col. Jones, unable to telephone to Companies whose lines were all cut, finally sent the S.O.S. The reply was prompt and terrific. There was plenty of ammunition, and all the gunners, wakened by the bombardment, were only too anxious to shoot, so that within a few minutes every weapon, from an 18 pounder to a 12″ gun on railway mounting, was raining shells into Monchy and its surroundings. It was very effective, but none the less there had to be an enquiry into " who had dared to use the S.O.S.," and, when the facts were all brought to light, the F.O.O., Lieut. Cave, partly responsible for the initial mistake, earned the name of " S.O.S. Cave," which stuck to him till he left the Division.

The raid was not a great success. For several days " C " Company, who were chosen for the task, carried out continuous practices at Pommier, first under Capt. Mould, and later, when he had to go to Hospital with septic tonsilitis, under Capt. Shields. Capt. Moore was at the Army School at the time. The Infantry arrangements were made satisfactorily, but there was little or no opportunity for the Gunners to observe the result of their wire-cutting, with the result that, when the party went over on the evening of the 5th, they found no gaps. The raiding party advanced in four groups, each group with bombers, bayonet men, and sappers for demolition work, and each under an officer—2nd Lieuts. Steel, Barrett, Heffill and Morris. The party removed all marks of identification, but wore their collars turned up, and a small patch of white on the back of their collars for mutual recognition.

At 11-0 p.m. the party left our trenches and lay out in front of our wire, waiting for our bombardment, which 15 minutes later opened on the enemy's front line. The shooting was excellent, but the backward burst from our 6 inch Howitzers caused several casualties ; amongst others 2nd Lieut. Steel was badly wounded in the leg. At Zero, 11-25 p.m., we advanced, but found no means of getting through the wire, while the Boche sent numbers of bombs and rifle grenades along the whole front. The party acted very coolly and searched carefully for gaps, but, finding none, threw their bombs and returned, guided to our lines by rockets and lanterns. Six men were missing. A curious thing happened when our search party, under L/Cpl. Archer, went out to look for them. A German machine gun, hearing the movement, opened fire, and, at the same moment, our "Flying Pig"—240 mm. trench mortar—which had jammed during the barrage, suddenly went off and dropped its shell exactly on the gun team. The following night Cobley's body, one of the raiders, was found in a shell-hole, and soon afterwards two others, Worth and Sommers, returned to our lines, having been lost the previous night. Barkby was found dead a day later, and Duckett's body was buried by a patrol which found it during the following tour. The sixth was Private "Arty" Carr, who returned unhurt at 11-0 p.m. on the 8th, after three days. During the raid he had left his party, and, while they worked to the left, looking for a gap, had gone to the right, where, outside the raid area, he found the wire thin. He had entered the German lines, had some exciting times with a post which he bombed, and then tried to get out, only to find that he had moved away from his original gap, and was now confronted by some very strong wire. He did not get through until dawn on the 6th, so then lay in a shell hole until dark, when he started to return. Tired and somewhat exhausted, he lost his way in the waste of shell holes and mortar craters round the Monchy Salient, and did not finally find our lines until the 8th.

Our total casualties were three killed and one officer and 15 wounded. To these must be added Captain

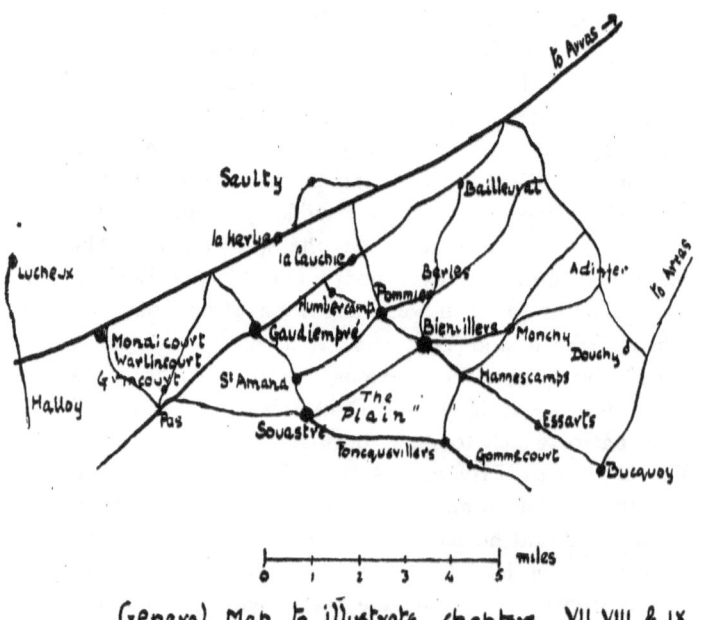

General Map to illustrate chapters VII, VIII & IX.

Barton, who had a most unfortunate accident. Always wanting to be "up and doing," he watched the raid and helped the wounded, standing on our front line parapet, but, turning to re-enter the trench, slipped and bayonetted himself in the thigh. It was not a very serious wound, but would not heal, and he had to be sent to England. With him we lost another valuable officer, 2nd Lieut. Williams, who, while acting as bomb instructor at Brigade Headquarters, met with an accident, and was wounded in the head. Not long afterwards, Serjt. Goodman, our chief N.C.O. Instructor, who was wounded, and lost one of his legs and part of an arm as the result of a bombing accident at the Divisional School. During this first month our casualties, "holding the line," were very slight, though we lost three good N.C.O.'s through shell fire. Serjt. Shreeves, of " C " Company, died of wounds, Cpl. Ambrose, of " B " Company, was killed outright near Hannescamps, and later Serjt. W. Gartshore, of " C " Company.

Between raids and gas attacks we were kept hard at work repairing our trenches. General Kemp was a sapper before he became an Infantry Brigadier, and we were soon instructed in the mysteries of sump-holes, " berms " and " batters," interlocking trench floor boards, and the correct angles for the sloping sides of a trench, while anyone who dared to undercut a parapet for any purpose had better not be present the next time that the General appeared. As far as possible all the carpentry work was done by the Sappers out of trenches and sump-frames were sent up ready made, also small dug-outs in numbered parts, easily put together; all we had to do was to dig the necessary holes. At the same time some genius invented the " A " frame, a really wonderful labour saving device. Hitherto floorboards had been supported on piles and crossbars, while further and longer stakes were driven in to carry the rivetment. The new frame shaped like a flat-topped letter "A," was put in the floor of the trench upside down. The legs held the revetment against the sides, the floorboards rested on the cross-piece, and the space between the cross-piece and the flat top formed a good drain. These were first used in communication trenches only, where the Monmouthshires were at work for us; later we used them in all trenches wherever possible.

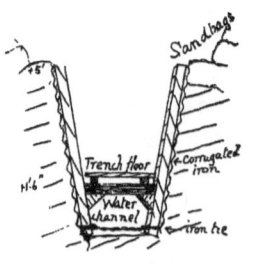

Meanwhile, when not in trenches, we rested, first at Bienvillers and later at Pommier. Bienvillers had many good billets, but was too full of our heavy artillery to be pleasant, for the noise was often very disturbing. The enemy, too, used to shell the place, and 2nd Lieut. Shipston had a most remarkable escape one day when standing in front of a first floor window, shaving. A whizz-bang hit the window sill and carried itself, sill and many bricks, between his legs into the room; he himself was untouched. Another early morning bombardment found the Doctor in his bath. He left it hurriedly and hastened, dripping and unclothed, to the cellar, which he found already contained several officers and the ladies of his billet. But this stay in Bienvillers is most remembered on account of a slight fracas which occurred between Col. Jones and a visiting Army Sanitation Officer. A full account is given in two entries in the War Diary. The first, dated the 23rd July, says simply—"Major T———, Sanitation Officer, IIIrd. Army, came to look at billets. We received him coldly, and in consequence got a bad report, see later." The second entry, a week later, is dated 30th July. "The Sanitary report referred to came and we replied. The report detailed many ways in which we, as a Regiment, were living in dirt, and making no attempt to follow common-sense rules, or to improve our state. It stated that we had been in the village *three days*, and thus implied that there could be no excuse. Our reply asserted that the inaccuracy of the report made it worthless. That, though the Regiment had been there three days, the Army, which the gallant Major T. represented and worked for, had been in the village some months. That Major T.'s party had done nothing to put or keep the billets in order, to put up incinerators, or in any way to make suitable billets for soldiers resting from trench duty. It suggested that Major T. had neglected his duty, and thus was not in a position to judge a Regiment."

Pommier was much pleasanter, and was very seldom shelled. Brigade Headquarters lived there, and, with the aid of an energetic Mayor and our invaluable interpreter, M. Bonassieux, had done much to improve the billets. There were plenty of civilians who were good to us, though, to quote the War Diary again, 26th August, "A complaint was made by the Maire that certain of our officers were bathing in the open, and that this was not counted amongst the indecencies the French permitted." At about the same time, during one of our rest periods, we were inspected by General Thwaites—a full ceremonial inspection, the first of many of these much dreaded ordeals. Again it is impossible to improve on the account given by the War Diary. "At 2-30 we were drawn up in close column in

Ceremonial—Companies sized. We received the new G.O.C. with several salutes, the last was probably the worst. The Battalion was then closely inspected, and a few names taken for unsteadiness, dirty buttons, badly fitted packs, and the like. A slight confusion between the terms packs and equipment led us to take off equipment, and we then formed up as a Battalion in Brigade. We saluted again, this time we had no bayonets, and then marched past by Companies and back in close column several times. Then, by a questionable, though not questioned, manœuvre, we came back again and advanced in review order. The Brigade Band was in attendance and played the Brigade March in place of the Regimental March, because it did not know the latter. While still in Ceremonial order, we finished by doing Battalion drill, under the general idea 'keep moving.' We kept moving for two hours in all, and it was universally conceded that the men moved very well. One or two of the newly arrived officers were unequal to the occasion. It was a good day in the country, and, in the senior officers, stirred up pleasant memories of old peace time annual inspections." The exceeding fierceness of the General on this Inspection had an amusing sequel when, a week later, two of our soldiers were repairing a road outside the Brigade office. One regarded the other's work for a few minutes critically, and then exclaimed fiercely, "Very ragged, very ragged, do it again!" It is only fair to add, that, terrible as was the ordeal of a Divisional Inspection, the General kept his original promise, and spent many hours in the foremost trenches, "that he might know us well."

The evening of this same inspection was one of the few occasions on which Pommier was bombarded. A sudden two minutes' "hate" of about 40 shells, 4.2 and 5.9, wounded three men and killed both the C.O.'s horses, "Silvertail" and "Baby"; both came out with the Battalion. We still, however, had some good animals left, as was obvious at the Brigade Sports and Race meeting held on the 11th September at la Bazéque Farm. This was a most successful show, and the only pity was that we were in trenches at the time, and so could only send a limited number of all ranks to take part. The great event of the day was the steeplechase. The Staff Captain, Major J. E. Viccars, on "Solomon," led all the way, but was beaten in the last twenty yards by Major Newton, R.F.A. Lieut. L. H. Pearson was third on "Sunlock II.," the transport Serjeant's horse. It was a remarkable performance, for he only decided to ride at the last moment, and neither he nor horse had trained at all. The Battalion did well in other events, winning 1st and 2nd places in both obstacle and mule races, and providing the best cooker and best pack pony; the two last were a great credit to the Transport Section. One of the features of the day was the Bookies' G.S. wagon, where two officers disguised with top hats, yellow waistcoats and pyjamas, carried on a successful business as "turf accountants." At a VIIth. Corps meeting, held a fortnight later on the same course, we secured two places for the Battalion: Capt. Burnett came home 2nd in an open steeplechase, and Capt. Moore 3rd in one for Infantry officers only.

During September our Mess, already up to strength, was considerably increased by a large draft of Officers.

First we were glad to see Major Griffiths back as Second in Command, though sorry for Captain John Burnett, who had to go back to Transport for the time. With Major Griffiths came 2nd Lieuts. J. R. Brooke, S. Corah, and W. I. Nelson, while within the same month, or shortly afterwards, 2nd. Lieuts. L. A. Nelson, J. H. Ball, P. Measures, T. L. Boynton, W. C. Walley, W. Lambert, M. F. Poynor, and J. A. Wortley all arrived. In October also Serjeant Beardmore, M.M., of " C " Company, who had latterly being doing exceptionally good work with the Battalion Scouts, was given his Commission in the Field, and reposted as a platoon Commander to the old Company. Capt. Barton's place as M.O. was taken by Captain T. D. Morgan, of the 2nd Field Ambulance. At the same time a stroke of bad luck robbed us of 2nd Lieut. Coles, who was badly wounded. During a raid of the 4th Lincolnshires in October it was our duty to cause a diversion by blowing up some tubes of ammonal in the Boche wire. The party, led by 2nd Lieut. Coles, was about to leave our trenches when a rifle grenade or " pine apple " bomb dropped in their midst and exploded one of the tubes, doing much damage.

During these long months of trench warfare a considerable advance was made in the work of the Intelligence department of the Infantry Battalion. A year ago one officer did duty for a whole Brigade, now each Battalion had its Intelligence officer, its scouts and observers, and its snipers, sometimes the last under a separate officer. The duties of the Intelligence section were many. They must see and report every little thing which happened in the enemy's lines, no small detail must be omitted. The number and colours of his signal lights on different occasions, the relative activity of his different batteries and their positions, the movement of his transport, the location of his mortars and machine guns, the trench reliefs, all these must be watched. The immediate purpose was of course retaliation, counter battery work, the making of our bombardments more effective by picking out the tender spots in his lines, and generally harassing the enemy; but there was a further purpose. It was particularly necessary that the higher commands should be kept informed of all the big movements of troops, the state of the enemy's discipline, etc., and often some little incident seen in the front line would give the clue to one of these. Lieut. L. H. Pearson was at this time Intelligence officer, helped by Serjt. Beardmore, M.M., L/Cpl. Wathey, Pte. A. E. Gilbert, and others. There was of course also the humorous side to their work, and many amusing things were seen, or said to be seen, through the observers' telescopes. The old white-haired Boche, digging near Monchy, who looked so benign that no one would shoot him, became quite a famous character, until one day his real nature was revealed, for he shook his fist at one of our low-flying aeroplanes, and obviously uttered a string of curses, so one of the snipers shot him. Then again there was the lady of Douchy, who could be seen each evening coming out to hang up the washing; she was popularly known as Mary, and figured in the reports nearly every day.

With the observers worked the snipers. After nearly two years, telescopic sights at last appeared, and we tried to train the once despised "Bisley shot."

They were very keen, and had much success, of which they were duly proud, as their individual reports showed. "We watched for ¾ of an hour until our viggillance was rewarded by seeing a Boche; he exposed half of himself above the parapet, I, Pte. ———, shot him," so said one report, the name has unfortunately been lost. Some snipers even kept a book of their "kills," with entries such as "June 1st, 9-30 a.m. Boche sentry looking over, shot in shoulder, had grey hair almost bald very red face and no hat." It was just the right spirit, and it had its results. Autumn, 1915, saw us hardly daring to look over the top for fear of being sniped; Autumn, 1916, saw us masters, doing just what we pleased, when we pleased.

CHAPTER IX.

GOMMECOURT AGAIN.

29th Oct., 1916.   15th April, 1917.

MANY Divisions were now taking part in the Somme battle for the second time, and as we suddenly left Pommier on the 29th October—our final destination unknown—we naturally thought it probable that we, too, should soon be once more in the thick of the fighting. However, our fears were groundless, and we moved due West, not South. Our first night we spent in Mondicourt, and then moved the next day in pouring rain to Halloy, where we stayed two days. On the 1st November we marched 14 miles through Doullens to Villers L'Hôpital, on the Auxi le Chateau road, where we found our new Padre waiting for us, the Rev. C. B. W. Buck. The march was good, and no one fell out until the last half mile, a steep hill into billets, which was too much for six men; as we had done no real marching for several months, this was very satisfactory. There was only one incident of interest on the way, a small collision between the heavily laden mess cart and the level crossing gates at Doullens, due to the anxiety of the lady gate-keeper to close the gates and let the Paris express through, a feat which she accomplished, despite all the efforts of our Transport, which was consequently cut in half.

The following day it rained again, and we marched to Conteville, stayed a night, and went on to Millencourt the next morning. Here we found good billets and, as we were told we were likely to remain a month, fixed up a Battalion Mess in the Farm Chateau.

We were soon informed that we had not come to Millencourt to rest, but to carry out "intensive training" to fit us for offensive action. This meant very hard work all the morning, many afternoons, and two or three nights a week as well. The idea was to devote the first week to Platoon and Company work, the next to Battalion drill and training, and to finish our course with some big Brigade and Divisional days. The weather was not very good, but we managed to do many hours work, the usual physical training, bayonet fighting, steady drill, and extended order work, night compass work and lectures. The most exciting event was one of the night trainings, when Col. Jones combined cross country running with keeping direction in the dark. The running was very successful, but the runners failed to keep direction, and ran for many miles, getting in many cases completely lost; far into the night the plaintive notes of the recall bugle could be heard in the various villages of the neighbourhood.

Soon after our arrival a Divisional Sports Committee drew up a programme for a meeting to be held at the end of our training, and to consist of football, boxing, and cross country running. Eliminating heats and events had to be decided beforehand, and, with Lieut. Heffill and Serjt. J. Wardle to look after the boxing, and Capt. Shields as "O.C. Football," we started training without delay. At the football we had our usual luck, for, after a good victory over the 4th

GOMMECOURT AGAIN.

Lincolnshires, we were once more beaten by our own 4th Battalion. The last game was very exciting, and feeling ran so high that the language on the touch line became terrible, and would have shocked even a Brigadier. The finals of the boxing and cross country running could not take place until later when we had left the area. On one or two of the spare afternoons we managed to get some Rugby football, and had some excellent games, during which we discovered that our Padre was a performer of considerable merit.

On the 22nd November we started back Eastwards, and, after a night at Prouville and two at Fortel, arrived in the pouring rain at Halloy, where we were told we should stay for about a week. We were put into the huts, which were unfinished and entirely unfit for habitation, while to make matters worse, the field in which they stood had become a sea of mud. After the good billets of Millencourt, this change for the worse produced the inevitable sickness, and, in addition to many N.C.O.'s and men who went away with fever and influenza, we lost for a short time Col. Jones, and several of the officers. Amongst them was 2nd Lieut. J. R. Brooke, who had long ago been warned against the danger of again getting nephritis, but in spite of this refused to stay away from the Battalion, and insisted on braving even the worst weather and the wettest trenches. About the same time, Captain Burnett went to England, going to Hospital from the Army School.

The week in these horrible surroundings was lengthened to a fortnight, and we were at last able to hold the finals of the cross country run. Many of the Battalion entered, and over two hundred came home in the time, a very good performance, though not good enough to win. The boxing tournament was held still later at St. Amand, and we sent two entries. In the heavy weights, Boobyer was beaten on points after a plucky fight, and in the feather weights, O'Shaugnessy knocked his opponent all over the place, and won in the second round.

On the 6th December we marched to the Souastre huts, where the Colonel returned to us, and we once more began to feel fit; the huts here were not palaces, but were far better than those we had left at Halloy. On the 11th we moved up through Bienvillers and went into our old trenches opposite Monchy. But the recent heavy rains had undone all the good that we had done in the early autumn, and they were now in a very bad state. On the right of the Hannescamps road they were particularly bad, and Liverpool Street, which ran from Lulu Lane to the front line, was almost impassable. There was the same terrible clinging mud, feet deep, that we had found at Richebourg a year before, and the old troubles of lost gum boots began again. Fortunately we were now prepared, and were able to combat the dangers of "trench foot." Each Company had its drying room—a dug-out occupied by the Stretcher bearers, and kept warm by an ever burning brazier. Here at least once in every 24 hours every man who could possibly have got wet feet, and every man wearing rubber boots, came, had his feet rubbed, and was given dry socks and boots, while at Headquarters and in Bienvillers were large drying rooms where the wet boots could be dealt with. In this way we were able to keep almost free from the complaint, and the few men whose feet did fail were all men who had had "trench feet" the previous winter, and were consequently always liable to it.

All this time it was not only wet, but cold, and after Christmas it became colder until the first week in January, when heavy snow fell. Thenceforward, until the middle of February, there was continuous frost with occasional heavy falls of snow, though generally the days and nights were fine and clear. For several feet down, the ground was frozen hard, and digging became absolutely impossible. There was now solid ice instead of water in the trenches, and the front line sentries found their task a particularly cold one. Fortunately by this time the trench cook-house was not only an established thing but had become a very successful affair, and four times a day hot meals were carried in tanks and food containers from Battalion Headquarters to the front line. For this purpose the rectangular tanks from the cooks' wagons were used, being carried by two men, on a wooden framework or stretcher. Along a road or up a well made communication trench this was a comparatively light task, but to carry a tank full of hot tea over slippery shell holes and through knee-deep mud was a difficult matter, and on more than one occasion a platoon lost its hot drink at night through the disappearance of the carriers into some shell hole. The wonderful thing was that both tea-less platoon and drenched carriers would laugh over it all.

Christmas Day was spent in trenches. We were relieved in the afternoon by the 4th Battalion, who had their festivities on Christmas eve, and went back to Souastre, where the following day we, too, had our dinner. Pigs had been bought and killed, and we all gorged ourselves on roast pork and plum pudding, washing them down with beer—a very satisfactory performance. There were also the usual games and Company dinners, and we all spent a very enjoyable few days. Later on we managed to arrange a Battalion concert which was a tremendous success, and voted by all a most excellent evening; the "star" turn was Colonel Jones, who gave a recitation.

The weather made raids and active operations impossible, and though we made all preparations for a rifle grenade demonstration to assist a Staffordshire raid on New Year's night, this had to be cancelled on account of the snow. Patrols, however, still continued to tour No Man's Land in the hopes of finding a stray Boche, or encountering a Boche patrol. In front of Essarts the lines were so far apart that there was plenty of room for a small pitched battle, and night after night Lieuts. Pearson, Creed, Poynor, and others visited such familiar haunts as the "Osier Bed," "Thistle Patch," "Lonely Tree," and other well-known places. The first to meet the enemy was Lieut. Pearson, who came upon a small party in the "Thistle Patch," who made off rapidly back to their lines. Our patrol used their rifles, but, though they hit one of the enemy, failed to take a prisoner, and for a week or two the Boche did not show himself. Then on the 10th January, 2nd Lieut. Creed, with a mixed party of scouts from all Companies, while reconnoitering the "Osier Bed" suddenly found that a party of the enemy was in their right rear and close to our wire, where four of them could be seen. Our patrol turned at once and ran straight at the four as fast as they could, coming, as they ran, under a heavy fire from a Boche covering party lying some 50 yards out. Pte. A. Garner was

GOMMECOURT AGAIN.

killed outright, but the remainder, led by 2nd Lieut. Creed and Pte. Frank Eastwood of " C " Company, rushed on and wounded and captured one of the four, who was found to be the officer. The remainder of the enemy took the alarm in time and made off. The officer proved to be an English-speaking subaltern of the 55th Regt.—our old opponents of Hohenzollern in October, 1915. He was led down to the Aid Post to have his wound dressed, much to the disgust of Captain Terry, the M.O., who would have liked to have killed him outright, though Serjeant Bent, the medical orderly, took compassion on his shivering prisoner and fed him on hot tea, and actually gave him a foot warmer!

This little affair caused the Boche extreme annoyance, and the following day he spent the morning shooting at Berlin Trench, the Bienvillers road and Bienvillers itself, round the Church. As we were relieved during the morning we had to march out through it all, and found it particularly unpleasant, especially when a shell hit the R.E. Dump, exploded an ammunition store, and sent the house at the Church corner several hundred feet into the air.

At this time there were again several changes in the personnel. Capt. G. W. Allen went to Brigade Headquarters and thence to the Corps School as an Instructor; Capt. J. D. Hills, who took his place, fell down and injured his knee so badly that it took him to England for six months; Capt. Knighton was made Town Major at St. Amand, and Captain Mould went to England. Capt. Wollaston rejoined us, bringing with him 2nd Lieut. Banwell and a new subaltern, 2nd Lieut. D. Campbell. 2nd Lieut. C. H. Morris acted as Adjutant. 2nd Lieut. J. R. Brooke paid one of his periodical visits to the R.A.M.C., driven thither by the M.O., who was afraid he would die on his hands, but returned to us again soon afterwards.

During the last fortnight of January we had several Units of the 58th (London) Division attached to us for instruction. They were one of the first " second-line " Territorial Divisions to reach France, and were followed by our own second-line, the 59th, who went for their initiation to the most Southern end of the British front, and we consequently did not see them. Nothing of any note happened during their stay, except a heavy gas shell bombardment on " D " Company's (Capt. Shields') trenches. The men were all warned in time and put on helmets, so that we had no casualties. The shells were almost noiseless, so that when the gas blew over the crest into " B " Company (Capt. Wollaston), who were in support, it was thought to be cloud gas and the Strombos horns were sounded. The flank Units sounded theirs, too, and Bienvillers took it up, much to the annoyance of the batteries and staffs who were thus unnecessarily disturbed, since the Strombos should never be used for gas shells only. It was a very natural mistake, but we were severely " strafed " by the authorities; however, as we had no casualties, and there had been many in other Units, we ended by being congratulated.

On the 14th February came the beginnings of the thaw, and with it the first rumours of a German withdrawal. Three days later the enemy shelled Foncquevillers heavily, apparently with a view to a raid, or possibly to deceive us into thinking that he did not mean to retire. Our guns replied, and the Right Half Battalion under Major Griffiths, who was already

GOMMECOURT AGAIN.

quartered in the village, stood to, but nothing happened. The remainder of the Battalion with the Headquarters was now in Bienvillers in Brigade reserve. The weather once more became frosty, and there was a thick mist almost every day. On the 23rd we relieved the 4th Battalion, and occupied some 2,500 yards of front line opposite Gommecourt, where the Huns shelled us at intervals all the next day, but did no damage. At midnight 24th/25th the Brigadier had reason to believe the Boche was going to leave his lines, and a strong patrol under Major Griffiths went out to reconnoitre. They cut many gaps in the wire, but found the German front line still held. At dawn it was very foggy, and there was some shouting heard in Gommecourt, which sounded like "Bonsoir," but at 7-10 a.m. the enemy opened a heavy bombardment which lasted $3\frac{1}{2}$ hours. Shells of every kind were fired and our trenches hit in several places; one man was killed. The next night patrols were again out and, though it was found that the Boche had evacuated Gommecourt Park, he was still in the village, where the following morning dug-outs were seen to be on fire. Wire was cut and everything prepared for the advance.

However, the Boche still hung on to his line, and on the evening of the 26th and at dawn the following morning our patrols still found him there. 2nd Lieuts. Banwell and Beardmore and Serjt. Growdridge were constantly out, waiting for a chance to enter his lines, but the chance never came, and, on the 27th, we were relieved by the 4th Battalion, and returned to Souastre. That evening the Boche retired, and the 4th Battalion entered Gommecourt. At this point we lost Captain J. W. Tomson, who had been far from well for some time, and now went to England with fever. He had never missed a day's work for two years. Lieut. D. B. Petch took his place in command of "A" Company.

The German withdrawal was very slow, and we spent the next day having baths in Souastre. On the 1st March we moved into the new front line, round the East edge of Gommecourt, while the Boche was still holding Pigeon Wood. The enemy was very alert, as General H. M. Campbell, the C.R.A., discovered; he went into the wood, thinking it unoccupied, and was chased out by a fat Boche throwing "potato mashers." In the evening the Headquarters moved into a German dug-out, but the enemy still occupied the "Z." The front line between there and Gommecourt was filled with deep dug-outs, all connected underground, so the Boche occupied one end, while 2nd Lieuts. Banwell and Barrett sat in the other, of the same tunnel. There were many booby traps, such as loose boards exploding a bomb when trodden on; trip wires at the bottom of dug-out steps bringing down the roof, and other such infernal machines. We were warned of these, and had no casualties.

On the 2nd March we continued to press the enemy, having as our objective a circle 900 yards round Gommecourt Church. 2nd Lieut. Corah was slightly wounded by a sniper, and one or two men were hit with splinters of bomb, but there were no serious casualties. Our bombing parties were very vigorous, and in one case consumed the hot coffee and onions left by a party disturbed at breakfast. In this bombing work, Serjeants A. Passmore, Cave and Meakin, Cpl. Marshall, and L/Cpls. Dawes and A. Carr all distinguished themselves. Gommecourt wood was soon cleared, and by the evening we had gained the whole of the circular objective. The next morning early the 8th Sherwood Foresters came up to relieve us, but, though the other Companies were relieved, "A" Company (Petch) refused to be. They were busy chasing the Boche, and were quite annoyed when told that they must come away. Relieved, we marched back to Souastre.

We stayed at Souastre until the 11th March, and then moved up once more to the line, taking over 2,600 yards of frontage from the la Brayelle Road to the Hannescamps-Monchy Road. Our time in reserve had been spent almost entirely in lectures on the attack, and on lessons drawn from the enemy's recent withdrawal from Gommecourt, and we had more than once been congratulated on our patrol work, which was excellent throughout this time. Between Essarts and Monchy the Boche was still holding his original line, and though expected to retire at any time, he made no movement during the three days we stayed in the line. On the 13th we were ordered, during the afternoon, to make certain that the enemy were still present, so 2nd Lieut. T. H. Ball marched up the Essarts Road with two platoons, until fire was opened on them from more than one direction, and the strength of the enemy was apparent. That evening we were relieved by the Lothian and Border Horse, and marched on relief to Foncquevillers. The same night, just before midnight, the Staffordshires made an attack on Bucquoy Graben, a strong Boche trench, and the outskirts of Bucquoy village. It was very wet and dark, and the operation altogether most difficult, so that the Staffordshires, though they made a very gallant attack, lost heavily and gained little ground.

At dawn the following morning, 14th March, we were ordered to be ready to go and support the Staffordshires, but, after considerable uncertainty and waiting, this order was cancelled. Instead, a flagged plan of the Bucquoy trenches was made on the plain N.W. of our village, and here we practised the attack. The weather was bad, but we managed to make all the necessary arrangements and do some attack drill. In the village we had a singular stroke of ill luck. One solitary German Howitzer shell dropped amongst a party of ' D " Company, killing Pte. J. T. Allen, who had done good work in the bombing at Gommecourt, and wounding six others, one of whom, W. Clarke, died of wounds afterwards. The practised attack, which should have taken place from Biez Wood on the 16th, never came off, for it was made unnecessary by the rapidity of the German retirement.

After this the weather improved, and it was bright and warm when, on the 17th, we moved during the afternoon into Gommecourt and came temporarily under orders of the 139th Brigade. The following day we moved again, this time to dug-outs and fields 500 yards North of Essarts, country which the enemy had now entirely evacuated. The villages and farms had all been very badly battered by our Artillery, and the Boche had found time to destroy almost everything before he went, except at Douchy, where there was some good dug-out timber. Needless to say, the famous Mary of that village was not to be found. The French were immensely pleased at regaining part of their lost territory, though it was a pathetic sight to see some of the old people coming to look at the piles of bricks which had once been their homes. Two ladies came to Gommecourt with a key, little thinking that so far from finding a lock they would find not even a door or door-way—there was not even a brick wall more than two feet high. Those officers who could get horses rode round to look at the country which for nine months we had been watching through telescopes, and the concrete emplacements of Monchy and le Quesnoy Farm were all explored, while No Man's Land, the only place free from wire and shell holes, provided an excellent canter. The Companies were largely employed in road mending, filling up German mine craters, and making tracks across the trenches for our Artillery. The enemy seemed to be really on the move at last, and we were all looking forward to seeing some new country, but on the 20th the weather broke, there was another fall of snow, and we were not sorry to be ordered back to Souastre, where we went into the huts for two nights.

For the rest of March we were constantly on the move, mostly by march route. First, on the 22nd, we marched via Couin and Bus-les-Artois to Bertrancourt, where we found some huts and much mud. One very large "Nissen" hut provided an Officers' Mess, but was completely devoid of all furniture until the Colonel invented some wonderful hanging tables—table tops hung from the ceiling on telephone wires. Here we were joined by 2nd Lieuts. C. C. Craggs, S. R. Mee, and B. G. Bligh, all new-comers. 2nd Lieuts. R. C. Broughton and A. Ramsden had joined a week or two before, so we now had our full complement of Platoon Commanders. Soon afterwards, however, 2nd Lieut. and A/Adjt. C. H. Morris went to the Indian Army, and his place was taken by Lieut. L. H. Pearson. In

Bertrancourt we found some German prisoners working, one of whom obviously received the latest news from London quicker than we did, for he told us that as the result of an air raid "London was in bits"! After one night here we marched via Acheux, Lealvillers and Arquèves to Raincheval, where we again stayed one night—a hard frost. The next day we moved on again, passing through Puchevillers, Rubempré and Pierregot to Rainnevillers. The march was made particularly uncomfortable by the number of different Units on the road, marching in all directions, and we had to keep big intervals between Companies.

Rainnevillers was only six kilometres from Amiens, and many officers availed themselves of this opportunity of visiting the town. The mysteries of Charlie's Bar, Godbert's, the Café du Cathédral, and other haunts were revealed for the first time, and proved so attractive that two senior officers made a very wet night the excuse for staying in a Hotel. They returned at dawn, but did not realise how early the Colonel rose, and met him at the breakfast table, to be congratulated on their (most unusual) earliness! We stayed here two days, and the G.O.C. came and presented medal ribbons to those who had been awarded decorations at Gommecourt. On the 26th March we "embussed" with the 4th Leicestershires, and were taken through Amiens to Dury, whence we marched a short distance to St. Fuscien, and went into billets. We were still near enough to Amiens for those who wished to "joy ride" into the town.

Two days later, on the 28th March, we marched to Saleux and entrained for the North. Passing through

Doullens we arrived at Lillers early the next morning, and marched thence to Laires, twelve miles through the driving rain. We reached billets all wet through. "B" Company followed by a later train, and joined us in billets just after midnight.

We were now in the 2nd Corps, and, before we had time to look round our new billets, the Corps Commander, General Jacob, came and was introduced to all officers, speaking to us in the village school room. After that we looked round our new quarters and found them excellent, so settled down to have, if possible, an enjoyable rest. Marie, of the "Cheval Blanc," provided a room where officers might meet and drink beer, subalterns, of course, champagne, and her name must be added to the long list of Tina's, Bertha's, and others who all over France welcomed the British officer so cordially at their estaminets. Meanwhile, we spent our days training, and particular attention was paid to route marching, in which we were severely handicapped by the bad state of our boots. For some reason there was at the time a shortage of leather, so Serjeant Huddleston, our shoemaker, could do nothing to improve matters, and we had to make the best of a bad job. It was really remarkable on some of the longer marches how few men fell out considering that many had practically no soles to their boots. However, the pleasant billets at Laire amply repaid us for our other troubles, and we were all sorry when on the 13th April, 2nd Lieut. Brooke and the rest of us bade farewell to Marie and marched to Manqueville.

Here we continued training so far as the weather allowed, but a considerable amount of rain rather hampered us. On the 15th we lost Colonel Jones who went to England for three months' rest. With the exception of a few weeks in 1915 he had been with us since the beginning, and there was not an officer or man who did not regret his going. There was never a trench or post which he did not visit, no matter how exposed or how dangerous the approach to it. Moreover, he was never downhearted, and while he was in it, the Battalion Headquarters of the 5th Leicestershire Regiment was known throughout the Division as one of the most cheerful, if not the most cheerful, spot in France. Major Griffiths took temporary command until, on the 23rd, Major Trimble, M.C., of the E. Yorks. Regt. arrived from the 6th Division and took over from him.

CHAPTER X.

LENS.

16th April, 1917. 10th June, 1917.

ON the 16th of April we learnt that we were once more to go to trenches, and the same day we moved to Annezin, just outside Béthune. The march will always be remembered on account of the tremendous energy displayed by Captain Shields, who was acting second in command. Just before the start he insisted on the reduction of all officers' kits to their authorised weight, thereby causing much consternation amongst those whose trench kits included gramophones, field boots, and other such articles of modern warfare. However, on arrival at Annezin all such worries were dispersed by the radiant smiles of the ladies at the C.O.'s billet, with whom all the Subaltern Officers, and one or two Captains at once fell in love.

Two days later Major Griffiths and some of the Company Officers went to reconnoitre the area round Bully Grenay and the western outskirts of Lens, which we were told would be our new area. The capture of Vimy by the Canadians a few days before, had made an advance on Lens more possible than it had ever been before, and there were many who thought that the Boche would be compelled to evacuate the town. But the Germans had not yet any intention of doing this.

Though the Vimy heights were lost to them, they still held "Hill 70" on the North side, and due West of Lens, near the Souchez river, Fosse 3 and "Hill 65" were naturally strong positions. South of this again, and just the other side of the river, was another small rise, on which stood an electric generating station, another commanding position held by the enemy. Our line ran through the houses of Liévin, across the Lens road, round the Eastern edge of Cité St. Pierre, and through Cité St. Edouard to the slopes of "Hill 70."

The whole neighbourhood was covered with coal mines. Each had its machine buildings, its slag heap, and its rows of miners' cottages, called "Corons," all in perfectly straight lines. The mine complete was known as a "Cité," and a Cité in the case of a large mine, covered a considerable tract of country, and had several hundred cottages. As the mines increased in number or grew in size, these Cités became more and more numerous, until when war began the country was fast becoming one large town. The trenches ran from cellar to cellar, through houses, along roadsides, were very irregular, and mostly short, unconnected and isolated lengths. Streets were the only means of communication, and these could not be used except at night. We were at a great disadvantage in this area. The Boche had but lately occupied the line we were now holding; he knew its whereabouts exactly, knew every corner of it, and could observe it from his heights on both flanks. We on the other hand never quite knew where the Boche was living, had no observation of his front line, and were consequently unable to retaliate as effectively as we should have wished to his trench mortars.

On the 19th of April Lt. Col. J. B. O. Trimble, M.C., arrived and took command, and the same night we marched through Béthune and Noeux les Mines to the "Double Crassier"— a long double slag heap near Loos— where we lived for two days in cellars and dug-outs, in Brigade Reserve. The day after we arrived an attempt was made by the Division on our left to capture "Hill 70." It failed, and during the enemy's retaliatory bombardment our positions were heavily shelled, and five men wounded. The next night we moved back to Maroc and Bully Grenay, where we stayed until the 23rd, when we relieved the 4th Battalion in the front line.

Our new sector was one of the worst we ever held. The front line, "A" Company (Petch), consisted of "Cooper Trench"—an exposed salient in front of Cité St. Pierre, overlooked and shelled from every direction and absolutely unapproachable during daylight, except for those who were willing to crawl. "B" and "C" Companies (Wynne and Moore) were behind in cellars, and "D" (Shields) and Battalion Headquarters still further back in the Cité. On the left could be seen the low slag heap and railway line of St. Pierre coal mine, held by our 1st Battalion, under which the 6th Division a few days previously had lost an entire platoon buried in a collapsed dug-out.

The tour lasted six days, and at the end of the second "D" Company relieved "A" in Cooper trench. It was originally intended to relieve "D" in the same way two nights later, but this was impossible, because we had to take over a new sector of line on the right, where "B" Company now relieved the 4th Lincolnshires, astride the Cité St. Edouard road. The new sector was not so exposed to view, and consequently to shelling as Cooper trench, but had other disadvantages, chief among which was its peculiar shape. A sharp pointed salient ran out along the Cité St. Edouard road, while South of this the line bent back to the right until it reached the outskirts of St. Pierre.

The shelling was very hot throughout the tour, and, at night particularly, there was plenty of machine-gun fire up the streets, which made ration carrying a dangerous job. "D" Company suffered most in casualties, nearly all of which were caused by shell fire on Cooper Trench, where they were unlucky in losing, in addition to some twenty others, Serjeants Williams, Queenborough and Goode, all of whom were wounded. The other Companies had some ten casualties between them.

All this time the enemy were inclined to be nervous after our attack on "Hill 70," and almost every day the columns of smoke in Lens showed us where he was burning houses and stores in case he should be forced to retire. His Infantry remained comparatively inactive in the front line, and when one night 2nd Lieut. Banwell and his platoon of "C" Company raided Cité St. Edouard Church they found no enemy there.

One humorous episode is handed down concerning this otherwise rather grim tour. Battalion Headquarters lived in a very small cellar—mess and office below, clerks and signallers and runners on the stairs. The Boche, the previous occupants, had left a suspicious looking red and black object on one end of the table which we used for meals and work. This took up a large part of our very scanty room, so an R.E. Specialist was called in to examine it. He

examined the object, at once condemned the cellar as
dangerous, and advised our immediate departure.
Cellars were hard to find, we consulted another
specialist. His actions are best described in the words
of one of those present: " He (R.E.) clears dug-out,
or rather dug-out clears itself, and ties string gingerly
to object; the string he leads upstairs and along a
trench to what he considers is a safe distance. When
all is ready the string is pulled. Nothing happens.
Suspense—a long pause—two hours—several drinks—
R.E. proceeds to examine result lying on floor—an
improvised lantern used for photography !"

On the 29th, after a big gas bombardment against
the enemy's positions in Cité St. Edouard and St.
Theodore, we were relieved by the 4th Battalion, and
went into the St. Pierre cellars—in Brigade support.
The whole place was under direct observation, and
movement by day was impossible, which made our
existence very unpleasant. It was while here that we
began to realize what a magnificent man was Padre
Buck. Nothing worried him, and even Cooper trench
formed part of his parish, to be visited each night. In
St. Pierre he held a service every evening in one of
the cellars, undeterred although on one occasion a shell
burst in the doorway, scattering its bits inside, but
doing no damage.

On the 3rd of May we again relieved the 4th Battalion
and stayed for three days in the Cooper trench sector.
We had a quieter time than before, and only lost one
killed and nine wounded during the tour. Amongst
the latter were L/Cpl. Waterfield and " Pat " Collins
the runner, who were both hit by a shell, which burst
on the orderly room. Our chief difficulty was the water

supply. With the hot weather the demand for water increased, and it all had to be brought to the line in petrol cans. Fortunately the limbers could come as far as Battalion Headquarters, and cans had to be carried forward from there only; even this took many men, and our numbers were by no means large.

At the end of this tour, the Brigade went into Divisional reserve, and we, relieved by the Sherwood Foresters, went back to Fosse 10, near Petit Sains. Here we stayed for six days training, playing games, and, by way of work, wiring a new line of defence. During this time we lost several officers. Capt. Wollaston and Lieut. H. E. Chapman went to Hospital, Lieut. Petch, 2nd Lieuts Clay and Bligh had already gone, and 2nd Lieut. Hepworth left a few days later to join the Indian Army. Captain Shields went on leave and "D" Company was commanded by Captain John Burnett, who, on his return from England, had been sent to the 4th Battalion, but soon worked his way back to us.

It was now our turn to go to the right Brigade sector, previously held by the Staffordshires, and on the 12th May we marched up to Red Mill, between Angres and Liévin. It was a disastrous march, for we were heavily shelled, and lost L/Cpl. Startin and Pte. Norton killed, and three L/Cpls., Ellis, Richardson and Roper, wounded—four of these were "No. 1" Lewis Gunners. Once at Red Mill all was well, and for the next two days we had an enjoyable time. The Mill proved to be a large red-brick Chateau, now sadly knocked about, on the banks of the Souchez river. The weather was bright and warm, so a dam was built, and we soon had an excellent bathing pool, much patronized by all ranks.

2nd Lieut. J. C. Barrett was the star performer, and never left the water, so that those who had nothing better to do used to " go and see the Signalling Officer swim "—it was one of the recognised recreations of the place.

At night we provided carrying and wiring parties, all of which had to go through Liévin, a bad place for shells. The Church stood at a particularly hot corner, and here, on the 14th, 2nd Lieut. T. P. Creed, M.C., was wounded in the head and foot and had to be sent to England, a great loss to " D " Company. We had two killed and nine wounded about the same time, and lost amongst the wounded one of our old soldiers, O'Shaugnessy, the boxer.

On the 15th May we relieved our 4th Battalion in the right sub-sector, staying there for ten days, with a three days' holiday at Red Mill in the middle. We were very weak, and our strength in trenches was barely 450, for in addition to casualties we had to send many away on leave or to courses. Our new sector lay between the Souchez river and the Lens-Liévin road, while across the river were the Canadians. Opposite them and our right flank, was the ridge with the generating station, opposite our centre Fosse 3 and " Hill 65." Fosse 3 had a large group of mine buildings standing on a slag heap, which ran Southwards from " Hill 65," ending above the river with a thirty foot slope. The Western face was the same height, and at its foot on our side was a large lake. The Corons were on the slopes of the Hill and round its base on the Western side. Those at the bottom we held, but the enemy had those on the slopes, and one building in particular, the " L-shaped house," was very strongly fortified. The right Company had its outposts in the cellars and shell-holes round the N. and W. edges of the lake, the centre and left companies had cellars and trenches, through the Cités de Riaumont and du Bois de Liévin, down to the main Lens road. Left Company Headquarters had a beautiful chateau, with a fruit and asparagus garden, known after its first occupant as "John Burnett's Chateau." There were two communication trenches, one each side of the Riaumont Hill: "Assign" on the South, shallow and unsafe in daylight, and "Absalom" on the North. "Hill 65" dominated everything, and gave the Boche a tremendous advantage. We had the Riaumont hill, 500 yards West of our front line, and could use the Bois de Riaumont on its summit as an O.P., but this was always being shelled, and though the view was excellent, one was seldom left in peace long enough to enjoy it. Battalion Headquarters had a strong German concrete dug-out in Liévin, said to have been formerly occupied by Prince Ruprecht of Bavaria.

The enemy confined his activity to his artillery, which hammered our back areas, and his trench mortars, which constantly bombarded our outposts. A row of houses along an absolutely straight street forms a comparatively easy target, and a cellar is no protection against a 240lbs. Minenwerfer shell. On one occasion the enemy, starting at one end, dropped a shell on every house in turn down one side, smashing each cellar; it was a nerve-racking performance for those who lived in one of the cellars and had to watch the shells coming nearer, knowing that to go into the street meant instant death at the hands of some sniper. The headquarters of No. 15 Platoon had a direct hit, but fortunately 2nd Lieuts. Brooke and Ramsden were both out crawling about somewhere, and the only damage was to their dinner. Every mortar, whose position was known, was given a name and marked on a map, so as to simplify quick retaliation. Captain Burnett spent much time at the telephone demanding the slaughter of "Bear," "Bat," "Pharoah," "Philis," "Philistine," "Moses," "Aaron," etc. etc.

It was impossible to visit any of the outpost line by day, and those from Battalion Headquarters who wanted to do so had perforce to go at night. Nights were dark; the ground was covered with shell-holes, some of them of great size. Once Major Griffiths, going out with Grogan, his runner, suddenly disappeared from view in an enormous hole which had apparently amalgamated itself with some well or sewer. The Major was almost drowned, but came to the surface in time to hear Grogan say: "You haven't fallen in, have you, sir?" He was fished out and scraped down and went on his way to "John Burnett's Chateau," where he was given warmth and comfort, and whence he eventually returned to Liévin—taking care to rob the asparagus bed before leaving.

Towards the end of the tour the enemy attempted a small raid against our somewhat isolated right post, but was easily driven off by our Lewis guns, and made no other attempts. On the 25th of May the Sherwood Foresters took our place, and we marched out to Marqueffles Farm. The tour had cost us twenty-four casualties, three of whom were killed; we had some narrow escapes in the cellars, and were fortunate not to lose more. "D" Company had had a particularly bad time, and owe much to Serjeant Burbidge, who seemed in his element in the midst of terrific explosions and rocking cellars, and saved many casualties by his calmness.

Marqueffles Farm stands next to Marqueffles coal mine, at the foot of the Northern slopes of the Lorette ridge. The Companies were all billeted in the farm, and the officers in tents outside, while a home-made marquee formed an excellent mess. After our first difficulty, which was to find the place at all in the utter darkness of relief night, we spent a very happy twelve days in beautiful weather. After coal mines and squalid narrow streets, the woods of Lorette, the little village of Bouvigny, and the open country were delightful, for the scenery to the south was all very pleasing. Games of all descriptions were our programme for the first two days, while our chief amusement was to watch the enemy's attempts to hit the observation balloon above us. His shells, fitted with clockwork fuzes, burst very high, and were quite harmless.

But our stay in Marqueffles was not merely a rest, we were there to practice for an attack to be made shortly on Fosse 3. A plan of the Fosse and its trenches was marked out, and each day the assaulting Companies, "B" and "C," practiced their attack over it, until each man knew his task exactly. In addition to this "C" Company were able to scale the Marqueffles slag-heap, and so prepare themselves for Fosse 3, whose 30 feet they would have to climb in the battle. General Kemp had had to go to Hospital with a poisoned foot and Colonel Thorpe, the Divisional Staff Officer, who took his place, came often to watch our practice, making on the last occasion a very encouraging, if somewhat bloodthirsty speech. Through it all we enjoyed ourselves immensely. For a change canteen stores were plentiful, and a generous supply of cigarettes, beer, and other luxuries, did much to raise our spirits. The officers, too, had many pleasant evenings, and, on more than one occasion, the night was disturbed by the old familiar strains of "Come Landlord fill the flowing Bowl," "John Peel," and other classical ditties.

On the 6th of June we moved up to Liévin and took over the line from the 5th Sherwood Foresters. For the first time the officers were clothed exactly as the men. " D " Co. (Burnett) was in front, " A " Co. (Broughton) in support, and " B " and " C " (Wynne and Moore) in the row of houses just west of Riaumont Hill. These had hardly settled down before a shell burst in the doorway of " C " Company Headquarters killing Serjeant Harper, the Lewis Gun N.C.O., and wounding six others, amongst them another Gunner, L/Cpl. Morris. At the same time 2nd Lieut. A. L. Macbeth had to go to Hospital with fever; Capt. Wynne was also far from well, but refused to leave his Company on the eve of the attack.

The final preparations were made on the night of the 7th/8th, when two parties went out to cut wire, 2nd Lieut. Banwell and 2nd Lieut. C. S. Allen. The first party found some thick wire, placed their ammonal tubes and successfully blew several gaps. The others, under 2nd Lieut. Allen, found no uncut wire, so brought their tubes back. Everything was ready by dawn on the 8th, and Zero was ordered for 8-30 p.m. the same day.

For several days the Monmouthshires had been at work deepening " Assign " trench, and had done much, but it was still shallow, and there is no doubt that as

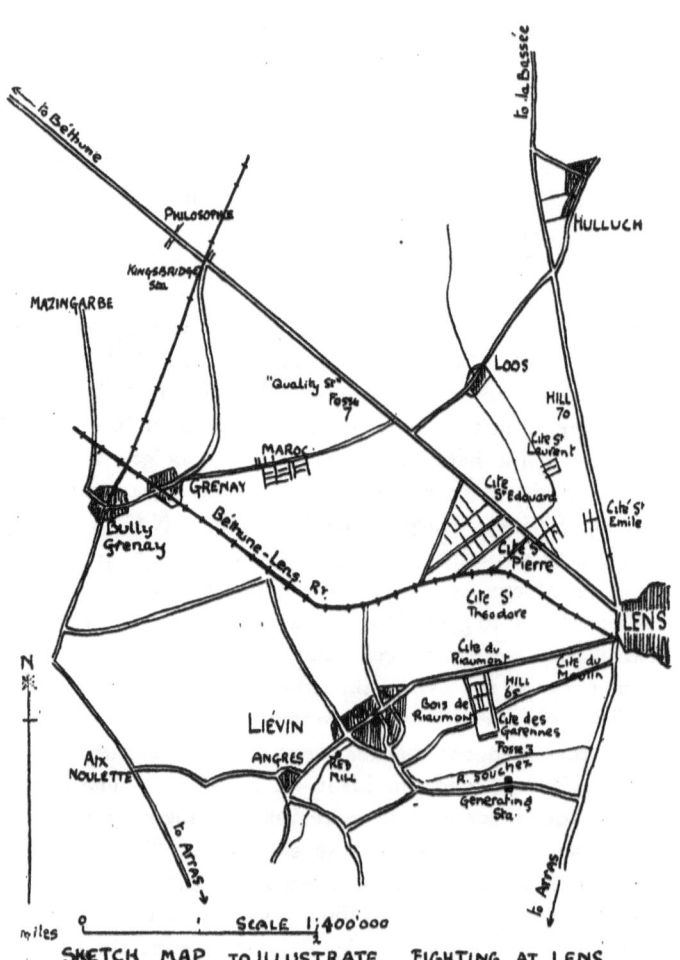

SKETCH MAP TO ILLUSTRATE FIGHTING AT LENS
– MAY, JUNE 1917 –

"B" and "C" Companies came up it between 5.0 and 6.0 p.m., they were seen from the top of "Hill 65." For as "B" Company passed the group of cottages South of Riaumont Hill, the Boche opened a heavy fire on the trench and dropped a shell right amongst the Company Headquarters. Capt. Wynne was untouched, but his Serjeant-Major, Gore, and his runner, Ghent, both first-class soldiers, were killed by his side. Assembly was complete by 6.0 p.m. and "B," "C," with "D" Co. in close support, waited for Zero in some short lengths of trench, dug amongst the houses at the East end of "Assign" trench. "A" Co., who were to carry ammunition and stores for the attackers, formed up near Battalion Headquarters, in the group of houses half way up the trench. Capt. Wynne, though worn out with fever, and hardly able to stand, still stuck to his Company.

At 8.30 p.m. the barrage opened, and the attack started. Almost the first shell exploded some ammunition dump on the far side of the slag heap, and the whole battle was lit up by the gigantic fire which followed. Against the red glow the black figures of "C" Company could be seen swarming up the slag-heap, clearing the two trenches, "Boot" and "Brick," on its summit, and sweeping on to clean out the dug-outs beyond. There were many Germans on and around the heap, and in a short time between 80 and 100 were killed, nearly all with the bayonet. Serjeant Needham stormed a trench mortar emplacement, himself accounting for most of the crew. Serjeant Roberts, formerly of the Transport, and with his Company for the first time, was much annoyed to find a bayonet through his arm, but did not stop until he had dealt with its owner and any of his friends he could find. Pte. Tookey and many others showed splendid dash, bombing dug-outs, bayonetting stray Huns, and occasionally taking a prisoner or two. But the central figure of the fight was 2nd Lieut. Banwell. Armed with a rifle and bayonet he simply ran amock and slaughtered some eight of the enemy by himself, while their leader he ran to the edge of the slag-heap and kicked over the side into the lake, where he broke his neck and was drowned. Altogether this Company took eight prisoners and destroyed three machine guns and two trench mortars.

Meanwhile the attack on the left had failed. At Zero Captain Wynne led " B " Company from their trenches and advanced towards the " L-shaped " building. They had hardly started before their ranks were swept from end to end with machine gun fire from the houses to their left and front. Capt. Wynne and 2nd Lieut. R. B. Farrer were killed, 2nd Lieut. W. I. Nelson was wounded, and the company had no officers left. Still, under the N.C.O.'s, they tried to push forward, only to meet with more losses. They were compelled to stop, and, under Serjeant Martin, the senior N.C.O. left, began to dig a line a few yards east of their starting trench. Serjeant Passmore, who was acting Serjt.-Major, Serjts. Kemp, Thorpe and Hibbert were all wounded, L/Cpl. Aris and nine others killed, and more than half the Company wounded. For some time Battalion Headquarters knew nothing of this disaster, and it was only when the Signaller L/Cpl. Woolley came back to report, that Col. Trimble heard what had happened. He at once ordered " D " Company to fill the gap, so as to protect the left flank of

"C" Company, which he knew must be seriously exposed.

"A" Company, carrying ammunition, had also had their casualties, and 2nd Lieut. Broughton, after being hit more than once, eventually had to leave them. He had been personally organizing most of the parties, and during the battle was everywhere, quite regardless of danger. Consequently, when he went, "A" Company became scattered; parties which had delivered their ammunition did not know where to go; and some of them, a few under Serjeant Putt and Pte. Dakin, wandered into the slag-heap and took part in the battle, helping to kill some of the Boche there. "D" Company lost two killed and ten wounded, for their position, joining the two flanks, was exposed to a considerable amount of enfilade fire.

As soon as they had cleared the summit of the slag-heap "C" Company started to consolidate "Boot" and "Brick" trenches, while the most forward of the attackers formed a protective screen. Their position was precarious. They were exposed to heavy fire from the generating station and "Hill 65," while unable to keep a watch on the low ground of the Souchez river valley or East of the slag-heap, where numbers of Boche could assemble unseen. The "L-shaped" building, too, was a thorn in their left flank. Still they were well established, when Col. Thorpe and Captain Wade, the Brigade Major, came round the line and looked at our new positions. They left the slag-heap just before dawn, and a few minutes later, when they were talking to Capt. Moore in his headquarters in the cottages below, a runner came in to announce a big Boche counter-attack. It was still too dark to see much, but our sentries could make out large numbers of men closing in on them from three sides, and fire was opened. The Boche dropped into shell holes, but continued his advance steadily, making use of all available cover. "C" Company, finding their rifles useless and very short of ammunition, waited until they came near enough to start bombing, and then gave them a volley of Mills grenades. But once again we were ruined by the inefficiency of those in rear; the bombs had no detonators. In a few minutes the Company would have been completely surrounded, so slowly and in good order they withdrew, first to the edge of the heap, and then down to the cottages at the bottom. One group of men stayed for an incredibly long time on a ledge partway down the face, but in the end they too had to come away. During the night the Company lost one killed and twenty-eight wounded, five of whom stayed at duty; two others were badly wounded during the counter-attack, were subsequently captured, and died as prisoners in Germany—Privates A. Beck and R. Collins. At the time, the withdrawal from the slag-heap seemed like a defeat, but, had we stayed, our casualties would have been far worse and the result the same; for with daylight, nothing could have lived on the heap, so long as the Generating Station and "Hill 65" remained in German hands.

The night after the battle we were relieved by the 5th Lincolnshires and marched out to Red Mill again for a few days' rest. We were congratulated by the General on the fight, and Captain Moore and "C" Company came in for special praise for their work with the bayonet. Capt. Wynne and 2nd Lieut. Farrer were buried in Bully Grenay, and Lieut. N. C.

Marriott took over "B" Company. For the last twenty four hours it had been commanded by Lieut. Petch, who returned from Hospital in the middle of the battle. He now went to "A" Company again, and was promoted Captain. Lieut. Marriott got his Captaincy a few weeks later. Capt. Shields returned from leave and took command of "D" again, while Capt. Burnett went to Headquarters.

CHAPTER XI.

HILL 65.

13th June, 1917.   4th July, 1917

THOSE who had hoped for a rest after the battle were disappointed, for, on the 13th of June, we once more went into the line opposite Fosse 3. The enemy seemed to have recovered from our attack on the 8th, and we spent a quiet five days, gaining no ground and suffering practically no casualties. Towards the end of the tour the Canadians gained a footing on the Southern corner of the slag-heap and established a post there, and at the same time took the whole of the Generating Station and the high ground round it. It seemed improbable that the Boche could hold Boot and Brick trenches much longer, so the General brought the 5th Lincolnshires into the line on the evening of the 18th to make a new attack on Fosse 3. This attack was to take the form of a large raid.

Leaving " A " Company (Petch) in close support in Cité des Garennes we went out to Red Mill while the attack took place, and the following day, the 19th, the Lincolnshires sent us down 24 prisoners to guard. Their raid had been a great success, they had cleared the slag-heap and the machine buildings and killed many Boche as well as taken prisoners. As a result of this the Lincolnshires were able to move into Boot and Brick for their outpost line, and here on the 20th we relieved them. Twice during the relief the S.O.S. Signal was fired by our posts in the front line on account of suspected counter-attacks, but our artillery replied so promptly and so efficiently that nothing materialized.

Our second night in the line was disastrous. During this fighting round Lens, any progress made was the result of minor operations, raids and even patrol fights, and there was seldom a large scale battle. It was naturally difficult to keep all units informed of the latest progress, and this difficulty was particularly great in our case, when trying to maintain liaison with the Canadians. The Souchez river was the boundary between the two corps, and made it impossible for us to visit their front line troops. We had therefore to rely on Division and Corps headquarters keeping each other posted as to the latest progress, and on more than one occasion this liaison broke down, and we suffered very heavily.

At dusk on the 21st we received a message, and at once warned all ranks, that the Special Brigade R.E. were going to carry out a gas bombardment of the mine buildings of Fosse 3. Projectors would be fired by a Company operating with the Canadian Corps, from whose front the buildings could be best attacked. The wind was satisfactory, and the buildings were at least 150 yards away from our nearest trenches, so there seemed no need of any special precautions. "C" Company, occupying Boot and Brick trenches, heard the familiar explosion as the projectors went off, and waited to hear them fall in the buildings. Instead, they fell in our trenches, several hundred of them; in a few seconds, and before any warning could be shouted, the trenches were full of phosgene, the deadliest of all gasses. Officers and men worked hard to rouse those resting, and, in particular, 2nd Lieut. Banwell taking no heed for his own safety, went everywhere, rousing, rescuing and helping the badly gassed. But it was too late, and all through the night and next morning casualties were being carried out to Liévin and down the line. 2nd Lieuts. Craggs and Macbeth both went to England, and, almost the last to leave the slagheap, 2nd Lieut. Banwell. His great strength had enabled him to survive longer than the others, but no constitution could stand all that phosgene, and during the morning he suddenly fainted, and had to be carried down. By the time he reached Liévin he was almost dead, and the Doctors held out no hope of his recovery. However, fed on oxygen and champagne he lasted a week, and then, to everybody's surprise, began to recover. The greatest surprise of all was when this marvellous man refused to go to England, but preferred to remain in Hospital in France until fit enough to rejoin his own Battalion. With the exception of Capt. Moore, who was fortunately on leave at the time, " C " Company was wiped out and temporarily ceased to exist. Twenty-four died from the poison, and in all sixty-two others of the Company went to Hospital. Most of these found their way to England, though one or two, such as Serjt. Needham and L/Cpl. Tookey, both fighting men, preferred to remain and return to us. " D " Company also had their losses, and Serjeant Sullivan and nine others were gassed, ten others wounded. The rest of the Battalion escaped untouched.

The following night the 8th Sherwood Foresters came into the line, and we went back to Marqueffles Farm.

HILL 65.

Our losses had been heavy and so far we had had practically no reinforcements, so had to reorganise our three remaining Companies with three platoons each instead of four. We were also becoming short of officers, having lost eight and only received one reinforcement—Lieut. R. J. H. F. Watherstone, who came to us from England.

We spent two days resting and cleaning ourselves, and trying to recover from the effects of the battle, before starting on any more serious work. On the Sunday, at Church Parade, General Thwaites came and spoke to us, congratulating us once more on the 8th, and praising especially "C" Company for their bayonet work. He was very angry indeed about the gas disaster and explained the cause. It appeared that the Company carrying out the operation had never been informed of our occupation of the trenches on the slag heap, and that, when they said they were going to bombard the mine buildings, they meant the whole area, including these trenches, which they imagined were still held by the enemy.

The whole Division was now very weak, for the series of small battles during the past six weeks had been expensive. However, the higher authorities considered we were still fit for battle and decided to give us one more show, before sending us to some quiet trenches to recuperate. The objective this time was "Hill 65," "Adjunct," "Adjacent" and "Advance" trenches and the outskirts of the Cité du Moulin—the last of the Cités outside Lens itself. Three Battalions would attack, ourselves on the right, our 4th Battalion in the centre, and the 5th S. Staffordshires on the left. Practice started at once over a flagged course, and our new Brigadier, General F. G. M. Rowley, C.M.G., of the Middlesex Regiment, came to watch us at work. Our formation differed slightly from that used in previous fights, for we gave great prominence to the "Moppers." Several times lately the leading waves of an assault had gone straight to their final objective, consolidated, and then found themselves cut off by parties of the enemy, over whom they had passed during the advance. Now a line of "moppers" was detailed to follow ten yards behind each wave, with orders to mop up everything and leave no living Boche anywhere behind the assaulting troops. In our case "D" Company (Shields) would mop up, "A" and "B" (Petch and Marriott) would make the attack, while two Companies of the 4th Lincolnshires were detailed to assist us with carrying parties.

While we were practising this, on the 25th the troops in the line made further progress, somewhat lightening our task, but not necessitating any alteration in our plans of attack. The battle was ordered for the 28th June, and the previous evening we moved up Assign trench to our assembly positions, Boot and Brick Trenches on the slag heap. We were to relieve partly Lincolnshires and partly Monmouthshires, and for some reason or other there was confusion among the guides. Those detailed for "A" Company wanted to lead them to the right instead of the left of the assaulting frontage, while "B" Company had "A's" guides. Fortunately Capt. Petch was able to catch his platoons in time, and, dismissing the guides, sent each to its correct position. Serjeant Putt, who had started first, he could not warn in time, but fortunately this N.C.O. knew enough of the plans to know that he was being led wrongly, and so retraced his steps and rejoined the rest of his Company on the slag-heap. "A" Company were in position by 10.0 p.m., but the other companies were seriously delayed and wandered about most of the night under guides, who took them the wrong way. To add to the confusion our liaison with the Canadians again broke down, and without any warning the Division on our right suddenly launched an attack. Barrages followed by both sides and the noise continued throughout the night. Long after the attack was over the noise went on, for every few minutes some post would get nervous and send up an S.O.S. signal, immediately calling down a barrage, to which the other side would reply in kind. All this took place on the other side of the Souchez river, but we came in for much shelling, and the relief was not finally complete until 5.0 a.m. At dawn we were all in position. "B" Company (Marriott) was on the right with a frontage from the Souchez river to the Southern edge of the mine buildings; "A" (Petch) was on the left, with the length of the buildings as their frontage; "D" (Shields) assembled under the slag-heap behind them. Zero was ordered for 7.20 p.m.

The original plan had been for the assaulting Companies to leave their assembly trenches a few minutes before Zero, and, moving forward carefully, to form up for the attack a few yards in front. At 7.0 p.m. it was still, of course, bright daylight; the enemy had two observation balloons up, and there were several aeroplanes about. It seemed that any such movement must be noticed. However, fate was on our side, and at 7.15 p.m. a rain storm burst over the country, completely obscuring the view, and by Zero the assaulting troops were lying out ready. They had not been seen.

At 7-20 p.m. the rain stopped, the barrage started, and we went forward. At the same time real and dummy gas attacks were made North of the Liévin-Lens road, and the enemy must have wondered very much where the main attack would be. The result was satisfactory; we met no real barrage and no very heavy machine gun fire, though there was a considerable amount of scattered shooting of both kinds. This did not delay our advance, though 2nd Lieut. Dawes was wounded and had to leave his Company. Our only difficulty was the mine building, through which "A" Company were supposed to advance; this was found to be impenetrable, and Captain Petch had to send half his Company through "B" Company's frontage, and half through the 4th Leicestershires, so as to avoid it. "Adjunct" and "Adjacent" trenches were reached practically without loss, but the enemy did not stay to receive us, and we found them empty. At 7.40 p.m. Yates, the "A" Company runner, reached headquarters with the news of the success of the battle.

Adjacent trench was organised as our new outpost line and several strong points were built along it. We also secured the Western end of "Almanac," a communication trench running N.E. alongside the railway. Halfway up this trench a deserted Boche machine gun post would have provided us with an excellent forward post, but unfortunately it was in our defensive barrage line and we were not allowed to occupy it. We had, therefore, to content ourselves with collecting the souvenirs, which included a telephone, and to come away. We had several casualties while consolidating, and lost another officer, 2nd Lieut. M. J. S. Dyson, who was slightly wounded by a stray shell. "B" Company lost Cpl. Baker wounded, and L/Cpl. Snow of "A" was also hit, in addition to two killed and twenty-five others wounded in the Battalion. The scattered shelling became somewhat more concentrated after our arrival, but did not stop our consolidation, which went forward rapidly with only one pause. About 8.0 p.m. there was a terrific rainstorm and everyone stopped work to put on waterproof sheets. The enemy must have done the same, and it was curious to notice how the battle stopped while everybody sheltered, for while the rain lasted there was complete silence, and neither side fired a shot.

Our task the next morning was to discover how far the Boche had retired. The Canadians South of the river had pushed on to the outskirts of Cité St. Antoine, almost in Lens itself, and, with "Hill 65" in our hands, the German positions in the Cité du Moulin were overlooked from everywhere. Patrols were sent forward to investigate, and 2nd Lieut. Brooke, with some of "D" Company, pushed forward up "Almanac" trench as far as the Arras road. Here they caught sight of a Boche patrol, which promptly fled as fast as possible. Except for this, the day passed quietly, as did the following morning.

The afternoon of the 30th, however, was far from quiet, and for several hours our new line was heavily shelled. In addition to the usual field batteries, there was one heavy gun which fired continuously on "A" Company's lines, obtaining a direct hit on Company Headquarters. Capt. Petch and 2nd Lieut. Campbell were both buried but not seriously hurt. Serjt. Ault, the acting Serjeant-Major, Wheeldon and Stevenson, the two runners, all three old soldiers of exceptional ability, were killed. Raven, another runner, was wounded, Downs had already been hit, and was again severely shaken, but both these stayed at duty, while they helped Lilley and Balderstone, who pluckily came along, to dig out those who were buried. In all twenty-eight were wounded, making our casualties for the battle three officers and ninety other ranks. That night the 4th Lincolnshires relieved us, and we went into Brigade reserve, two Companies in Cité des Garennes, the other in Liévin.

A few hours after relieving us the Lincolnshires made another attack, but failed to gain much ground, and met with considerable opposition from the neighbourhood of the Arras road. Their casualties were consequently heavy, and they asked to be relieved again the following night, so we were ordered to go up once more and take over their new line. Guides were to have met us at the " Broken bridge " near " Adjacent " trench, but only those for " A " and " B " Companies arrived, and for several hours Captain Shields waited with " D " Company, not knowing where to take his men. Apparently there had been some further operations, and the Lincolnshires had been shelled, in any case no guides appeared, and it was nearly dawn. At last, Capt. Shields, knowing that in a few minutes he would not have time to reach the front line, even if guides did arrive, gave the order to " about turn," and marched back. This caused considerable discussion at Battalion Headquarters, and Brigade finally decided that Col. Trimble should take over the line with two companies of the 4th Lincolnshires in front in the outpost line, two of our Companies in "Acorn" and "Adjunct," and one Company of ours under the slag-heap. We were all well dug in, and consequently did not lose very heavily when the following day, the 2nd of July, we were shelled continuously for several hours. Our telephone lines were almost all cut, so that messages had to be sent by the runners, whose task was far from pleasant on these occasions. Throughout these two months of fighting in Lens the runners, both Battalion and Company, had proved themselves to be very fine soldiers. We relied on them almost entirely in battle, for telephone wires never lasted long, and pigeons, once released, did not return. But the runners never failed, and what is more were always cheerful. Cheerfully they crawled along some exposed street, or dodged round houses in the Cité St. Pierre, cheerfully they faced Assign trench and Liévin corner, and equally cheerfully they crossed the slag-heap, often having to go actually through a barrage to reach their destination. Grogan, Collins, Sullivan, Raven, Kilcoyne and others, always ready and always willing, they would work till they dropped, and the Battalion owes much to their courage and endurance.

The 3rd of July passed quietly, and that night we were relieved by the 25th Canadians and marched to Aix Noulette, where we embussed and went to Monchy Breton for a rest.

CHAPTER XII.

ST. ELIE LEFT.

4th July, 1917.   23rd Nov., 1917.

WE stayed for three weeks at Monchy Breton and enjoyed ourselves immensely, with good weather, good billets and plenty of games. The Headquarters lived and messed at M. le Curé's, where they consumed a disgraceful amount of strawberries and cream, while the other officers under Captain Burnett messed together in another house. But the chief feature of this period of rest was the Divisional Rifle meeting, a regular Bisley meeting, which took place at the end of it. It was a triumph for the 5th Leicestershires, for we carried off amongst other trophies the G.O.C.'s Cup. R.S.M. Small, D.C.M., had one "first" and two "seconds," Corporal F. H. J. Spencer, M.M., one "first" and one "second," in the individual competitions, while Serjt. Clancy and Pte. F. Bindley won the assault course and individual "pools." On the second day "A" and "B" Companies each got third place in the Company Assault Course and Snap-shooting Competitions, and "C" was second in the Company "Knock-out" and third in the "running man" competitions. In this last Pte. Pepper won third place in the pool. Finally our officers' team won the revolver shoot. The rifle shooting throughout both days was of a very high order, but the same cannot be said for the revolver work, and we only won this last competition by being not quite so terribly bad as anybody else.

On the 20th of July we received orders to go into action again—this time to a quiet sector near Hulluch— and the following day we moved to Vaudricourt. The C.O. and most of the officers went by motor-'bus through to Philosophe to reconnoitre the new line; the rest of the Battalion set out under Captain Burnett to march. The previous evening had been spent in celebrating our rifle-shooting victories and we felt like anything rather than marching twenty miles under a blazing July sun. Those who took part in it will never forget that march; it was worse than "Luton to Ware" in 1914. Packs seemed heavier than ever before, the hill at Houdain was too much for many, and the beer and white wine of the previous evening proved stronger than march discipline, and many fell out. We finally crawled into Vaudricourt at 4-0 p.m. —tired out.

The following evening our Transport lines and Quartermaster's Stores moved to Labourse and we went into the line, relieving the 2nd York and Lancaster Regiment in the Hulluch right sector. For six days we lived in tunnels, with a front line which consisted of odd isolated posts at the end of each passage. The old front line trench seemed to have disappeared entirely. We were not much worried by the enemy, in fact, except for one trench mortar near Hulluch, called the "Goose," he kept very quiet. At the end of the tour we were relieved by the 4th Battalion and went into billets at Noeux les Mines.

Noeux was not shelled during our stay, so we had a peaceful time, though one officer was somewhat troubled on waking the first morning to find attached to his house the following notice: "THIS CROSS ROADS IS REGISTERED. NO PARTIES TO HALT HERE." We did not stay long, however, for on the 30th July we were suddenly ordered to move to Fouquières to prepare for a coming raid, and marched there during the afternoon, Battalion Headquarters to the Chateau, Companies to the village. For some reason best known to himself the billeting officer had billeted all officers with the wrong companies, but this was soon rectified, and we were very comfortable.

Our coming raid was to be carried out against the enemy's trenches West of Hulluch on a frontage of 300 yards. The sector chosen was bounded on the North by Hendon and on the South by Hicks Alley, while Herring Alley was in the centre. There were three German lines, and on the left a small extra line between the first and second, which we named Hinckley Trench. The scheme was for two Companies to take and hold the German third line, one Company to mop up behind them, and the fourth Company to follow with some Engineers to demolish dug-outs. One of the forward Companies would have to send a special party to deal with the "Goose" trench mortar. All wire cutting would be done by the Artillery, who were allowed a fortnight for it, so that they might not excite the enemy too much by heavy shooting. During this time we were to detail an officer to stay in the line, watch the shooting, and patrol the gaps at night. We would also practise the attack over a flagged course.

The flagged course was set out very elaborately at

Hesdigneul, and not only was each trench shown, but small notice boards denoted the position of every supposed machine gun, trench mortar, or deep dug-out. Practices took place first by day and finally by night, for the raid was to be a night attack, and various lamp signals were arranged to assist the withdrawal. The position of Hulluch village was indicated on the practice ground by a large notice board—HULLUCH—which probably gave any spies there might be in Hesdigneul a very fair idea of what was intended.

Meanwhile, we received various reinforcements. Lieut. G. E. Russell returned, 2nd Lieut. W. M. Cole came from the Artists' Rifles, 2nd Lieuts. R. W. Edge, T. R. L. Gibson, R. B. Rawson, C. P. Shilton, R. W. Sanders, L. W. Mandy, and J. S. Plumer came to us for the first time from England. At the same time a large party of men, arriving at Monchy Breton, had enabled us to reconstitute " C " Company, so that we now had four Companies of three platoons each, and enough officers for two Battalions. Lieut. Pearson went to Hospital and thence to England, and Capt. Wollaston acted Adjutant. The Company Commanders were unchanged.

For the second week of our fortnight we slightly relaxed the vigour of our practices, and devoted more time to musketry, bombing, and training the demolition parties for their work. The officers to take part in the raid were also chosen, and various tasks allotted to the others. Capt. Shields with 2nd Lieut. Cole and " D " Company would make the right attack; Capt. Petch with 2nd Lieut. Gibson and " A " Company, the left. " B " Company (Capt. Marriott and 2nd Lieut. C. S. Allen) would be the supports, and the two demolition parties would be found by "C" Company under 2nd Lieuts. Lowe and Edge. 2nd Lieut. Plumer was detailed to take a party of "D" Company to destroy the "Goose." Lieut. G. E. Russell was "O.C. Searchlight," and various other officers were chosen to count the raiding party when they returned.

Meanwhile, up in trenches the most wonderful work was being done by 2nd Lieut. Brooke and six other ranks of "D" Company—L/Cpl. Clapham, Ptes. Haines, Hanford, Johnson, Mason, and Rolls. This was the party left in the line with the Staffordshires to observe the wire cutting and patrol the gaps. At first, 2nd Lieut. Brooke spent his days with the F.O.O. and confined his patrolling to the hours of darkness, but later he was out in front both day and night. On two occasions he came into contact with the enemy. First, on his very first patrol, he had just reached the enemy's wire, and was trying to find a way through, when the enemy opened a heavy fire at close range. L/Cpl. Clapham was killed, shot through the head, and it was only with the utmost difficulty that the rest of the party escaped with their lives. The second encounter was in daylight. The Staffordshires had reported that they believed the German front line to be unoccupied, so on the 13th August, in the middle of the afternoon, 2nd Lieut. Brooke crossed No Man's Land, passed through the wire and entered the Boche front line. He was just exploring it when a very surprised German came round a corner and saw him. 2nd Lieut. Brooke at once left the trench and took shelter as quickly as possible in a shell hole outside. A perfect shower of bombs and rifle grenades were thrown after him, but he was untouched, and regained our lines without a scratch.

ST. ELIE LEFT.

On the 14th August, after a very happy fortnight at Fouquières, we moved to the huts at Noyelles, where the special stores for the coming raid were issued. At the same time all pay books, badges, identity discs and personal kits were handed in, and to each man was issued a small round cardboard disc with a number on it. The following morning we paraded at 10 a.m., and marched through Vermelles to Lone Trench and Tenth Avenue, where we were to wait until it was time to assemble. On the way, "B" Company had a serious disaster. A shell, intended for one of our batteries West of Vermelles, fell on the Company as they were passing the Mansion House Dump. They were marching in fours and had practically a whole platoon wiped out, for eleven were killed and fourteen wounded. Amongst the killed was Freddie Chambers, self-appointed Company humorist, and one of the best known and most cheerful soldiers in the Battalion.

Our Patrol party was waiting for us in Lone Trench, but their report was far from satisfactory. 2nd Lieut. Brooke declared that there were by no means enough gaps, in fact none at all on the left, and Colonel Trimble asked for the raid to be postponed. Meanwhile, 2nd Lieut. Brooke went off to the front line, where he finally was able to convince the Divisional Intelligence Officer that there were not sufficient gaps, and at the last moment, as the Companies were preparing to move to their assembly positions, the raid was postponed for 24 hours. Accordingly we spent the night in our somewhat cramped surroundings in Lone Trench, and the following day the Artillery continued to cut the wire, this time with better success.

One of the original objects of the raid had been to detract attention from a Canadian attack on "Hill 70" to be made at the same time. This attack we watched from the back of Lone trench, and later in the day were able to give material assistance. The German counter attack came from behind Hulluch, near Wingles, and the troops for it assembled and started their attack in view of our posts. Captain Ellwood and his machine gunners at once got to work and did terrific execution, being chiefly responsible for the failure of the enemy's efforts, and enabling the Canadians to hold the Hill.

So successful was the wire cutting on the 16th, that our patrol reported all ready for the raid, and accordingly we moved at dusk to our assembly positions. One alteration in the plan of attack had to be made at the last minute. It had originally been intended that the attacking platoons, after passing in file through our wire, should spread out in No Man's Land into lines. As the German wire was only cut into gaps and not obliterated, it was now decided that platoons should keep in file until through that belt also, and spread out on entering the front line. Bridges were placed over our front line, all faces were blackened, and by 10-30 p.m. all were ready for Zero, which was to be 10-58 p.m.

The barrage started promptly, and the advance began. The enemy's wire was a little thick on both flanks, but all passed through fairly easily and entered the front line, where, as arranged, each man shouted to show he had arrived. Two enemy were found and killed, but much of the trench was full of wire. The attackers passed on rapidly to the second and third lines, finding the wire thicker in front of each line, but finally reaching their objective and building bombing blocks. It was a dark night, and to avoid losing touch, Captains Petch and Shields had arranged to call each other's names as they went forward. Suddenly Captain Shield's voice stopped with one last cry, and Captain Petch hurrying to the spot found he had been hit by a shell and terribly wounded in both legs. However, his Company reached the third line, and the party under 2nd Lieut. Plumer set out to destroy the Goose.

Meanwhile, the mopping up and demolition continued behind the attack. Several Germans were found and killed in the second line, but on the whole very few enemy were seen, somehow they had managed to escape. Probably there were many tunnels, and in the dark it was quite impossible to tell what was a tunnel entrance and what merely a dug-out. Many of the latter were destroyed by "C" Company, though they lost 2nd Lieut. Lowe, who was slightly wounded, through being too keen to watch the effect of one of his own Mills bombs. Corporal Tunks and Pte. Baker did particularly good work with these demolition parties.

Back at Battalion Headquarters was a listening set, and this managed to overhear the German Company Commander's telephone report to his headquarters. "We are being attacked, ... front line penetrated, ... second line wrecked . . . . third line entered . . . . send up two sections." The two sections came in two parts. A strong bombing attack was made up Hicks Alley which was held by our bombing party at the newly built block; at the same time our left was attacked over the open. "A" Company were ready for them, and Lilley, the Lewis Gunner, soon accounted for many and broke up the attack. "D" Company also had some fighting, in which both 2nd Lieut. Cole and Serjeant Growdridge distinguished themselves.

The time finally came for the withdrawal, and the special flare lights were fired. Unfortunately they failed to light, and messages had to be sent at once to the raid area. The enemy were held off while the withdrawal was carried out, and by 2-0 a.m. the 17th the majority of the raiding party had returned. Captain Shields was carried in by C.S.M. Passmore, who very gallantly stayed out some time after the others were all back, but nothing could be found of Capt. Marriott or 2nd Lieut. Plumer and the "Goose" party. Capt. Marriott had been last seen in the second German line, but he had been missed in the withdrawal, and was never seen again. We brought no prisoners and no identifications, though one man brought back a rifle and another some papers from a dug-out. Several of the enemy had undoubtedly been killed, but no one had thought to cut off shoulder straps or search for pay books. At 3-0 a.m. we returned to Noyelles, where we spent the day cleaning and repairing our clothing.

The raid had not been a success. We lost Captain Marriott, 2nd Lieut. Plumer, and seven men missing, whom we never heard of again. Three more men were known to be killed, and three others were afterwards reported prisoners, while no less than fifty-one were wounded. Capt. Shields, the most cheerful, strenuous, and popular of Company Commanders, would never fight again. He reached Chocques hospital with one leg almost blown off and the other badly shattered, and the Doctors decided to amputate the one at once. It is still recorded as a unique feat, that throughout the operation neither the patient's pulse nor temperature altered, thanks to his wonderful constitution. The other leg soon healed, and within a few months he was hopping over fences in England in the best of spirits. "B" Company had lost their second Company Commander in two months. Like his friend Capt. Wynne, Captain Marriott had soon won his way to the hearts of his Company, with whom he rose from Platoon Commander, while in the Mess he was one of the merriest of companions and the friend of all.

There is no doubt that the enemy had been prepared for us. The rapidity with which his barrage started, the partly wired trenches, empty dug-outs and absence of garrison all pointed to this. He probably waited for us at his tunnel entrances, and hurried away as soon as we arrived; the few we found were those who had been too slow in getting away. As far as we ourselves were concerned, we only made one mistake—failing to bring back any identification. Apart from this all ranks had worked well, and we were congratulated by General Thwaites on our efforts.

Five days after the raid we relieved the 4th Leicestershires in a new trench sector, the "St. Elie left," and for nearly three months the Brigade remained in this same part of the line. The sector had its name from a much battered coal mine, the Cité St. Elie, which stood just inside the German lines opposite. About five hundred yards on our right, the Vermelles-Hulluch road crossed No Man's Land, while a similar distance on our left, Fosse 8 and its slag heaps formed the chief feature. All through 1916 active mining operations had been carried out along the whole front, and though there was now a deadlock underground, the craters still remained a bone of contention; each side tried to retain its hold on the near lip. Our right Company held a line of six of these craters, joined together, called " Hairpin " on account of their shape on the aeroplane photographs. The centre Company held another group called Border Redoubt, consisting amongst other things of two enormous craters, the Northern and Southern. Between these two groups lay " Rats' Creek," a short length of trench, 200 yards from the enemy, and without a crater. The left Company held another isolated post—" Russian Sap "—500 yards from the centre and not connected with it by any usable trench. The old front line between Border and Hairpin, via Rats' Creek, a distance of 400 yards, could be used by liaison patrols at night, but was impossible by day.

The various posts in " Hairpin " were connected by an underground tunnel with four exits to the trench, while another with two exits did the same for Border Redoubt. From each of these, a 300-yard tunnel ran Westwards to what had been the old support line, where they were connected underground by another long passage—Feetham Tunnel. A branch of the Border tunnel led to " Rats' Creek." At various points along these tunnels exits were built up to fortified shell holes, occupied by Lewis gun teams; these were our only supports. Down below lived Company Headquarters, the garrison, one or two tunnelling experts and the specialists, stokes mortars, machine gunners and others. It was a dreadful existence. The passages were damp and slippery, the walls covered in evil-looking red and yellow spongey fungus, the roof too low to allow one to walk upright, the ventilation practically non existent, the atmosphere, always bad, became in the early mornings intolerable, all combined to ruin the health of those who had to live there. But not only was one's health ruined, one's " nerves " were seriously impaired, and the tunnels had a bad effect on one's moral. Knowing we could always slip down a staircase to safety, we lost the art of walking on top, we fancied the dangers of the open air much greater than they really were, in every way we got into bad condition.

The entrance to this tunnel system was at the end of our only communication trench, Stansfield Road, a deep well-gridded trench running all the way from Vermelles. Battalion Headquarters lived in it, in a small deep dug-out, 200 yards from the tunnel entrance, and at its junction with the only real fire trench, O.B.1, the reserve line. In this trench the reserve Company lived in a group of dug-outs, near the Dump, called Exeter Castle. The left Company, with one platoon in Russian Sap and the remainder back in O.B.1, alone had no tunnels. But after our first few tours, the system was altered, and the support Company, living in tunnels, provided the Russian Sap garrison. Battalion Headquarters had a private tunnel, part of the mining system, leading to Feetham, which could be used in emergency, but as this was unlit, it was quicker to use the trench. The main tunnel system was lit, or rather supposed to be lit, with electric light. This often failed, and produced of course indescribable chaos.

Although the tunnels had all these disadvantages, it is only fair to say that they reduced our casualties enormously, for during the three months we lost only three officers slightly wounded and eighteen men; of these at least four were hit out on patrol. We also managed to live far more comfortably as regards food than we should otherwise have been able. Elaborate kitchens were built in Stansfield Road, and hot tea, soup, the inevitable stew, biscuit pudding, and other "luxuries," were carried up in hot food containers to the most forward posts. The only difficulty was with Russian Sap, for its approach, Gordon Alley, was in a bad state; but as the garrison was there at night only, they needed nothing more than "midnight tea," and this could be taken to them over the top.

A light railway ran all the way from Sailly Labourse to Vermelles, and thence to the various forward dumps, ours at Exeter Castle. Rations and R.E. material were loaded at Sailly, taken by train to the Mansion House Dump at Vermelles, and then by mule-drawn trucks to the front. The Exeter Dump was lively at times, especially when a machine gunner on Fosse 8 slag heap, popularly known as Ludendorf, was pointing his gun in that direction. But beyond a mule falling on its back into O.B.1, we had no serious troubles, and got our rations every night with great regularity.

The enemy were not very active, although they were reported to be the 6th Bavarians, "Prince Rupprecht's Specials." An occasional patrol was met, and our parties were sometimes bombed, but on the whole the Boche confined his energies to machine gun fire at night, scattered shelling at any time, and heavy trench mortaring, mostly by day. Fortunately there was not much mortaring at night, and what there was we managed to avoid by carefully watching the line of flight, as betrayed by the burning fuse. These heavy mortar shells with their terrific explosion and enormous crater were very terrifying, and few soldiers could face them with the indifference shown to other missiles. One exception was L/Cpl. Robinson of "B" Company who, with his Lewis gun team, treated them with the utmost scorn, and used to fire "rapid" with a rifle at them, as they came through the air.

All this time the system of holding the Brigade sector was to have two Battalions in the line, one in Brigade support, and one resting at Fouquières. Thus, one rested every eighteen days for six days, while one's trench tour was broken by six days in the middle in Brigade support. This last meant Battalion Headquarters and two Companies in Philosophe, the remainder in Curly Crescent, a support trench several hundred yards behind O.B.1. Philosophe was a dirty place, but had the advantage of being much less shelled than the neighbouring Vermelles, and we were not much molested.

Fouquières was always pleasant. The Chateau and its tennis court and grounds made a delightful Battalion Headquarters, and the Companies had very comfortable billets in the village. We played plenty of football, and were within easy reach of Béthune, at this time a very fashionable town. The 25th Divisional Pierrots occupied the theatre which was packed nightly, and the Club, the "Union Jack" Shop, and other famous establishments, not to mention the "Oyster Shop," provided excellent fare at wonderfully exorbitant prices.

During these three months we received many new officers, some of them staying for a few days before passing on to Tank Corps, Flying Corps, or Machine

Gun Corps, others proving themselves worthy of our best traditions. One party in particular, 2nd. Lieuts. F. G. Taylor, H. C. Davies, G. K. Dunlop, and W. R. Todd, provided four who came to stay, a very valuable asset, when so many merely looked in for tea and then went away. Others who came to fight were 2nd Lieuts. W. Norman, A. J. Mace, J. S. Argyle, C .D. Boarland, J. G. Christy, A. Asher, A. M. Edwards, and, later, Lieut. P. Measures, who had been with us in 1916 for a few weeks. Col. Trimble and Capt. Moore each had a month's leave, and Major Griffiths, after commanding during the Colonel's absence, went to Aldershot for a three months' course. Capt. Burnett became 2nd in Command with the acting rank of Major. Capt. Hills, the Adjutant, returned from England and resumed his duties, while Captain Wollaston took charge of " B " Company for a short time, and then went to the Army School, where he stayed as an Instructor and was lost to us. Captain Barrowcliffe came to us for a short time in command of " D " Company, but then went to the Army School, and handed the Company over to Lieut. Brooke, who had been granted an M.C. and three weeks' leave for his Hulluch patrols. 2nd Lieut. Campbell went to Hospital with the results of gas poisoning and had to go to England, whither also went 2nd Lieuts. Rawson and Gibson who were invalided. A great loss to us was our Doctor, Captain Morgan, who had been with us for many months and was now sent to Mesopotamia, and was replaced by a succession of stop-gaps until we finally got the invaluable W. B. Jack. There were changes, too, in the ranks. Most important was the departure of R.S.M. Small, D.C.M., our Serjeant Major since mobilization. He had been unwell for some time and at length had to go to Hospital and home to England. Debarred by his age from taking a Commission, for which he was so well suited, he had rendered three years' very faithful service to the Battalion, untiring alike in action and on the parade ground, and popular with all, officers, N.C.O.'s and men. He was succeeded by C.S.M. H. G. Lovett, formerly of " B " Company, and latterly serving with the 2nd/5th Battalion. At the same time, Serjt. N. Yeabsley, a very capable horseman and horse master, came to us from the 4th Battalion as Transport Serjeant.

This long tour of trench warfare was not entirely devoid of interest, and several little incidents occurred to break the monotony. The first was a big " strafe " on the 25th of August, when for some unknown reason the enemy shelled Stansfield Road very vigorously, and obtained a direct hit on " C " Company Headquarters. Lieuts. Banwell and Edge were occupying the dug-out at the time, and were both shaken, though the former as usual did not take long to recover. Lieut. Edge, however, was sent to the Stores for a time and for some months acted as Transport Officer. On another occasion, 2nd Lieut. Norman was firing rifle grenades from " Hairpin " craters, when he received one in reply, and had to go to England with one or two pieces in him.

Except for these two incidents, all other excitement occurred in No Man's Land, where we had patrols every night in the hopes of catching a Boche. The first to meet the enemy was 2nd Lieut. Mandy, who was almost surrounded by a large party of them just North of Northern crater. He managed to fight his way out, though for a time he lost one of his party, Pte. Brotheridge, who did some fighting on his own and returned to us at dawn. After a time, tired of finding no one, our patrols became more venturesome, and most nights entered the German lines at some point or other. "A" and "C" Companies worked mostly round the Hairpin craters, and Lieuts. Banwell and Russell, 2nd Lieuts. Dunlop and Norman, all explored the enemy's front line. On one occasion Capt. Petch himself accompanied Lieut. Russell and Serjeant Toon to look at the enemy, and for a change found his front line held. They were caught peering over the parapet, and got a warm reception. Both officers were slightly wounded and had to go to England. Meanwhile, Lieut. Banwell took command of "A" Company. He, too, on another occasion explored the same piece of trench and found it empty, nor could he attract any enemy, though he and his party shouted, whistled and made noises of every description.

Border Redoubt and Rats' Creek were the hunting ground of "B" and "D" Companies, and here Lieuts. Ball and Measures more than once nearly captured a Boche post. But the enemy was too alert, and slipped away always down some tunnel or deep dug-out. But the best patrolling was done from Russian Sap, by 2nd Lieut. Cole and his gang from "D" Company, including Serjt. Burbidge, Cpl. Foster, L/Cpl. Haynes, Ptes. Thurman, Oldham and others. They had very bad luck, for on two occasions they lay in wait for the enemy in his own front line and he never came, though he had occupied the post the previous night, and the party, wet through and frozen, had to return empty handed except for a bomb or two.

ST. ELIE LEFT. 223

There was one other unusual occurrence before we left the St. Elie sector. We were visited one day by a local newspaper reporter, Mr. Wilkes of the "Leicester Mail," who came to see us in trenches, and was introduced to the tunnels and all the "grim horrors" of trench warfare. It seemed curious to see a civilian in a grey suit, adorned with a steel helmet and box respirator, wandering about the communication trenches.

On the 14th of November, while in Brigade Support at Philosophe, we were ordered to reconnoitre the "Hill 70" sector, with a view to taking over the line from the Sherwood Foresters. The same day we moved to some particularly cold and uncomfortable huts at Mazingarbe, going to the line the next night. Our route lay along the main Lens road past Fosse III. and Fosse VII., then by tracks past Privet Castle to Railway Alley. This endless communication trench led all the way past the famous Loos Crucifix, still standing, to what had been the front line before the Canadian attack. Thence various other alleys led to the front line. Our new sector was by no means luxurious. There was a front line trench and portions of a reserve line, all rather the worse for wear, while the communication trenches, "Hurrah" and "Humbug" Alleys, were unspeakably filthy. The whole area at the top of the hill was an appalling mess of tangled machinery from Puits 14 bis, battered trenches, the remains of two woods, Bois Hugo and Bois Razé, and shell holes of every size and shape. There was mud and wet chalk everywhere, and a very poor water supply for drinking purposes. What few dug-outs existed were the usual small German front line post's funk holes, and all faced the wrong way. It was a bad place. There was, however, one redeeming feature. From the hill we could see everything, Hulluch, Wingles, Vendin and Cité St. Auguste lay spread out before us; we could see the slightest movement. Behind the hill, Support Companies were out of sight, and those not actually in the front line could almost all wander about on top without fear of being seen. Furthermore, there were no tunnels.

We spent all our time working, for there was much to be done. Our chief tasks were clearing out existing trenches and digging new communication trenches where they were wanted. Digging was both difficult, for the ground was sodden, and dangerous on account of the number of " dud " shells and bombs everywhere. Two men of ' B " Company were injured by the explosion of a grenade which one of them struck with a shovel, and the next day Captain Moore had a miraculous escape. Clearing the trench outside his Company Headquarters, at the junction of " Horse " and " Hell " Alleys, he put his pick clean through a Mills bomb; fortunately it did not explode. Padre Buck also had a busy time, for there were many unburied dead still lying about. Hearing of one body some sixty yards out in No Man's Land, where it had been found by a patrol, the Padre went out with his orderly, Darby, to bury it. It was a misty morning, and they were unmolested until suddenly the mist lifted and they were seen. Darby was wounded in the head, and they were heavily fired on, but this did not worry the Padre, who brought his orderly back to our lines, and came in without a scratch.

We remained only seven days in this sector, and did not come into contact with the enemy at all at close quarters. A few bombs were thrown in the Bois

Hugo trenches, and a raid by the 11th Division on our right caused a considerable amount of retaliation to fall on our heads, but on the whole the enemy was quiet, and we had practically no casualties. There was not time to learn the ground well enough to do any extensive patrolling, though Lieut. Watherstone earned the Divisional Commander's praise for a bold reconnaissance from the Bois Razé. The transport had as bad a time as anyone, bringing rations on the light railway through Loos, which was never a pleasant spot. Once again a mule succeeded in falling into a trench, and it took R.S.M. Lovett and a party of men more than an hour to extricate it.

The 4th Battalion took our places at the end of the tour, and we marched back to Mazingarbe. Our billets had been slightly improved, and Headquarters now had a house in the Boulevard, commonly called "Snobs' Alley." While here a new horse, a large chestnut, which arrived for the Padre, caused considerable commotion in the Regiment. First he bolted with the Padre half-way from Mazingarbe to Labourse, when he finally pulled him up and dismounted. He then refused to move at all, and went down on his knees to Padre Buck, who was most disconcerted, especially when the animal moaned as though truly penitent. The next day the Adjutant tried to ride him, and once more he bolted. This time his career was short, for horse and rider came down on the Mazingarbe cobbled high road, and the Adjutant had to go to Chocques hospital with a broken head, and was away for a week.

During his absence we lost Colonel Trimble, who, much against his will, was ordered to take command of his own Battalion, the 1st East Yorkshires. He had been with us for seven months, and we were all very fond of him and very sorry indeed when he had to go. Worse still, there seemed no chance of Col. Jones returning to us. For six weeks, September and October, he had been close to us in Noeux les Mines, attached to the 1st Battalion, and more than once had come over to see us, but now the 6th Division had moved away and we did not know their whereabouts. The matter was finally settled by the arrival of a new Commanding Officer in the same car which came to fetch Col. Trimble. Lieut. Colonel R. W. Currin, D.S.O., of the York and Lancaster Regiment, had come to take command.

CHAPTER XIII.

CAMBRIN RIGHT.

1st Dec., 1917.   12th April, 1918.

COLONEL Currin, our new Commanding Officer, was a South African, a large man of enormous physical strength. He at once terrified us with his language, which can only be described as volcanic, and won our respect by his wonderful fearlessness. Of this last there was no question. In trenches, he would wander about, with his hands in his pockets, often with neither helmet nor gas-bag, and quite heedless of whether or no the enemy could see him. More than once he was shot at, and more than once he had a narrow escape at the hands of some hostile sniper, but this appeared to have no effect on him, and after such an escape he was just as reckless as before. He had withal a kind heart and a great sense of humour.

A few days before his arrival we had moved from Mazingarbe to Drouvin and Vaudricourt, and here we were now warned that on the 1st December General Thwaites would inspect the Brigade in review order. A rehearsal was carried out in a field near Noeux les Mines, a rehearsal so amusing in many ways, that the Colonel loved to tell the story of what he called his first experience with the 5th Battalion: "On approaching the parade ground I sent forward A——, who was acting Adjutant, to find where we were to fall in. My Adjutant was in Hospital as the result of falling off his horse. When I reached the field, I saw an officer galloping about waving his arms, but whether he was signalling to me, or trying to manage his horse I could not tell, so sent Burnett to find out. Burnett's horse promptly stumbled, fell and rolled on him, so I went myself and found the luckless A—— quite incapable of managing his pony. I told him to dismount, while I marched the Battalion into place, but subsequently found he had not done so because he couldn't! Eventually the Serjeant-Major seized him round the waist, someone else led the pony forward, and A—— was left in the Serjeant-Major's arms and lowered to the ground. All this in front of the Brigade drawn up for a ceremonial parade!" The parade itself also had its amusing side, chiefly owing to the ignorance of certain Staff Officers on matters of drill. However, a friendly crump, arriving in the next field, put an end to the proceedings, and we marched home.

After all this bother the actual inspection was cancelled and we went into trenches again instead. Our sector this time was Cambrin, called after the village next North of Vermelles, and the sector immediately on the left of our last—St. Elie. On the morning of the 1st of December we marched to Annequin, on the Beuvry-La Bassée Road, and relieved some Loyal North Lancashires, Worcestershires and Portuguese in the Brigade support positions. The Headquarters and two Companies were in Annequin village, the other two Companies in two groups of dug-outs, "Maison Rouge" and "Factory," about 500 yards East of Cambrin. We only stayed here twenty-four hours and then went into the front line, " Cambrin Right " subsector.

Cambrin Right was very like St. Elie Left with the good points left out. The right Company had tunnels but they were not safe, though just as smelly as our old ones. It was the same on the left, while in the centre, there were deep enough tunnels, but they were unconnected with anything and unlit. The front line consisted mostly of craters, a large series of which occupied what had once been the Hohenzollern Redoubt. At intervals along the lips were odd posts, each at the end of a short trench leading back into Northampton trench or the tunnel system. The right group of tunnels, the Savile tunnel, started half-way up Savile Row, a communication trench which had originally run from the Reserve line to Northampton trench, but now stopped at the tunnel entrance. The centre group had no name, started from Northampton trench, and had no proper communication trench. The left group was the " Quarry " tunnel system, starting from the old quarry and running leftwards from the Northern edge of the Hohenzollern craters almost to our posts opposite Mad Point. The left Company had no posts actually on crater lips, though they had one or two craters in No Man's Land. " Quarry " Alley led to the " Quarry " and a newly dug trench ran from this to Northampton near the centre tunnels, but it was in bad condition and seldom used. As a rule, those who wished to visit the centre went through either Savile or Quarry tunnels to get there. One other trench led forward from the Reserve Line, Bart's Alley, but this ended in a large pile of sandbags and one of the Tunnelling Company's private entrances to the mining galleries. Between the Reserve Line and Northampton a few ends of gas piping, sticking out of the ground, showed where our 1915 front line had been, from which we had attacked on the 13th October. The two flank Company Headquarters were in the tunnels, the centre Company in a deep dug-out in Northampton trench. The Reserve Company, with one platoon of each of the front line Companies, lived in the Reserve Line.

The Reserve Line was about the best trench in the sector. It was deep, well traversed, and had many good dug-outs. It also contained our cook-houses and dumps. The light railway from Vermelles, on which came rations and "R.E. material," ran along behind it, so that Company Quartermaster Serjeants could deliver their rations to the reserve platoon of their Company, and there was no fear of a carrying party from another Company "pinching" some of the rum. Westwards from this trench ran three communication trenches, all in good condition, Bart's Alley, Left Boyau and Quarry Alley, all leading to the Vermelles broad guage railway line, whose hedges concealed Sussex trench. Here, in some very elegant, but not very shell-proof dug-outs, lived Battalion Headquarters. The officers' bedrooms, and the Mess were on one side, the offices on the other. Here, Corporal Lincoln and Pte. Allbright, the Orderly Room clerks, took it in turn to look after the papers, keep the fire alight and generally make a happy home out of a crazy shanty with a wobbly roof and a door facing the Boche. Many would have preferred to go elsewhere in case of shelling, but these two never left their papers, though more than once the roof came perilously near being whisked off by some whizz-bang.

Philosopher James Lincoln was particularly imperturbable, as he sat surrounded by pipes and beautifully-sharpened pencils, discussing the weather and the crops with any who chanced to pass by.

Further down this same trench Serjeant Archer and "Buller" Clarke looked after the bombs, not quite such a popular weapon now-a-days, and the Pioneers under Serjeant Waterfield and L/Cpl. Wakefield had their home next door. Here also was Serjeant Wilbur and that very hard working body of men the Signallers, "strafed" by everybody when telephones went wrong, and seldom praised during months and months without a mishap. Then came Serjeant Major Lovett in a small dug-out by himself, and near him Serjeant Bennett and the Regimental Police; the latter in trenches became general handy men, carrying rations, acting as gas sentries, and doing all the odd jobs. Round the corner a large dug-out with two entrances provided the Canteen with a home large enough to contain, when it was procurable, a barrel or two of beer. L/Cpls. Hubbard and Collins and the runners lived wherever they could find an empty shelter, and as usual spent most of their time carrying messages or showing visitors round the lines.

There was one other trench, Railway Alley. This, like its namesake to "Hill 70," was of enormous length. It started at Cambrin, passed the Factory and Factory Dug-outs, and, following the Annequin-Haisnes Railway to its junction with the Vermelles Line, acted as dividing line between the two halves of the Brigade Sector. From the left Battalion Headquarters to the front line, an often much battered part of it, it belonged to the left sector. Our Headquarters had a private trench running to it, "Kensington Walk," deep and completely covered with brushwood by way of camouflage.

In the St. Elie sector we had been three months almost without an incident of any importance; we were only six weeks in Cambrin, and every tour contained some item of interest. We started disastrously. On the night after relief Lieut. Watherston was visiting "B" Company's posts in the centre sector, when a party of the enemy crept up to and suddenly rushed the Lewis Gun Section he had just visited. Lieut. Watherston turned back, drew his revolver, and rushed into the fight, but was himself shot through the head and killed instantaneously. He had fired three shots with his revolver, but was unable to stop the enemy, who, having wounded the sentry and blown the N.C.O. off the firestep with a bomb, now escaped, taking the Lewis Gun with them. The N.C.O., Cpl. Watts, got up and gave chase, but lost touch with the enemy amongst the craters, and after being nearly killed himself had to return empty-handed. Our predecessors in the line seemed to have made no effort to wire this part of the line at all, presumably thinking the line of craters a sufficient protection. A few nights later 2nd Lieut. Boarland reconnoitred the whole area with a patrol, and found that not only had the Boche got a well-worn track across No Man's Land between two craters, but close to the raided post had fitted up a small dug-out with a blanket and a coat in it. This would, of course, have been impossible had the previous occupants of the line done any patrolling; we suffered through their gross negligence.

Towards the end of the same tour, the enemy made

another very similar attempt against our extreme right posts held by "A" Company. L/Cpl. Beale and Pte. Foster were with their gun on the parapet, when they were suddenly rushed by three or four of the enemy who had crept close up to them, and were on top of them before they could open fire. L/Cpl. Beale used his fists on a German who seized him round the throat, but was then shot in the chest and fell backwards on the rest of the section who were coming to help. The Germans tried to carry off the gun, but Foster put up a fight, and they dropped it just outside the trench. However, one of them managed to knock Foster on the head, and, before help could arrive, he was carried off as a prisoner. Once again we suffered through the carelessness of our predecessors, for in this case, too, there was no protective barbed wire. We spent every night of the tour wiring hard, but could not of course finish the whole sector in five days.

The tour also contained a very severe Artillery and Trench Mortar bombardment, which seriously damaged our left and centre trenches. But more serious than this was the loss to "B" Company of L/Cpl. J. T. Pawlett, one of the best Lewis Gun N.C.O.'s in the Battalion, who was mortally wounded during the shelling. A few days later we lost another excellent Lewis Gun N.C.O., L/Cpl. Stredder, of "D" Company, who went to England wounded, fortunately not very seriously.

The tour ended on the 8th, and for the next six days we remained in Brigade Support, Annequin, Maison Rouge, and Factory Dug-outs. Even here we were not left in peace, for on two occasions the enemy opened very heavy bombardments against the Cambrin sector. The second occasion, the night of the 12th/13th of December, this was so terrific, and so much gas was used, that we had to "stand to" at midnight, while many messages, "Poison Cambrin" etc., were flying about. The damage to trenches, and more particularly to the tunnels, caused by this bombardment was very great, as we soon learnt when, two nights later, we returned to the line. Savile tunnel was blown in in several places, and the Company Headquarters completely cut off and unusable. The tunnel entrances were shattered, and the whole system so badly damaged as to be almost useless except as dug-outs for the various posts. Quarry tunnel was not so badly damaged, but several of the left posts had been isolated by having the main connecting tunnel blown in behind them. Fortunately the front line trench on the left was still in existence, and could be used instead of the tunnels. Finally, Northampton trench was literally obliterated in the centre, and a famous "island" traverse, no small earth-work, so completely wiped out that we could never afterwards discover its exact whereabouts.

Once more we had bad luck at the start of the tour, for we had only been a few hours in the line when a shell on Quarry Alley caught a small party of men coming down. Signaller Newton and Stretcher Bearer Cooke were killed outright, and Serjeant Woolley, acting Serjeant Signaller while Serjeant Wilbur was away, was wounded and had to go to Hospital. In addition to the wiring we now had the tunnels to dig out, and there was so much work to do that we had to have assistance from Brigade; this took the form of a Brigade Wiring Platoon and a Company of Monmouthshires. On one occasion these two parties, both of course working " on top," saw fit to imagine each other were Boche, and a small fight ensued. Fortunately no one was injured, though one of the Monmouthshires was only saved from a bullet through the head by his steel helmet.

The rest of the tour passed off quickly, and the irrepressible Capt. Brooke and 2nd Lieut. Cole of " D " Company started once more wandering about No Man's Land and the enemy's lines. They did the most incredible things, and gained invaluable information about the enemy, though awkward questions were often asked about the name of the " one other rank " who, according to the patrol reports, accompanied 2nd Lieut. Cole on these expeditions.

Our Christmas " rest " was spent in Beuvry, and here we arrived on the 20th of December at the end of our second tour. Our first duty was to inspect a large draft of 140 N.C.O.'s and men who had come to us while we had been in the line. Most of them came from the 11th (Pioneer) Battalion of the Regiment, and were men of good physique, very well trained, and excellent alike at drill, work, games, and in the line. During the whole time we were in France we never had a better draft than this. Meanwhile, although the enemy were apparently willing to allow us a Christmas rest, and kindly refrained from bombarding our billets, the higher command were not so gracious, and we had much work to do. Ever since the defection of Russia, the Staff had realized the possibility of a German offensive on a large scale, and every effort was being made to organize our defences. With this object, a new " village line " had been built, including Cambrin,

Annequin, Vermelles and other villages, and this had now to be wired. Accordingly, on the night of the 22nd/23rd December, the whole Battalion marched up to this line by parties, and worked hard for several hours putting out a "double apron fence." So well had Major Zeller and his Engineers organized the work, and so well did the Battalion work, mainly thanks to the newly arrived Pioneers who were experts, that we did an incredible amount during the night, and received the congratulations of the G.O.C. on our efforts.

The actual Christmas festivities had to be held on Christmas Eve, as we were due to go into trenches on the morning of Boxing Day. Everything combined to make the day a great success. Plum puddings arrived from England, large pigs, which Major Burnett had been leading about on a string for some days, were turned into the most delicious pork, and there was plenty of beer. The Serjeants' Mess also had a very lively dinner in the evening, though one Company Quarter Master Serjeant spent much of his time dragging the Beuvry river for his Company Serjeant Major whom he had lost. This Warrant Officer was eventually discovered asleep in an old sentry box, with his false teeth clenched in his hand. The Germans, in spite of their boast, dropped in a message from an aeroplane, "to eat their Christmas dinners in Béthune," caused no disturbance, and did not show the slightest sign of being offensive. Christmas, 1917, was unique in one respect. We produced a Battalion Christmas Card for the first and last time during the war. It contained a picture, drawn by 2nd Lieut. Shilton, of a big-footed Englishman standing on a slag-heap, from which a Hun was flying as though kicked. It was very popular.

Boxing Day, for us "Relief Day," was bitterly cold, and an occasional blizzard made getting into trenches all the more difficult. The ground was covered with snow, and each night there was a bright moon, so that the snipers of both sides were on the watch day and night for the slightest movement. Our snipers claimed to hit several of the enemy during the tour, but we, too, had our losses. First, F. Eastwood, M.M., of "C" Company, a soldier who had scarcely missed a day since the beginning, was shot through the head and killed outside "C" Company Headquarters in Northampton trench. A few nights later, on the 30th December, Lieut. P. Measures, commanding "B" Company, was sniped while fixing a sniper's post in the front line, and also killed instantly. He had not been with us very long, but both he and Lieut. Watherston had proved themselves very keen subaltern officers, and both had been praised by the General for their work on patrol. Lieut. T. H. Ball temporarily took command of "B" Company.

Whenever work was possible—it was often too light even at night—we worked at two new trenches, "Cardiff" and "Currin," connecting Bart's Alley with Savile tunnel, as an alternative to Savile Row. These had been dug by the Monmouthshires, and now had to be wired, and here, also, we suffered at the hands of a German sniper. Serjeant W. E. Cave, a very fine N.C.O. of "A" Company, was killed with a wiring party, and one or two others had narrow escapes. The New Year, 1918, was ushered in with several bursts of machine gun fire at midnight, but nothing of importance occurred.

Our stay at Annequin was once again disturbed,

this time more disastrously than before. A curious accident occurred on the 6th of January, when three of our aeroplanes collided and fell near the village. The enemy as usual opened fire at once with one or two batteries, and an unlucky shell fell amongst our Headquarter runners as they were leaving their billet. The two Corporals escaped, Collins with a slight wound and Hubbard untouched, but W. Raven, M.M., was killed outright, and A. Grogan, D.C.M., F. Smith, H. Eady, and H. Kirby, so badly wounded that they died soon afterwards. It is impossible to estimate the amount of work that these runners had done for the Battalion, not only as message carriers, but some of them as personal orderlies to the C.O. and other Headquarter Officers. In Lens they had proved themselves not only capable of wonderful endurance, but to be possessed of the greatest courage, fearing neither the enemy himself nor his barrages. To lose so many at one blow was indeed a severe loss for the Battalion.

After this, there followed two comparatively quiet tours in trenches with the usual six days at Beuvry in between them. The enemy's snipers were mastered, and we suffered no more casualties at their hands, but our bad luck still pursued us, and on the 10th and 11th January the left of the Reserve Line was badly battered by trench mortars. The left half Battalion cook-house was blown in, and Serjeant Growdridge of " D " Company was killed, while several others were wounded. In Serjeant Growdridge, " D " Company lost a most capable platoon Serjeant, the leader of many a daring and successful patrol, and of the highest courage in battle. On the 20th of January we were relieved by the 11th Division, and, after spending one night in

Beuvry, marched through Béthune to Busnettes, between Chocques and Lillers, for a long rest.

We stayed at Busnettes for three weeks, training and playing games, and doing our best to recover from the ill effects of tunnels and wet trenches. Our training was carried out on various areas round Chocques and Allouagne, and near the latter was a good rifle range, over which we practised for the Associated Rifle Association (A.R.A.) Competition. This competition was for a platoon, and included rifle and Lewis gun shooting and bayonet fighting, fire discipline and control, and the general principles of the advance. The platoon had to fire at various ranges, advancing from one to the other, and bayoneting sacks on the way. There were Battalion, Brigade, and Divisional Competitions, and to the Divisional winners the A.R.A. were to present silver medals. In the Battalion competition, No. 1 Platoon of " A " Company, under 2nd Lieut. Roberts and Serjeant H. Beardsmore, was victorious, but the other competitions could not be held until February, after our next move. Finally, this same platoon, beating the other Battalions in the Brigade, beat also the Staffordshires' and Sherwood Foresters' best platoons, and carried off the silver medals.

At this time there were several important changes in the Battalion. First, we were very glad indeed to see Captains Tomson and Petch back again with us, the former to command " B," the latter to " A " Company. At the same time, Capt. Barrowcliffe returned to the Royal Engineers. Lieuts. C. S. Allen and R. W. Edge went to England for six months, and 2nd Lieut. Todd became Transport Officer. We also received a large draft from the 2nd/5th Battalion. Finding that it was impossible to obtain sufficient recruits to supply all the Battalions formed at the beginning of the war, each Brigade was now reduced to three Battalions, and we lost from our Brigade the 4th Lincolnshires. In the 59th Division, the 2nd/5th Leicestershires were broken up and divided into drafts for the 4th Battalion and ourselves. Capts. J. A. Ball and W. H. Oliver, Lieuts. S. G. H. Steel and A. D. Pierrepont, 2nd Lieuts. A. B. Bedford, H. Coxell, K. Ashdowne, and, later, A. E. Hawley and Everett came to us, bringing with them 200 N.C.O.'s and men. Amongst the latter were several Serjeants, one of them, Serjeant T. Marston, M.M., destined to add further laurels to the honours he had already won with the 2nd/5th. There were also several "old hands" who returned to us, amongst them, Privates Garfield and Law of "D" Company, both original members of the 1914 Battalion. These reinforcements enabled us to form again four platoons per Company, and we became once more a full Battalion.

Another batch of reinforcements, which arrived at Busnettes, contained several drummers of the 1st and 3rd Battalions. We already had a few, and L/Cpl. Perry was given the rank of Serjeant Drummer and formed a Corps of Drums. With Drummer Price, an expert of many years' service with the side drum, and L/Cpl. Tyers, an old bandsman, to help him, he soon produced an excellent Corps, and all of them worked hard and keenly to make a good show. Within a week they played us on route marches and appeared at guard-mounting. Within two months they played at Mess, and the Fifes gave several very good concerts.

While in the Busnettes area, we were in Reserve for the 1st Army, and in case of attack were liable to be sent to support the Portuguese on the Neuve Chapelle-La Bassée front. In case of this, the C.O. and Adjutant spent a day reconnoitering the Locon, le Hamel, le Touret area and its keeps and strong points, many of which we afterwards occupied when the Portuguese had been driven out.

On the 8th of February, we moved to Fiefs through Lillers, and the following day marched to Reclinghem in the Bomy training area. The march took the form of a tactical field day, and we ended by taking up an outpost position on the river Lys at Reclinghem, where " B " and " D " Companies and Headquarters were billeted. The other two Companies were at Vincly, a little more than a mile further South. A fortnight later, to the great regret of all ranks, Colonel Currin had to leave us, after being only three months in command. During this time we had become very fond of him, and there is no doubt that his never-failing cheerfulness, his reckless courage, and the atmosphere of " the fighting spirit " which always accompanied him, did more than anything else could have done to raise our " fighting spirit " to a high pitch. His successor, Lieut. Col. G. B. G. Wood, D.S.O., of the Lancashire Fusiliers, had commanded the 2nd/5th Battalion until he was wounded, and now, returning to France, was sent to us as his Battalion had been broken up.

Towards the end of February, the Staff became more than ever convinced that the enemy intended making a big spring offensive, and our training was devoted almost entirely to counter-attack practice and the re-

taking a line of trenches which had been temporarily
lost. We had several large field days near Bomy, with
this as the general idea, and would have had several
more had not the Division been suddenly recalled to
the line. On the 1st March, in a snow storm, we
marched to Ligny-les-Aire, and the next day moved on
again to Ecquedecques, where we stayed three days.
Our billets were fairly comfortable, but there were very
few for the officers; this, however, was soon righted
after the first night, when we discovered many officers'
billets occupied by Serjeants of an A.S.C. Company
who were permanent " garrison " of the village.

On the 5th of March we marched through Lillers and
Béthune again to Beuvry and, after staying one night
there, moved the following day to Annequin and Sailly
Labourse, where we were responsible for the defence of
the Annequin locality. The 1st Corps scheme of defence
was a series of fortified localities, Philosophe, Cambrin,
Annequin, Noyelles, and many others further West as
far as Vaudricourt. Each locality had its trenches,
dug-outs, stores of ammunition and rations, and was
ready for defence at any moment. The German
offensive was expected to start any day, and the
" wind " was terribly " up." This, however, did not
prevent the Infantry from amusing themselves whenever possible, and though the higher authorities may
have been sleeping in their boots, we managed to get
some football. General Rowley gave a cup for a
Brigade Company Competition, and, while at Sailly, our
" A " Company beat Brigade Headquarters in the
" final," after which " Tinker " Evans, the captain of
the team, received the cup from the Brigadier.

The following morning we went once more to the

line, back into the familiar Cambrin right sector. Unfortunately there was now a change. The Engineers, in an endeavour to make Headquarters less elegant and more shell-proof, had thrown up so much white chalk, that they had attracted the attention of the German artillery, who had promptly shelled the place out of existence. The Headquarters now lived in the old left Headquarters under Railway Alley. We had only two Companies in the line, one in support, and one in Reserve near the Factory; we were thus organized " in depth " to meet the coming offensive.

The enemy's artillery had certainly become more active during our two months' absence, and he was now using far more gas shells than before. These were of three sorts: " Green Cross," the most deadly, was filled with phosgene; " Blue Cross," the least harmful, with arsenic; both these were very light gases and soon blew away. Far more dangerous were the " Yellow Cross," mustard shells, which now made their appearance in ever increasing numbers. The mustard hung round the shell holes and was not blown away; in cold weather it had no effect, but as soon as the sun came out it became exceedingly powerful. A mustard shell falling on frozen snow might have no effect until the thaw came several weeks later, when it would be just as powerful as if it had only just been fired. A very little of this gas was sufficient to cause temporary blindness and loss of voice, burns and bad blisters. Much of it was fatal. During this tour, however, we did not suffer any casualties, and nothing of any importance occurred until our last morning before relief, the 16th of March.

At about 1-0 a.m. on this morning, Privates Culpeck

and Johnson were sentries together at one of " D " Company's Lewis gun posts. Hearing a noise in the wire, one of them challenged, and, receiving no answer, fired his Lewis gun. Two minutes later, two Boche, one an unwounded warrant officer, the other a wounded soldier, were being escorted down Railway Alley to Headquarters. Neither of the two prisoners would say much, but what they did say still further confirmed the opinion of the Staff that the attack was soon coming.

" Brigade Support " now consisted of the Headquarters and two Companies in Sailly Labourse, the remainder at Windy Corner near Factory Dug-outs. To this last area went Major Griffiths and the Right Half Battalion. They had an unpleasant time and were more than once heavily shelled, on one occasion having a narrow escape. The officers were sitting in a dug-out when an armour piercing field gun shell passed through the roof and out of the door, hurting no one. Major Griffiths and 2nd Lieut. Dunlop received slight scratches, as also did Adams, one of the batmen, but no serious damage was done. After four days of this, the 5th Lincolnshires relieved us, and we marched to Beuvry to be in Divisional Reserve. While here, the new Battalion distinguishing marks arrived from England, and were taken into use—a half-inch yellow ring, two inches in diameter—worn just under the shoulder on the sleeve. They were rather bright at first, and earned us the name (amongst other ruder epithets) of the " Corn-plasters."

On arrival at Beuvry we were told that the Major General would inspect us at Fouquières two days later, the 22nd of March. This was considerably more alarming than the prospect of the German offensive, and we at once started training, cleaning equipment, and revising our platoon organisation. Meanwhile, the offensive did begin in the South, and the Boche on the morning of the 22nd actually launched a big raid against the Divisional front. However, the Inspection was not postponed, as we had hoped, and for several hours we performed at Fouquières. Our ceremonial was by no means bad, considering we had done none for months it was very good, but what most pleased General Thwaites was our organization. In vain he tried to find mistakes. Soldier after soldier was asked "Who is your Section Commander?" "Who takes charge if he is killed?" "When will it be your turn to take charge?" etc. etc., and soldier after soldier answered promptly and correctly. The result was a good word for all of us, and we went back to billets much relieved and feeling quite elated.

Meanwhile, the morning's raid had left a prisoner in our hands, and he had now caused about as much sensation as one man could, by stating quite definitely that the Boche would attack from the la Bassée Canal to "Hill 70" on the 25th of March with three Divisions. We went into the Cambrin sector again on the 24th, this time with three Companies in the line. News of the disaster to the 5th Army in the South had reached us, and what with Generals coming round to pay farewell visits, and conferences every few hours, everything was as depressing as possible. Curiously enough we were not depressed, and, though most of us regarded the attack as a certainty, the private soldiers were particularly more cheerful than usual. Late at night we were ordered to withdraw all except the tunnel sentries from the front line, so as to minimise the casualties during the enemy's preliminary bombardment, and to concentrate everything on the defence of the Reserve Line, which must be held at all costs. Some of the N.C.O.'s and men grumbled a little at what they called giving up the front line, more especially as patrols reported that the enemy was busy strengthening his wire, which did not seem the prelude to an attack. Finally, by 2-0 a.m. on the 25th all was ready. The Staff at Corps Headquarters, ten miles back, slept in their boots, all support and reserve Battalions moved to "battle" positions and stood to, we in the line behaved very much as usual. All waited for dawn.

Dawn came at last—the quietest since war began, not a shot was fired. Morning followed and high noon, still no movement; the Staff breathed a sigh of relief, the Infantry groused, and we occupied our front line, preparing to pass a normal night. However, this was not to be. We had scarcely posted our night sentries when at 8-30 p.m. came another message to say that the prisoner who had originally caused the alarm had remembered that the attack was for the 26th, not the 25th. All precautions were to be taken as for the previous night. With this arrived a long epistle from the Intelligence department, showing that various new dumps and camouflaged screens had been seen in the German lines, motor transport had been increased, etc. etc. etc.—all tending to confirm their wretched prisoner's statement. Once more we evacuated our front line, once more we waited and once more we were disappointed. The 26th was as quiet as the 25th, and, except for a humorous telephone message from "C" Company, which caused much laughter as far back as

Divisional Headquarters, there was nothing to disturb the morning's peace.

The following evening the 11th Division took over our sector, and we marched out—the Headquarters and Left Half Battalion to Sailly, Right Half to Labourse. It was a cold and rather miserable night, for, owing to a sudden move of our Q.M. Stores to Noeux les Mines, we had no blankets. Meanwhile, all schools and classes were closed, and those students who had not been taken to stop the German advance on Amiens returned to us. The situation was serious, and another blow was expected at any moment in the neighbourhood of Vimy. The Canadian Corps was chosen to oppose this, and we were consequently ordered to relieve any units of that Corps still left on "Hill 70." But on the 28th March before relief had started the expected attack came—at Oppy. It was a miserable failure, we lost a few front line trenches, but our line stood firm; however, the Canadians were wanted in a hurry and we were sent up to relieve them at once. The other Battalions went into the front line, we relieved the 46th Canadians in support round Loos Crassier and Railway Alley. Relief was complete by 10-35 p.m., an almost incredible performance, considering that there had been no time for reconnaissance and practically no arrangements made for guides.

It had rained hard throughout the relief, but our first two days in the line were dry and warm, and we managed to dry our clothing and make ourselves fairly comfortable. The enemy after the failure at Oppy was very quiet on our front, though his documents captured in that battle showed that, had he succeeded in his first day's attempt, the second day was to include an attack on the Hulluch front. So the "state of readiness" in the Cambrin sector had not been entirely without justification. On the 31st the weather broke again, but this did not prevent the Padre holding his Easter services at each of the Company Headquarters. The following evening we relieved the 5th Lincolnshires in the "Hill 70" right sub-sector.

Our new sector was very much the same as the "Hill 70 left," which we had held in November. The reserve line was the main line of defence, and was in fairly good condition; the front line was shallow, wet, and dangerous. Opposite our right and centre was Cité St. Auguste, strongly held by the enemy; opposite the left, Bois "Dixhuit" and a broken down farm. There was one tunnel, "Hythe," leading from the reserve line to a railway cutting in the front line, but except in cases of extreme emergency this was not intended to be used by the Infantry. Battalion Headquarters occupied a small and evil smelling German dug-out on the reverse slope of the hill. Our tour lasted eight days, and almost every hour was eventful.

We started the tour with a gas bombardment soon after relief on " C " Company's support platoon, who occupied an old "pill-box" near Cité St. Pierre dynamite magazine. The gas appliances were defective at the dug-out entrance, and several men were slightly gassed. At 8-0 a.m. the following morning, the 11th Division on our left carried out a very successful raid. This did not in itself affect us very much, but a bomb-dropping aeronaut during the raid observed large bodies of troops massing near Meurchin, a large town behind Hulluch. Immediately the old alarm about a coming attack was renewed, and we once more were ordered to be in readiness. However, by evening as nothing had happened, we resumed normal conditions.

This same evening we were given an entirely new scheme of defence, consequent upon the failure of our trench system to stop the enemy's advance in the South. The front line was to be held by isolated observation posts only, and there was to be no garrison within effective trench mortar range of the enemy. We were to consider the Reserve or "Red" Line the line of defence, and this must be rebuilt if necessary, to ensure that it was everywhere out of reach of the enemy's minenwerfer. Our chief difficulty was to find accommodation for the front line troops as they were withdrawn; however, we cleared out old dug-outs, and, after a few days of terribly hard work, were able to comply with the order.

Meanwhile, the enemy's artillery became very active, and in addition to frequent gas bombardments of Loos and the Crassier, he harassed our transport very badly as they came along the main road. Some of this gas blew back over our lines, and for several hours we lived in an atmosphere of gas, scarcely noticeable, but none the less dangerous.

The 5th of April was particularly noisy. At 3-0 a.m. we discharged a large number of gas projectors on to Bois "Dixhuit" and Cité St. Auguste, to which the enemy replied by shelling our reserve line, fortunately doing no damage. In the evening, however, he replied in earnest, and, just after "C" Company had relieved "B" in the front line, he put down a "box barrage" round their posts. Coloured lights were fired in all directions, the noise was terrific, and Captain Moore, expecting a raid, sent the "S.O.S." This was promptly answered, and within a few minutes the gunners were hammering away vigorously at the enemy's lines, until he stopped shooting. Our front line was damaged in many places, but by extraordinary good fortune we escaped without a casualty. During the day, however, " A " Company lost another very good N.C.O. in Serjeant Putt, who was wounded and had to go to Hospital.

Throughout the 6th the shelling of Loos continued, and the following morning, in retaliation to a heavy gas projection on our part, the enemy turned his attention again to our front line. This time we were less fortunate, and a Lewis gun post of " D " Company was wiped out by a direct hit: two of the gunners, C. H. Payne and T. P. Hardy, were killed. In the evening, in spite of a slight West wind, the enemy poured blue cross gas shells into Loos, and much of the gas again drifted back across the lines. During the night, Lieut. Banwell, exploring the enemy's lines, single-handed ran into three of the enemy, who were almost on top of him before he could use his weapons. However, he managed to make his way out, and returned to our lines, having lost nothing worse than a little breath.

On the 8th of April, the enemy's artillery was never silent. Mustard gas was fired into the plain East of Vermelles and Philosophe almost without intermission, while Mazingarbe and Les brebis were similarly bombarded, only with larger shells. 2nd Lieut. Todd and Serjeant Yeabsley were both gassed with the transport, the latter so badly that he was several weeks in Hospital. The following morning in a thick mist the enemy attacked the Portuguese and drove them from their trenches, pushing his advance Westwards towards Estaires and Locon. The mustard gas bombardment of the plain still continued, but the front lines were comparatively quiet. That night we were relieved by the 4th Battalion, and went once more into Brigade support. After relief, Capt. A. G. Moore, M.C., and forty-three other ranks were sent to Hospital with gas poisoning. This was not due to any one bombardment, but to the fact that for the past week " Hill 70 " had hardly ever been entirely free from gas, and though never in very large quantities this had gradually taken effect. Capt. Moore was sent to England, where for some months he was seriously ill with gas poisoning, and never returned. He and Capt. Shields commanded Companies longer than any other officers in the Battalion. No amount of tedious trench warfare could shake their enthusiasm or damp their spirits, " soft jobs " and six months' rest were not for them; they simply stayed with their Companies until wounds took them to England—a really magnificent record.

For three days we remained in support, and the whole time the plain behind us was full of gas. The Artillery suffered most heavily, for they could not always wear their masks, and after the first 24 hours there was a continuous stream of blinded gunners helping each other back along the road to Philosophe—a terrible sight. We too had several casualties, for the platoons, on their way to bath at Les brebis, had to pass across the plain. At Philosophe we lost two mules, through a direct hit with a heavy shell, and the driver, H. Gamble, was very lucky to escape with nothing more than a bad wound. It was a miracle he was not killed. On the 12th the battle became quieter, and that night, relieved by the Canadians, who arrived very late owing to a railway accident, we marched out to Bracquemont. Before we went the Germans to the North had advanced so far that we could see their lights in our left rear. Béthune, too, was in flames, so we were not sorry to be leaving the sector. Most thankful of all were the transport drivers, for there are not many worse places than the Loos road, and few more desolate spots than Philosophe coal mine on a dark wet night, when the wind is making the loose sheets of iron rattle, and the horses have "got the wind up."

CHAPTER XIV.

GORRE AND ESSARS AT PEACE.

12th April, 1918.   10th Aug., 1918.

BRACQUEMONT was sadly changed. Instead of the gay, almost fashionable suburb of Noeux les Mines, with numbers of people in the streets, it was now a wilderness of empty houses; the only sign of life, the piteous little groups of women and children waiting by the roadside for some French car to come and take them to a place of safety. The miners alone remained. Inspired by Clemenceau, who had visited the place a day or two before, they were working day and night, regardless of bombardments and nightly bombing raids. The furnaces at the Noeux Mines could be seen for miles round, and were a constant mark for every German gun and aeroplane, but still the plucky miners carried on their work, knowing that on them alone depended the coal supply of France. We were billeted in the Convent formerly occupied by the Casualty Clearing Station. The following morning the Drums gave a short concert in the Bandstand, and after dinner we were taken by lorries to Hersin Coupigny.

Hersin Coupigny was still fairly thickly populated, but the news from the Merville and Kemmel area where the enemy seemed to be making good progress, together with the arrival each evening of a few high-velocity shells, were fast driving the inhabitants to seek safety further West. We remained here until the 24th of April, the first few days in huts, the remainder in the Tile Factory. It was not an enjoyable rest—in fact it was no rest at all. All ranks were ready to move at short notice, and one expected almost hourly to be sent forward to fill some new gap in the line.

Pamphlets poured in—" How to fortify farmhouses for defence "—" Notes on recent German offensives " —Plans of rear defences. Generals made speeches telling the troops to be brave, artillery officers reconnoitred new gun positions miles behind the lines, and the entire Labour Corps seemed to be digging " last ditches." It was all very depressing, and many men were heard to remark that they wished the Boche would attack, so that there might be an end of words, and a chance for a few deeds. No one doubted that the Division was perfectly capable of looking after itself and dealing with any German attack.

Then came Influenza, and with it the end of all chance of immediate action for the Battalion. Officers and men were attacked alike, and in a few days more than 250 were sent to Hospital. Fortunately a temporary place was fitted up at Bruay, and the majority of cases were dealt with there and not sent down the line, where they would have been irretrievably lost. The cause of the complaint will be for ever a mystery; its symptoms were temperature—weakness, fainting and loss of voice. Some blamed the gas, others the huts, and others the Bracquemont hospital buildings. The Medical Officer, wise man, would give no opinion. The weather was damp and raw and at times very cold. Consequently no one was very sorry when, on the 24th, the Brigade marched to

Bruay. The Battalion and a 9″ high velocity German shell arrived in Bruay about the same time and found the place deserted. Several houses had been hit, and the inhabitants had wisely decided to take no risks, so, with the exception of the colliers, had all gone. This made billeting very difficult. Buildings were all locked up and no one had the key. Eventually everybody was squashed into the Girls' School—the officers occupied one of the dormitories, and, though uncomfortable, all had at least shelter from the rain which fell in torrents. At intervals a tremendous roar followed by a crash announced the arrival of what became known as "another toute suiter"; fortunately no one was hurt. The following day the Brigade moved into Fouquières; the 4th Battalion occupied the old Hospital huts, and we shared the remainder of the village with the 5th Lincolnshire Regiment. Battalion Headquarters were in the Chateau, still occupied by the two ladies, now the only civilians left in the village. With the most wonderfully cheerful courage did these two remain, though their servants had gone, though food was almost unobtainable, and though there was seldom an hour without a shell falling in some part of the village or its surroundings. The Battalion was exceedingly lucky and escaped with practically no casualties; not so the 4th Battalion, which lost several men in the huts. Most of the influenza cases now returned, and we were once more strong enough to take the field. On the 26th we lost Captain and Quartermaster A. A. Worley who went to England never to return. For some time his health had been bad, but though unfit for duty he had refused to leave the Battalion until he had seen the stores properly organized for battle. Except for a short stay in England in 1917, he had been with us since the beginning. His one thought was always for the welfare of the Battalion, and no one ever gave more devoted service than he did. His place was taken in June by Captain and Quartermaster W. A. Nicholson, of the Essex Regiment. During the interval the duties were very ably carried out by R.Q.M.S. Gorse.

On the 24th of April the Sherwood Foresters and Staffords had taken over the line from Route "A" Keep to the Canal just South of Locon. Four days later we were ordered to relieve the Sherwood Foresters in the right half of the left sector. Various reconnoitering parties went up beforehand, and at dusk we moved off by platoons through Béthune and Essars. The former town had already suffered very badly. All roads through the centre were completely blocked, and troops had to find their way round its Western edge and past the Prison. Civilians had all been evacuated and the only permanent occupants were the Tunnelling Company assisted by some French colliers. The route to trenches was the main road through Essars, and parts of this were constantly "harassed" by the enemy's artillery. The Battalion was particularly unfortunate on this first relief. Headquarter Officers were riding, and, in passing the column, had just come level with the head of "C" Company, when the enemy suddenly opened fire on the road with a field battery. Captain Banwell was thrown from his horse which was hit, and the remainder of the chargers immediately bolted across a field. The plunging animals and the shells (about 50 of which were fired in two minutes) threw the leading platoon of "C" Company into confusion, and, as the ditch at the side of the road gave no cover, the casualties were high; but for the coolness of the Platoon Commander, 2nd Lieut. H. Coxell, they would have been higher still. The rear platoon of " B " Company also suffered heavily. The shells were gas, and those men who were hit had small or no chance of putting on their masks. Captain Jack, the Medical Officer, was as usual wonderfully calm, and quite regardless of his own personal safety, succeeded in getting several men under the wall of a house, where he was able to dress their wounds. The remainder of the relief was carried out without molestation.

Our new sector was very different from anything we had previously seen. The front line—practically the outpost line—marked the limit of the German offensive in April; on the right was Route " A " Keep, one of the old 1915 strong points with two concrete machine-gun emplacements. It was now a mere heap of shattered trees, shattered trenches and the usual remains of many fights, for in 20 days it changed hands nine times. The Staffords captured it for the last time on the 29th of April, and from then onwards it remained British. The line then ran between Loisne Chateau and Raux Farm —our old Brigade Headquarters of 1915, now a German machine gun and trench mortar nest—to the S.W. outskirts of Le Touret and on to the canal at Mesplaux. Except for the old keeps at intervals, it consisted entirely of a few small holes dug more or less at random, with little or no wire in front. Behind this, along the whole Divisional front ran the Liverpool Line or Reserve Line, slightly deeper and better sighted than the front line, and defended by the "Beuvry river," a small stream running between steep banks and reputed to be uncrossable by tanks. Gorre and Le

Hamel villages came behind this line, and provided Battalion Headquarters with cellar accommodation, and the Support Battalions with billets of a sort.

Farms in the front line were not too plentiful, and Company Headquarters usually consisted of a hole 4ft. by 2ft. by 2ft. into which the Company Commander could just squeeze himself, and curl up his feet to avoid having them kicked and trodden on by the men passing along the ditch outside. Rations came to Gorre and Essars by rail and limber, and were carried forward by hand over the top to the front line. Except for occasional bursts of fire on certain roads and villages, particularly Essars and Gorre, the enemy was on the whole quiet. These were small gas bombardments, and one or two really bad days, but for the most part it was a quiet sector, except round Route A.

Behind the villages came the La Bassée Canal with all the bridges mined and demolition parties ready to blow them up in the event of a hostile attack. The idea of course was that they should be blown after the last Englishman N. of the Canal had either been killed or had crossed it. That the bridges would get demolished all right, none of us ever doubted for a moment; we were equally certain that this would take place on the first alarm of any attack, and those of us who happened to be on the North bank would thus be compelled to fight to the end or swim. Fortunately these warriors were never called on to perform.

Vaudricourt Park was the rest area. At first, bell tents and a few bivouacs were all the available cover, but in time, as corrugated iron could be sent down from old horse lines in the forward area, messhuts, cookhouses and canteens were built. There were no long spells of wet weather and when it was fine the Camp in the Park was delightful. It was never shelled and never bombed, and it is hard to imagine a better place. Verquin and Vaudricourt provided the necessary estaminets and the soldiers could obtain as much vin blanc (or "Jimmy Blink" as it was more popularly called) as they desired; while one Bertha made large sums of money by inserting a slip of lemon peel into a glass as cheap champagne and selling it to officers at an exorbitant price as a "champagne cocktail." The country round provided good ground for a sports meeting, in which "A" Company were victorious, while "D" Company managed to finish a close second in most events. Lieutenants Everitt and Quint and Private R. O. Start were the chief runners, but large numbers took part and tremendous keenness was displayed by all. There was cricket almost every day in the Park, and great enthusiasm was shown in the Battalion Championship, won by Headquarters.

From the beginning of May to the middle of August the Brigade never left these two sectors, Gorre and Essars, and during this time there was no change in the front line. It was seldom that anything happened of sufficient importance to find its way into the day's communiqué, but every tour was full of interesting incidents, all of which show how the warfare was rapidly changing.

Our first relief was remarkable for the fact that we took over at Battalion Headquarters two cows (and with them a daily supply of fresh milk), for whom L/Cpl. "Pat" Collins was self-appointed cowman— while the left Company found a plentiful supply of eggs. A stray mule was found wandering round the outposts on the " wrong " side of the Beuvry river, while in the farm actually in the front line we discovered still alive after 21 days without food—a cow and calf, two bullocks, an old white horse and a pig; they were in a terrible condition of starvation and had to be killed by the Intelligence Officer, 2nd Lieut. Hewson, who found it a most unpleasant task. There were of course many dogs—one, at a cottage in no man's land, being particularly unpleasant for patrolling. In addition to Lance-Corporal Collins' cows, two others and a goat were led out by Private Muggleton. The goat came to an untimely end, being done to death in Vaudricourt Park by its Company Commander, outside whose tent it was noisily bewailing its captivity.

In front of us, there was little or no wire, and our first encounter with the enemy was on the 6th of May when a Corporal and three men of " D " Company went out to wire their post and marched straight on to a patrol of about 15 enemy waiting for them. The enemy opened fire at close range and the wiring party threw down their wire and replied. Two of the party were hit in the first few seconds and a third—Private Smith—who had come to us from the 2nd/5th in January—was attacked by two Germans and carried off struggling. The Corporal fired at the enemy who then made off, leaving one dead man behind them. The Platoon Commander (2nd Lieut. W. M. Cole) came up and, after assisting the wounded back, set off to look for Smith. Except, however, for the dead man, nothing could be found of the enemy, and by dawn the search was given up as hopeless. The following night Smith returned. It appears that the enemy meeting more opposition than they expected, made off as soon as they had got their prisoner, and, as there were plenty of bullets about, the remainder of the patrol, leaving prisoner and escort to follow as best they could, hurried back to their lines. Smith watched his chance; suddenly stooping, he kicked one man amidships, siezed his rifle, gave the other a jab with the bayonet, and ran for his life. He got away, but had to lie up until the next evening to get back. For this he was awarded the Military Medal.

The following tour, in the Gorre right sector, was very successful until the last two days when Battalion Headquarters received the just punishment for tempting fortune too far. Both 4th and 5th Battalions had their Headquarters in the cellar of Gorre Chateau—cramped and stuffy at any time, and in the hot weather unendurable. Our Headquarters, therefore, cleared out a room on the first floor for a mess—it had a carpet and other luxuries, and its only blemish was a shell-hole in the corner of the window. With great pride we invited Brigadiers and others to our new mess, until on the 17th of May the crash came. The enemy had fired several salvoes towards the Chateau during the afternoon, and at 8-15 p.m. he started in earnest. The wood, the Chateau and the corner by the Church were shelled unceasingly—first with 77 and 105 m.m. shells—later on with 5.9's. The mess was knocked in, the wood was filled with gas, the kitchen and signal office both had direct hits. The Transport had a terrible time on the road, and it was only the devoted work of the Transport Officer, 2nd Lieut. W. R. Todd, with his drivers, particularly Hill and Randall and the Provost Serjeant Bennett, which enabled rations to be taken up. An advance party of Stafford Officers got to the cellar and couldn't leave it for two hours, until finally Colonel Wood took them up the line himself, returning alone through the wood.

The Companies were comparatively immune except near the "Tuning Fork." General Thwaites was visiting the line at the time and had a narrow escape himself, while his A.D.C. was badly wounded. Towards morning the shelling somewhat subsided, but one very unlucky shot hit the cellar ventilator and filled it with gas. Then came the sun and with it the mustard; not very many mustard shells had been fired, but, as the day advanced, the heat kept drawing the gas out of the ground and the Chateau became a death trap. We all cleared out early and went into the fields, but even so it was too late; many men's clothes were tainted, and by 6-0 p.m. all the servants and more than half the other Headquarter details were blind and had to go. Serjeant Bent, of the Regimental Aid Post, and Allbright, the Orderly Room Clerk, were amongst those who went down. Our Medical Officer (Captain W. B. Jack), Intelligence Officer (2nd Lieut. J. A. Hewson) and Lieut. K. Ashdowne all went to Hospital, while the 4th Battalion lost all their Headquarter Officers. By night the Commanding Officer was unable to speak, the Adjutant half blind, and the Padre was doing everybody's job with his wonderful energy. It was a very sorrowful Battalion Headquarters that handed over to the Staffordshires and found its way slowly back to Vaudricourt.

Soon after that—on the 29th of May—"C" Company had another gas misfortune while in support in Gorre village. Their house was heavily shelled with mustard, and though all men were taken out as soon as possible 40% of the Company, together with 2nd Lieuts. H. Coxell and O. Darlington had to be evacuated. There was so much gas at this time that special compartments were set apart for gassed men and gassed clothing on the Fouquières-Le Quesnoy-Kantara Dump light railway.

Towards the end of the month the crops began to get very high, and by the first week in June hardly a day passed without some daylight patrol taking advantage of them. Captain Banwell first made the experiment. Accompanied by his runner, Smiles, he visited the "crashed" aeroplane just N. of the Rue du Bois and found a most elaborate German night post in a tree, with wires to machine gun posts. His example was followed on the 9th of June by 2nd Lieut. Cole, who went out one morning with Lance-Corporal Thurman and a party from "D" Company. They crawled through some wire and found themselves close to a German shell-hole post. 2nd Lieut. Cole himself reconnoitred this post, and finding the sentry dozing called up his Corporal. The latter hit the sentry on the head with his rifle "to attract his attention" (so read the patrol report), and leaning over the hole whispered "Ici yer ——er." The Boche, however, was too frightened to "ici" and looked like giving the alarm, so 2nd Lieut. Cole jumped down and fired his revolver to hurry him along. This caused a considerable disturbance. Two German Machine Gun posts only a few yards away joined in the fight and for a moment things looked bad for the patrol. The latter, finding they could not get a prisoner, made a note of his Regiment, shot him, and made off under a heavy fire from the machine gun posts. They all got away safely.

The Corps Commander described 2nd Lieut. Cole's work as " a very fine piece of patrol work, and called for courage, initiative and cunning of a high degree." Ten days later—on the 19th of June—the enemy suddenly shelled the " Tuning Fork Switch " trench, and this very gallant young officer was badly wounded in the arm. He was taken down to the Casualty Clearing Station at once, but in spite of all the Doctors' efforts, blood poisoning set in, and on the 29th Lieut. Maurice Cole died. The same evening he was awarded the Military Cross for his patrol fight. He lies now in Pernes cemetery. No officer was ever more loved by his men, and justly so, for he was not only their leader in danger, but their first friend in difficulty. In the Mess " Bill " Cole was as popular as in the field. Patrolling was not confined to these two Companies, and many officers and men spent quite a large proportion of their time crawling through the corn. Chief among these were 2nd Lieuts. Asher, Argyle, Boarland, Christy, Davies, Serjeants T. Marston, M.M., Haines, Foster, M.S.M., P. Bowler, T. Tunks, T. Needham, Clamp and others.

With the hot weather the La Bassée Canal became a very useful asset, and not only were there constant bathing parties, but it was actually possible at the end of July to hold a swimming gala in the " Brewery Reach." There were several well contested races and diving competitions, uninterrupted by hostile aircraft, and a very pleasant afternoon (considering the Boche were less than a mile away) was spent in this way. The chief race was won by Signaller Stanton.

Towards the end of July, as there was no sign of the long expected German attack, preparations were made for the coming winter. Houses were reinforced, and had concrete houses built inside them, and some very comfortable Headquarters were built in this way. Perhaps the best of these was the Battalion Headquarters of the Route A sector—a cottage on the banks of the canal and screened from any observation by the woods. It had its own bathing place (where Serjt. Wilbur nearly got drowned) and its own private approach by the tow path—incidentally, of course, its own mosquitoes, but one got used to them in time.

On the 13th of July we lost Captain Banwell, who went into hospital for a few weeks with his fifth wound—an aeroplane bullet in the stomach. It was not at all a slight wound, but he managed to persuade the Pernes Doctors that it was, and so contrived not to be evacuated beyond the C.C.S. He eventually returned in August, and after a few days as A.D.C. to General Rowley, who was then Commanding the Division, went off on a month's leave to get fit.

On the 6th of August the Staff had reason to believe that the Boche might be contemplating a withdrawal that morning, and we were asked to make sure that we could still get in touch with the enemy. Accordingly, Lieut. Pearson, Lance-Corporal " Anty " Carr and Pte. Ferrin, all of " A " Company, crawled out at dawn towards the ruined houses and battery positions opposite Route A Keep. It was the anniversary of Carr's 1916 experience and before they went several of his friends jestingly warned him not to be captured this time. The patrol crawled via several dykes and got close to the house without disturbing anyone, until, to get a better view Lieut. Pearson knelt up to use glasses. A machine gun then opened fire on them at close range, so they returned. On the way back they were suddenly fired at by a post in their path—the occupants must have been asleep on the way out. Pte. Ferrin was hit and died almost at once, but the others tried to bomb the enemy out, and, finding they could not, decided to lie still until evening. However, the enemy proved more resolute than usual and soon surrounded and captured the whole party. The fight was seen by several of the front line posts and also by a patrol of "D" Company under 2nd Lieut. Christy. This latter was quite unable to give any help as it was itself having very great difficulty in getting away from two large Boche patrols who were trying to cut it off. A few days later, while we were in support at Le Quesnoy, the enemy started his withdrawal, and the Gorre-Essars front once more became a battle sector.

CHAPTER XV.

GORRE AND ESSARS AT WAR.

10th Aug., 1918. 12th Sept., 1918.

THE enemy started his withdrawal North of the Lawe Canal, and it was not until the latter half of August that the Gorre sector was affected. However, all preparations for more open warfare were made, and the supply of rations and ammunition was reorganised in such a way that either limbers or pack animals could be used at short notice. During our tour in the Right Sector from the 14th to 18th of August all rations for " Route A " were taken up to forward Company Headquarters on mules and ponies; the latter, under the skilful handling of their drivers, showed a most admirable fortitude in the face of machine-gun fire. Each night a little column of heavily laden ponies under Corporal Archer or Lance-Corporal Foster could be seen moving slowly along the Tuning Fork Road, first with rations then with water; towards midnight they returned (" drivers up ") at a much brisker pace.

On the 18th we left trenches and came into support for three days at Le Quesnoy. Colonel Wood was away Commanding the Brigade for a short time and Major Griffiths was in Command. All available men were set to work cutting the corn, which was now ripe and would soon spoil if not cut and carried in.

Bayonets took the place of scythes as the latter were almost unobtainable, and it was surprising to find what progress was made with these weapons. In a few days several train loads were sent down on the light railway to Fouquières. All this time the news from the South was most encouraging. The great attack of the 8th had freed Amiens and each day brought us news of further successes. On the 20th the Staffordshires on the left found some of the enemy's advanced posts unoccupied, and the same day prisoners taken on the Lawe Canal spoke of an impending retreat to the Le Touret-Lacouture line. On the 21st the Commanding Officer returned, and the same day the Brigade moved into and occupied the old German front line near Cense du Raux Farm. That night we relieved the 4th Battalion in the old Right Sector and occupied the Liverpool Line as Support Battalion to the other two, both of whom were in and forward of the old front line. On the 22nd General Rowley decided to have one outpost Battalion for the whole frontage, and the following day we took over the line from the junction with the 55th Division (in the old front line E. of "Route A Keep") to the junction with the Sherwood Foresters N.E. of Le Touret village.

On the extreme right we had pushed forward across the road where they were opposed in the centre by Epinette East Post, and on the left by some houses in the Rue itself, to both of which the Boche was still clinging tenaciously. On the left the line was continued by "D" Company (Lieut. T. H. Ball in the absence of Captain Brooke) who held positions astride the Rue du Bois. The extreme left platoon was about 200 yards up the Rue de Cailloux and occupied one of the old keeps in the Sailly—Tuning Fork—Vielle Chapelle Line. Here, and on the Rue de L'Epinette, the enemy was active with snipers and trench mortars—in the centre things were very quiet. " C " Company (Hawley) and " B " Company (Tomson) were in Support in the old front line; Battalion Headquarters lived in Loisne Chateau, now " Railhead " for the light railway. There was no front line in the old sense—it was simply " outposts " as laid down in Field Service Regulations. Very few of the Company Officers had had any previous experience of this work, but Colonel Wood soon put us straight, and organized things himself. He was absolutely indefatigable and day and night was up in the line sighting good positions and studying the enemy. The latter were distinctly alert as they showed by their behaviour on the 24th and 25th when we not only made no progress, but had several casualties. First, on the extreme right, an " A " Company patrol tried to reconnoitre the Epinette East Post by night. They were seen and fired at heavily and had to come back leaving one of their number dead behind them. Soon afterwards, in an attempt to recover his body, Lance-Serjeant Clamp was himself hit and died a few hours later. " A " Company could ill afford to lose this N.C.O., who had shown himself as gallant a leader in battle, as he was an efficient instructor on the Parade Ground. The following morning, accompanied by his runner, Lance-Corporal Collins, and the Adjutant, the Commanding Officer started on a tour round the outpost line. He visited " A " Company's posts and passed on to " D " Company. On reaching the Rue du Bois he got on to the road, and, as it was misty, started to walk Westward along it. Whether the little party was seen or not will never be known; what happened would seem to show that they were. They had not gone seventy yards before a "whizz-bang" burst a few yards North of the road hitting a Stretcher Bearer. Another followed, this time the burst was only a few yards behind the party. The others escaped, but Colonel Wood was hit in the back of the head and was thrown stunned on to the road. More shells followed, and the three lay in a ditch till it was over, and then made their way back to Battalion Headquarters. The Colonel refused to be carried and walked all the way to the Aid Post, where the Doctor found that a shell splinter had grazed the back of his skull, and had only been prevented by the steel helmet from doing more damage. The Colonel wished to remain with the Battalion, but the Medical Officer was obdurate, and he was finally evacuated, and a week later sent to England. He had been in Command only a short time, but we had learnt in that time what a very gallant soldier he was, and how his one care was to make us the first Battalion in the Division. His place was taken by Major J. L. Griffiths who had been Second in Command since 1916, while Captain John Burnett took over the latter's duties.

The same afternoon we had further bad luck. On the extreme left No. 13 Platoon (Christy) had been very actively sniping the enemy on the Cailloux Road, and soon after midday, came the retaliation in the form of heavy shelling which lasted about an hour. There was little cover, and one post was wiped out, including a promising young soldier, Lance-Corporal Harries, whose name had been recommended for a Commission. 2nd Lieut. Christy managed, in spite of the difficulty of moving men in daylight, to get the majority of his Platoon out of the Keep, and took up positions on either flank; this action undoubtedly saved many casualties. Corporal Hamill, one of the old soldiers of the Battalion and a well-known long distance runner, was killed at the same time. The Platoon was naturally rather shaken, and its place was therefore taken by a Platoon of " C " Company. The following night we were relieved by the Sherwood Foresters and went back to Vaudricourt. The Relief was carried out without interference from the enemy except for Battalion Headquarter Officers, who had to leave Loisne Chateau at the gallop. Salvoes of whizz-bangs were arriving at frequent intervals, and there was just time to mount and gallop 300 yards down the road between the bursts.

The next six days at Vaudricourt were delightful; we all needed a rest, and the weather for once was excellent. At this time Major General W. Thwaites, C.B., who had Commanded the Division since 1916, was appointed Director of Military Intelligence at the War Office, and his place was taken by Major General G. F. Boyd, C.M.G., D.S.O., D.C.M. It is impossible even now to estimate all that General Thwaites did for the Division, and it was very bad luck for him that he had to leave just at the time when the Division was to reap the fruits of his training. He took us over after the Gommecourt battle, and we were tired and weak, as is to be expected after heavy casualties; if he had stayed another month he would have seen us doing as no Division had done before. There are many of us who would cheerfully have been " crumped " to escape a " G.O.C.'s Inspection," but we have lived to be thankful even for these; they made our Platoon and Company organisation perfect.

On the 30th we all went and listened to a lecture on Co-operation with Tanks, given by an Officer who had taken part in the recent fighting down South. It was a bloodthirsty and blood-curdling recital, and at the end of it we all felt ready for an enormous battle, provided we could have a tank or two to help. The following day, being the Brigade Boxing Tournament Finals, some of the N.C.O.'s and men got an opportunity of slaking their battle lust. This they did very successfully, as at the end of the day we were equal with the 5th Lincolns, who had previously always been winners. Serjeants Wardle, Ptes. "Mat" Moore and Martin, all won their weights, and in addition Serjeant Wardle won the open catch weight championship. This N.C.O. then challenged any one of the 5th Lincolns' side to fight a "one round" deciding bout, and, beating his opponent, won the day for the Battalion. The Brigadier gave away the prizes and also the Sports Cup which we had won. There was a very gratifying predominance of "yellow rings" throughout this part of the proceedings.

The following day—the 1st of September—we returned to trenches, and went into support with Battalion Headquarters in Le Quesnoy and the Companies in and around Gorre village. As the new Divisional Commander had not yet arrived Brigadier General Rowley was still in command of the Division and Lieut.-Colonel Foster, of the 4th Battalion, commanded the Brigade. The Germans were withdrawing very slowly, and by the 3rd the Staff decided that as soon as the 5th Lincolnshires had gained "Rum Corner" on the Rue du Bois, where the Boche had a strong pill box, we should go forward with a barrage with Princes' Road as our objective. Orders did not arrive until after midday and then Rum Corner had not fallen; it was, however, expected to fall by 4-0 p.m., and our attack was ordered for 8-0 p.m. the same evening. There was no time for reconnaissance and little for getting out orders, but we managed to arrange for an assembly position and a barrage, which was to advance in jumps of 100yds. every 4 minutes. Everybody had a hurried tea and set out between 5-0 p.m. and 6-0 p.m. for the line. It was not very satisfactory and we were all glad when, owing to the stout resistance of Rum Corner the advance was postponed until 5-15 the following morning—the 4th of September. It was a warm night and the Companies remained in the trenches round Loisne and were able to have a good meal before starting. Late that night the 5th Lincolnshires reported the taking of the "Corner," so that all was now ready for the battle. We did not expect much resistance. Shortly before midnight fresh orders arrived making our objective the old breastwork through Tube Station and Factory Post (the support line in 1915). If possible we were to push patrols on to the old British front line in front of Fme. Cour D'Avoué and Fme. du Bois.

Soon after 4-0 a.m. we were all in our assembly positions—the three attacking Companies along a line running N. and S. about 300 yards E. of Epinette Road, with our left just North of Rue du Bois; the Support Company 100 yards behind them. "D" Company (Brooke) was on the right with orders to protect that flank, if necessary facing right to do so as they advanced, "A" Company (Petch) was in the centre, and "B" Company (Pierrepont) left, astride the

Rue du Bois, " C " Company (Hawley) was in support. Battalion Headquarters were in Epinette East Post with an Orderly Room and rear Headquarters in Loisne. About an hour before we were due to start a curious thing happened: It was suddenly discovered that a considerable number of the 5th Lincolnshires were now some distance E. of our "jumping off line," and consequently beyond where the barrage was due to start. The Brigadier tried to get the barrage advanced, but it was found impossible to tell the Artillery in time, and in the end the Lincolnshires, much to their disgust, had to be withdrawn. As their leading men had gone as far as Princes' Road, it did not look as though we should have much opposition that far at all events.

Promptly at 5-15 a.m. the barrage came down and the advance began. Princes' Road was reached and crossed, the breastwork was found empty, and, after a short pause in the latter, the right centre Companies went on to the old front line. The left Company had slightly more difficult ground, and arrived half-an-hour later; nowhere had a German been met, though one or two had been seen making for the Aubers Ridge. It was a bloodless victory, and by 7-0 a.m. the Battalion was occupying the identical sector that it occupied in 1915. The barrage had not been needed, but it was none the less very useful, for we all learnt how close we could keep and how to judge the "lifts." Consolidation was not a difficult matter except on the right flank, where we could not until evening get touch with the 55th Division. It was consequently necessary for " D " Company to swing back their right through Tube Station and Dead Cow Post and face South. On the left Colonel Currin with his Sherwood Foresters was in touch with us at the Factory Keep. Battalion Headquarters moved up just before midday to a small shelter 200 yards west of Princes' Road. In most of the captured dug-outs the following notice was found:—

> Dear Tommy,—
>
> You are welcome to all we are leaving, when we stop we shall stop, and stop you in a manner you won't appreciate.   FRITZ.

It was neatly printed in English block capitals and caused much amusement. The whole day was in a way one great joke—the un-needed barrage, the empty trenches, these farewell notices, all combined to make us very happy.

At first we thought we were going to be let off without any retaliation at all, but the following morning at " stand to " a fairly heavy barrage came down for half-an-hour on the breastwork support line—presumably to break up any intended attack. " B " Company Headquarters most unluckily received a direct hit causing six casualties. Two Serjeants who could ill be spared, A. Cross and E. Bottomley were both badly wounded, the latter mortally; two servants, C. Payne and L. Brotheridge, were wounded not very seriously, and the two runners, G. S. Bott and G. Dewsbury were hit, Bott so badly that he died in Hospital. These two runners, inseparable friends, had long been associated with " B " Company Headquarters, and had always done yeoman service, for there was probably never a better pair. In the afternoon orders came that we should be relieved at dusk by the 19th Division, but that we must be certain that we were in touch with the enemy when handing over. Accordingly orders were sent up to Captain Petch to try and locate the exact position of the enemy. At first the patrol sent out was unable to draw fire, so, taking C.S.M. Passmore, Serjt. Bowler and others with him, Captain Petch went out himself, and the two waved their arms and shouted to imaginary platoons to make the enemy think an attack was coming. The ruse was successful, a machine gun opened fire from close quarters. The two dropped into a shell hole and started to crawl their way back; there was plenty of cover, and if they had been patient all would have been well. Unfortunately C.S.M. Passmore thinking it was sufficiently dark, got up and walked towards our lines. He was hit and killed outright. This warrant officer joined us at Gommecourt in 1917; his energy and fearlessness at once brought him to the front, and he soon rose from Serjeant to be Company-Serjeant-Major. His place in "A" Company was taken by Serjeant Wardle, of "C" Company. As soon as they were relieved Companies marched to Loisne Chateau, where they were to entrain. Trains were not ready, but after a long wait, the well-nigh frantic efforts of Captain Schiller produced them, much to everybody's delight, and somewhere about midnight we marched back to Vaudricourt Park.

Two days later the new Major-General was introduced to us, and at once won his way to our hearts by his wonderful charm of manner. He must have been surprised to see outside the mess a long line of horses and mules all waiting saddled up. We had arranged an officers' paper chase and every officer attended; those who couldn't find chargers had perforce to ride mules. The hares (Captain Burnett on "Mrs. Wilson" and 2/Lieut. Todd on the frisky black) were given ten minutes' grace and then, led by "Sunloch" (Lieut.-

Colonel Griffiths "up") the rest of us swung out of the Park and off towards Labuissière. The pace was very hot and most of us soon dropped behind, though the mules, keeping as usual all together and led by Padre Buck, managed to stay the whole course. Four riders, finding they were getting left behind, started to make a short cut through Hesdigneul and there on the village green met the hares on the way home. It was a dramatic moment witnessed by large crowds of gunners, and Lieut. Brodribb on the Colonel's pony, and Lieut. Hawley on the faithful and well-intentioned "Charlie," dashed after the hares. The effect, however, was somewhat spoilt by "Lady Sybil," unused no doubt to audiences, throwing the Adjutant over her head on to the middle of the green. The hares were finally caught after a 9-mile run within a few hundred yards of home. It was a great performance.

Our stay at Vaudricourt was not a long one, and we soon moved to Béthune, preparatory to entrainment for the South, for it was now no longer a secret that we were going down to fight a real battle at last. The new General introduced a "Blob" formation, which was both easy and effective, and we practised this once or twice outside the town. Our first line transport was also reorganised in such a way that each Company had its own two limbers with Lewis Guns and ammunition, bombs and all necessaries. On one small Field Day the Signallers with their flags turned out as Tanks, and we practised everything as realistically as possible. We were all very keen, and better still, very fit; in fact, the Battalion never looked in better form than on one of these training days when we marched past the Brigadier.

From the 9th to the 11th of September we remained in Béthune, a depressing town now, to those of us who had known it in its days of prosperity. We managed to have one very good concert in the Barracks and it was surprising how much really good talent we found, conjuror, humourists and sentimental singer were all ready to amuse us. At midnight 11/12th we fell in on the Parade Ground and marched to Chocques—the irrepressible Drums giving us one or two tunes on the way. It rained hard at the Station and there was a terrible shortage of accommodation. At length, with much shoving, swearing and puddle-splashing we got on board, and at 4-0 a.m. left the Béthune Area. We had been on the Lens-La Bassée Sector for seventeen months : we never saw it again.

CHAPTER XVI.

PONTRUET.

14th Sept., 1918.   25th Sept., 1918.

Our journey Southwards was uncomfortable and uneventful. The only remarkable feature was the acrobatic skill displayed by the mess staff, transferring meals from the kitchen-cattle-truck to the officers mess-cattle-truck. Even at the usual speed of a French troop train, it is no easy task to drop off the train with a pile of plates in one hand, a dish of potatoes in the other, walk fast enough to catch up the carriage in front, and finally, in spite of signal wires, sleepers and other pitfalls, deliver all safely at the "Mess." Yet this was done not once but often. We spent the whole day in the train passing St. Pol, Amiens, and Corbie, and finally towards evening reached Ribemont, where we found our billeting party waiting for us. Billets consisted of some distant dug-outs across a swampy moor, and the recent rains had made what few tracks there were too slippery for the horses. It was all very unpleasant, and we spent a cold and cheerless night. "A" Company, which had remained at Chocques doing loading duties, did not arrive until midnight—very wet and tired.

The next day was bright and warm, and we soon discovered that the two villages, Treux and Buire would hold Headquarters and half the Battalion, so moved into them without delay and evacuated all except the more sumptuous and easily approached dug-outs. We were now fairly comfortable, and our only grouse was the absence of any canteen or even French civilians for miles and miles, and the consequent lack of tobacco, beer and other little luxuries.

Our move had brought us into General Rawlinson's Fourth Army, and, as we were apparently not needed at once for a battle, we started vigorous training. Route marches, and even " field-firing " practices were carried out, and there was one big Divisional Field day, which ended triumphantly with the Brigade and Battalion Staffs picking mushrooms on the final objective. Meanwhile the Second in Command's Department under Major Burnett fixed up baths and other comforts for us and, by the 18th of September, we were really very comfortable. This same day we were ordered to move at short notice.

Motor lorries took us on to the main Amiens road at Corbie, and turning East along it we jolted and bumped and splashed our way through Brie-sur-Somme to Tertry. The country—what we could see of it in the dark—seemed to consist of a barren waste of shell holes with here and there a shattered tree or the remains of some burnt-out Tank standing forlornly near some dark and stagnant swamp. Villages were practically non-existent, and Tertry was no exception, but we soon settled down under waterproof sheets, corrugated iron and a few old bricks. The transport under Major Burnett and Serjt. Yeabsley came all the way by road, and arrived some hours later; but much of our stores had to be left behind with two storemen in Buire.

Many efforts were made during the following months to retrieve these stores, but it was not until after the armistice that we were finally successful.

We were now IXth. Corps, and found our neighbours were old friends from the Béthune area—the 1st and 6th Divisions. The Transport lines and "battle details" of the 1st and 11th Battalions of the Regiment were quite close to us, and we paid several calls. On the 20th, Captains Tomson and Banwell returned from leave, much to the delight of their Companies, for the following day we went into trenches, relieving the 14th and 45th Australians in the Hindenburg Outpost line, that they had so brilliantly captured a few days before. We were in Brigade support along Ascension Ridge, called after a farm of that name, and the other two Battalions held the line in front of us.

In their attack, the Australians had pushed forward further than anyone else, while the English troops on their right, after some very hard fighting, had been held up by the village of Pontruet. Consequently there was a sharp bend in the line, and the Australian right flank, though on high ground, was somewhat exposed. The line ran roughly as follows:—

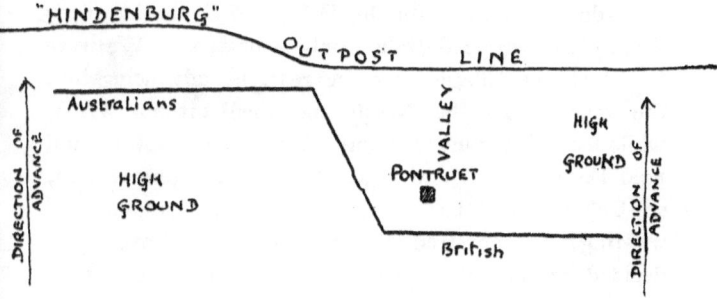

The enemy still held posts on the ridge close to the Australian front line, and were known to have several posts in Forgan's trench, which was the Southward continuation of our front line across the valley. Pontruet was overlooked from everywhere, and constantly bombarded by our Artillery, so it did not seem likely that it held many Boche. The Sherwood Foresters held the right of the Divisional line and joined with the 1st Division on the high ground South of the village. There was no sign of any intended operation, and it certainly looked as if we could not move until the troops on our right had advanced. Accordingly on the 22nd the Adjutant rode back to Brie to go on leave. Capt. Banwell, really a "battle detail," went up to assist the Headquarters, while the other "details"—Major Burnett, Captain Petch, Lieut. Pierrepont, 2nd Lieuts. Edwardes, Griffiths, Taylor, C.S.M.'s Cooper and Martin—remained with the Q.M. Stores.

No sooner had the Adjutant gone, than orders came for a battle. At dawn on the 24th the Division on our right was going to advance, and the 46th Division, by way of assisting them, was to capture Pontruet and hold Forgan's trench as a final objective. The 138th Brigade were chosen for this fight, and General Rowley decided to use one Battalion only—ourselves. We were to attack the village from the rear, by advancing into the valley from the North and then turning West, while one Company turning East would capture and hold Forgan's. There was little time for preparation, so Colonel Griffiths called a Company Commanders' meeting, reconnoitred the village from above, and decided on his plan of attack. At the same time a runner was sent after the Adjutant, and found him just boarding the leave train. It was a near thing, but not for anything would he have missed the next few weeks.

The Colonel's plan was as follows :—To assemble the Battalion in lines of platoons in fours facing South, just behind the right of our front line. " A " would be on the right, " D " on the left. At Zero all would move forward wth a barrage, keeping about 50 yards distance and interval between platoons. All would cross the Bellenglise road and finally, when the leading platoons were level with the farther, i.e., South, edge of Pontruet, " A " and " B " would turn to the right, sweep through and reform on the West side of it. " D " would turn left and capture Forgan's trench, having a platoon of " C " Company to help them. The rest of " C " would assist which ever party seemed to be in difficulties. The Headquarters would move to the high ground, whence the fight would be visible, and there was every hope of opening signal communication with the attacking Companies. Artillery arrangements were made accordingly, and bombardments ordered for the supposed posts in Forgan's. Unfortunately, much against our wishes, and in opposition to the Brigadier's scheme, a heavy smoke barrage was to be placed on the Western edge of the village. A West wind would make this a thick blanket and seriously hinder our advance, and West winds are very common; however, we could not alter this part of the scheme. The Sherwood Foresters were ordered to assist by pushing up to the village after we had captured it. Zero would be 5-0 a.m. on the 24th of September.

As soon as it was dark on the 23rd, Captain Banwell

taped out a "jumping off" line for the leading platoons. There was some unpleasant shelling at the time, but he completed his task successfully, and also taped out the route to this assembly position. At midnight, relieved by the 6th South Staffordshires (Lister), we mached off after an issue of hot tea and rum to the assembly ground, leaving great coats behind and wearing fighting order. On arrival we found that the Lincolnshires had been raided in their North end of Forgan's trench a short time before, and, as there might still be some of the enemy near the trench, "D" Company were ordered to form up in it, instead of on the top. It was not a dark night, and had we been seen assembling all would have been lost. There was some scattered shelling, and Lieut. Brodribb, commanding "A" Company, was wounded in the leg. He had it dressed at the R.A.P., and, finding he could still walk, rejoined his Company before the advance began. In absolute silence we lay in shell holes waiting for Zero. A mist had started to blow up from the valley, and the Battalion was almost invisible. Here and there a few heads, the muzzle of a Lewis gun, the end of a stretcher might be seen just above the ground, and occasionally one could see the tall figure of Capt. Tomson, imperturbable as ever, walking quietly round his Company with a word of encouragement for all. As the time went on, the mist became thicker and thicker, and by 4-50 a.m. platoons and Companies were unable to see each other. The shelling had ceased, it was very quiet.

Punctually at 5-0 a.m. the barrage opened, and the advance started. The timing of the Artillery was perfect and, with the road to guide them, "A" Company on the right swept across the Bellenglise road, keeping close to the barrage. By 5-14 a.m. No. 1 Platoon (Quint), which was leading, was ready for the right turn. The rest of this Company followed, and, though No. 4 Platoon (Dennis) slightly lost direction for a time, they soon regained their place, so that the whole Company was ready to turn together. It was still half dark, and, as we had feared, the smoke barrage blew across and shrouded us in a thick blanket of fog. During their advance, "A" Company had found the machine gun and rifle fire very hot from their left flank, apparently from Forgan's trench, and had already lost Serjt. P. Bowler, who was killed outright. They had met no enemy outside the village, and could not see more than a few yards through the smoke. The other Companies were out of sight.

Turning into Pontruet, "A" Company found it full of the enemy. Odd lengths of trenches here and there, cellars in every direction were filled with bombers and machine gun teams, some facing West, others, who had realised our intentions, facing East. Led by Lieut. Brodribb and their platoon commanders, "A" Company dashed in with the bayonet. Here and there a bomb was thrown down a cellar, or a Lewis gun turned against some party which resisted, but for the most part the bayonet was the weapon of the day. The enemy were scattered, a few tried to fight, but large numbers were killed trying to escape, while 120 were captured, and 50 more driven into the Sherwod Foresters' lines. The work on the North side was the easiest. Here, small parties led by 2nd Lieut. Dennis, who was slightly wounded, C.S.M. Wardle, Serjt. Toon, and others carried all before them, cleared the lower road

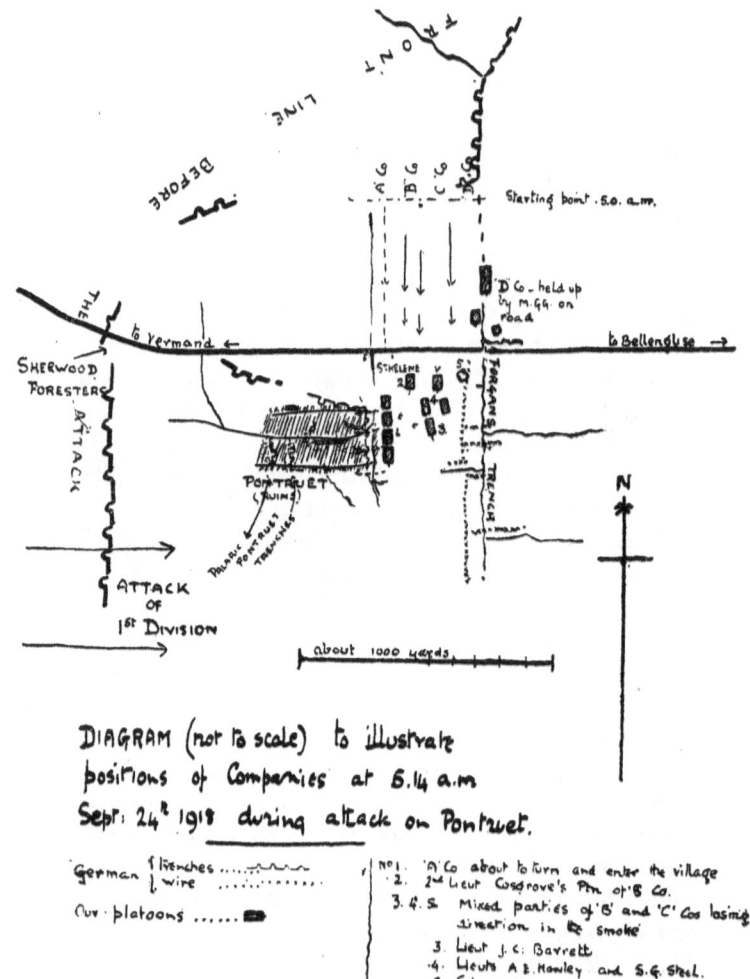

PONTRUET.

and the cemetery, and formed up outside the N.W. corner, where they were joined by their Company Commander.

In the centre there was more fighting, and while L/Cpls. Downs and Starbuck and Pte. Meakin led their parties through with tremendous dash, one Lewis Gun section under Dakin, a " No. 1 " Lewis Gunner, found itself held up by a strong German post. The " No. 2 " was killed, and Dakin himself was shot through both thighs almost at once, so that there was no one left to work the gun. However, Hyden, an untrained soldier, came forward and fired the gun, while Dakin, bleeding freely and with both thighs broken, lay beside him and corrected stoppages, until he succumbed to his injuries.

The Company's heaviest losses were on the Southern or upper side of the village. For, in the S.W. corner, the Germans had two lengths of well defended trench, supported by a block house, and against these 2nd. Lieuts. Aster and Quint and Corporal Tyers led their men. The two officers were killed almost together at the second trench, but the Corporal broke clean through, only to be shot through the head when almost outside the village. Seven others of this same gallant party were killed at this corner, and the remainder, unable to deal with the blockhouse, fought their way through to the main part of the Company.

Meanwhile, the rest, of the Battalion had been far less fortunate, and, with no road to guide them, had been baffled by the fog. 2nd Lieut. Lewin and Serjt. Harrison with a small party of " B " Company crossed the valley and, turning right, followed No. 1 Platoon into the Southern half of the village. They were too small a body to clear the blockhouse corner, and first Serjt. Harrison, then 2nd Lieut. Lewin were killed as they gallantly tried to get forward. Two others of their men were hit, and the rest were scattered.

One platoon of "B" Company remained intact. 2nd Lieut. Cosgrove, finding he could not keep direction and advance at the required pace, dropped behind. Stopping every few yards to take a compass bearing, this officer finally brought his platoon to its allotted turning point and entered the village. Following the lower road, the platoon split into two halves and "mopped up" anything left by "A" Company, making sure that the whole of this side of the village was absolutely clear of the enemy. 2nd Lieut. Cosgrove with his two sections joined Lieut. Brodribb outside the village. Corporal Barber with his Lewis gun section took up a position inside near the Cemetery.

The rest of "B" Company and the left half Battalion fared badly. Forgan's trench, supposed to be held by a few odd posts, was strongly manned from end to end. It was wired in front and lateral belts had been placed at frequent intervals across it. It would have been a stiff task for a Company to take it with a direct frontal attack; to "work up" it was impossible. None the less, "D" Company (Brooke) did their utmost. Led by their Company Commander in person, the Company left the trench at Zero and started to work along it. There was wire everywhere, and the going was very bad on top, so that many men of the rear platoons dropped back into the trench and made their way along it—a fatal mistake. On nearing the Bellenglise road this Company was met with a perfect hurricane of machine gun bullets from three guns in a nest near the road. Captain Brooke was hit but continued to lead his men, and, ably backed by Serjt. Darby, made a gallant attempt to rush the position. The men still in the trench could give no assistance, and though two prisoners were taken the rush failed, and the German machine guns remained unharmed. Captain Brooke was twice hit again and with 2nd Lieuts. Sloper and Buckley, who were both wounded, had to leave the fight. Serjt. Darby and L/Cpl. Smith had been killed close to the enemy's guns, Serjeant Sullivan was wounded, and for the moment the Company was leaderless. Lieut. Corah came up to take command, but by the time he reached the head of the Company it was too late to act, and Forgan's trench remained full of the enemy.

The occupants of Forgan's, mostly machine gunners, appear to have realised almost at once the direction of our attack, and opened a hot fire on our left flank as we crossed the Bellenglise road and set off across the valley. "A" Company felt this severely, but far more severe were the losses of "C" Company and those platoons of "B" which did not make their turn into the village. These were nearer to Forgan's trench, and both lost heavily. The mist and smoke were very thick, connecting files were useless, and the various officers, collecting what men they could find, made their way as far as possible in the right direction. Lieut. Hawley with the bulk of "C" Company found a few of the enemy still in the Eastern end of Pontruet, turned them out, and occupied a trench along the edge of the village, facing East. Further South along this same trench another party of "C" under Lieut. Steel made use of a small road bridge, and took up a position facing the same way. The rest of the Company followed Lieut. Barrett and Serjt. Spencer and reached the far side of the valley, being joined on the way by some of "B" Company. A few yards up the bank on the Southern side, Lieut. Barrett found to his surprise a trench across his route. The fog was still thick, and this puzzled him—it had been newly dug during the night—but, as it was full of Germans, he rushed it, got inside, and turned towards Forgan's. He was hit doing so. Reaching Forgan's, this party, in which Serjeant Spencer was conspicuous, quickly disposed of three German machine gun posts and their teams, but were then themselves fired at and bombed from several directions. Undeterred, Lieut. Barrett, though again wounded, drew his revolver and with it held up one bombing party, while Serjeant Spencer dealt with another. A bomb burst close to Lieut. Barrett's pistol arm and put it out of action, and by this time he was becoming exhausted. Calling his N.C.O.'s together, he explained what had happened and gave them careful directions as to how to get out, himself quite calm the whole time. Acting on his instructions, those of the party who were left cut their way out; Lieut. Barrett, refusing help, started to crawl through the wire, and was again wounded. He eventually reached the R.A.P. literally covered with wounds. Contrary to the Doctor's expectations, however, he not only lived to receive his Victoria Cross, but soon made a complete recovery.

At the same time, Captain Tomson, finding his Company now consisted only of his signallers, runners, and batmen, and unable to find out where the rest had gone, determined to try and rush the machine guns which were keeping up such a steady fire close to his left flank. His little party forced their way through some wire and found themselves opposed by three guns. With a shout of "Come along Tigers, show them what you can do," Captain Tomson led them straight at the enemy. Two of the gun teams were overcome, but the third could not be reached, and fired at them point blank. L/Cpl. Signaller J. Smith was wounded and fell, Captain Tomson, bending down to tie him up, was shot through the head. Only two men got away, leaving their leader, now dead, in a small shelter outside the trench. Smith, mortally wounded, refused to be taken away, saying "Leave me with Captain Tomson, I shall be all right"—and there he died next to his Company Commander. So perished the kindest hearted and bravest gentleman that ever commanded a Company in the Regiment. Calm, cheerful, with a friendly word for all, Captain Tomson was the father of his men, and a warm friend to his brother officers and N.C.O.'s.

By 6-30 a.m. it was daylight, but the fog and smoke still lay like a thick blanket along the valley, hiding the village and all that was going on there. It was not until 7-45 a.m. that the wind blew this away, and we were at last able to see how we had fared. The village, with the exception of the blockhouse corner, was in our hands. "C" Company were holding more than half its Eastern side, while "A" and part of "B" had reformed after the attack and were dug in just outside the N.W. corner. The only troops actually in Pontruet were those with Corpl. Barber at the Cemetery. The road leading West from the village was thronged with prisoners and stretcher bearers making their way towards the large crater on the main road, used as a Company Headquarters by the Sherwood Foresters. Captain Jack had established his Aid Post at the bottom of the little valley running down to the road, and here, helped by the never-tiring Padre Buck, was busily employed with our wounded.

In Forgan's trench there was a deadlock. Across the valley and on the Southern slopes it was still full of the enemy, who had many machine guns. Daylight made an attack over the open by "D" Company impossible, for as soon as anyone was seen to leave our lines he was at once fired upon. Every effort was made with bombs and rifle grenades to dislodge the German machine gunners from their posts on the main road, but, though Serjts. Marston and Haynes and L/Cpl. Thurman did their utmost, no progress could be made. Here, therefore, "D" Company had to stay throughout the day, almost powerless to help, except by harassing the enemy with stokes mortars from the high ground. With daylight, the enemy also had complete command of the Eastern edge of Pontruet, and Lieuts. Hawley and Steel had to lie very quiet; the slightest movement attracted the attention of the snipers in Forgan's.

At 8-0 a.m. the battle was practically at a standstill, and the C.O. sent the Adjutant forward to see what could be done to improve our position. The enemy's artillery was now fairly quiet, and, except for the one machine gun post near the blockhouse, there seemed to be no Germans in Pontruet. "A" and "B" Companies had exhausted all their grenades and Lewis gun ammunition in their efforts to capture this one post, but had failed, and our only hope was now that a 1st

Divisional Tank would do it for us. This Tank was seen coming up from the West, and, to attract its attention, we waved our helmets on our rifles. It turned towards us, but suddenly broke down, and soon afterwards was put completely out of action.

At the same time, efforts were made to signal to Battalion Headquarters for ammunition, but the signal apparatus had all been destroyed in the fight. The only flag available was one of the " red, white and black " Regimental flags, which the Adjutant happened to have in his pocket, and though this was vigorously waved, it could not be seen. A runner had to be sent instead.

Meanwhile, though we had practically cleared the village of the enemy, we were not, as far as we knew at the Western end of it, holding it very strongly. The only post known to "A" Company was Corporal Barber's at the Cemetery. "C" Company were supposed to be "somewhere at the other end," but no one quite knew where. However, with Corporal Barber was a "C" Company soldier—Coles—who undertook to find his way back to his Company. Our idea was to form a line through the village at once, and, when ammunition arrived, push the line through to the far side. Coles found "C" Company, but so hot was the sniping from Forgan's, that any idea of moving men in that direction had to be abandoned, at any rate until darkness. Coles himself was unable to return, so that the exact position of "C" Company was never known at Headquarters.

On the return of the Adjutant, Battalion Headquarters moved up to the valley next the R.A.P. At the same time a large supply of ammunition and bombs was brought up as far as the crater. Colonel Griffiths himself set off to visit " A " Company, but he had not gone many yards along the road before he was heavily sniped by the enemy machine gunners. The latter had established several posts on the high ground S.E. of Pontruet, and were now making the road impassable. For a long time the Colonel, making use of shell holes, tried to make his way to the village, but every time he was " spotted " and finally he had to return. Ammunition carrying parties lost very heavily and never got near our companies; the village seemed to be completely cut off from us. To add to our discomfort the enemy's artillery was again active and gas shells were fired wherever movement was seen. The Headquarters and the R.A.P. were frequently bombarded. At the same time the enemy's infantry started to dribble back by Forgan's and the new trench, into the S.W. corner of the village, probably to counter-attack. Observers saw this movement from the Tumulus Ridge, and, as soon as Corpl. Barber's post could be withdrawn, the suspected area was heavily shelled by our gunners, and no attack developed.

During the afternoon, the Headquarters, finding that in their new position they were in touch with neither Brigade Headquarters nor their Companies, moved back to the hill-top. Captain Jack and the Padre remained with the R.A.P., though their valley was almost continuously shelled, and never entirely free from gas. The devoted work these two did that day is beyond description and too great for praise.

At 4-0 p.m., as our position was materially unchanged, we received orders for a fresh advance, to be made in conjunction with one Company of the 6th Sherwood Foresters. Our objective was to be a line

along the Southern edge of the village, to link up with
" C " Company, or at least to extend to where we
imagined " C " Company to be. Captain Pink, of the
Sherwood Foresters, commanded the Company which
was to help us, and no one could have worked harder
than he did to make our advance a success, but the
uncertainty of " C " Company's exact position, and the
impossibility of sending them any orders, made our
task very difficult. Late in the afternoon we at last
got news of Lieut. Steel. In spite of shells and
machine-gun bullets, a runner came along the main road
from St. Hélène to the crater. This runner, Private
F. Lane, had had to crawl 250 yards across the open
under direct observation, had had to kill two Germans
before he could get clear of the village, and had then
run the gauntlet of shells and bullets along the road—
all this alone. Not content with having delivered his
message, he refused to rest, and, though exhausted,
made his way back by the same way that he had come.
We now knew where Lieut. Steel was under the bridge,
but still we knew nothing of the main part of " C "
Company.

At 7-30 p.m., as it was getting dusk, the combined
advance started without a barrage. It was a big
frontage for so small a force and parties lost touch with
each other amongst the ruins. " A " Company's left
kept close to the Sherwood Foresters, but the outer
flanks of both were " in the air," for " C " Company
could not be found. It was dark when the South side
of the village was reached, and it was found terribly
difficult to keep direction amongst the ruins and
trenches. A Lewis Gun Section, under C.S.M. Wardle,
disposed of the only party of the enemy who were
encountered, but the post near the Blockhouse could not

be found. Finally at 9-0 p.m. the Sherwood Foresters fell back to Fourmi trench near the main road, and 2nd Lieut. Dennis, now commanding "A" Company, ordered his platoons to return to their former positions. We had accomplished nothing.

The original plan had been that we should be relieved as soon as it was dark, but our present line was so uncertain that the relieving Battalion refused to take it over as we had it. The men were tired out, and it was impossible to expect them to make another attempt to form a line round the village. "C" Company were found, but too far North to link up with the others. Eventually, at 2-0 a.m. on the 25th, we were ordered to withdraw all our Companies and evacuate the village. This we did by 4-0 a.m. What was left of the Battalion then marched back to where we had left our greatcoats, while the Sherwood Foresters took over the line north and west of Pontruet. The Adjutant saw the last parties out of the village, and the Colonel, though tired out, insisted on going round the lines and visiting each platoon as it came in.

The following day we received this message from General Boyd :—

"Please congratulate Lieut.-Colonel Griffiths and the 1/5th Bn. Leicestershire Regiment on the good fight they put up yesterday, and tell them I am quite satisfied. They captured many prisoners and accounted for numbers of the enemy. Owing to unexpected reinforcements they attacked an enemy twice as strong as themselves, and moreover in a strong position. Although we did not reach our objective, the enemy was prevented from reinforcing the troops opposed to the Division on our right.

(sd.) G. F. BOYD, Major-General.

We had lost one Company Commander and three subalterns killed, one Company Commander and six subalterns wounded. Of the rank and file, thirty were killed, of whom three were Serjeants, one hundred were wounded, and eight were missing. But we had proved that five platoons could clear a village held by three Battalions (so said one of the prisoners) of the enemy; we had shown that when N.C.O.'s became casualties, private soldiers were ready to assume command and become leaders, and, most important of all, the battle had proved to each individual soldier that if he went with his bayonet he was irresistible.

CHAPTER XVII.

CROSSING THE CANAL.

25th Sept., 1918.   4th Oct., 1918.

THE two days following this action were spent in refitting and re-organizing what was left of the Battalion. All available officers from the "battle details" were ordered to join us, and Captains Petch and Banwell resumed command of their Companies, while Lieuts. Hawley and Corah took over "B" and "D." Major Burnett also came up and, though we were still in trenches and holes in the ground, managed to produce hot baths for everybody. The line was very quiet, the weather warm, we needed a rest, and for two days we had it. The Brigade was to be relieved by the Staffordshires on the evening of the 27th, and our first orders were to go into various trenches and dug-outs round Grand Priel Farm. These orders, however, were cancelled before relief, and we were allotted instead a quarry and some trenches just North of le Verguier.

Up to the evening of the 26th all had been very quiet and there was not the slightest sign that any active operations were intended. However on this evening, the Transport drivers, bringing up rations, told us that all the roads behind the lines were thick with guns, lorries and waggons, all moving up. At the same time Colonel Griffiths returned from a Conference, with some orders so secret that they were told to no one. The following day we saw that during the night many new batteries had taken up positions on the Ascension Ridge, guns had been carefully camouflaged, men hidden away in copses, and all was still very quiet. The same day, officers of another division came up reconnoitering—all with considerable secrecy—though one was seen to be carrying a map with a red line on it, somewhere four miles East of the St. Quentin Canal. The following night more batteries silently took up their positions; large bomb, water and ammunition dumps were made wherever a house or copse would screen them from the enemy's aircraft, everything was being prepared for some gigantic enterprise. As we went out to le Verguier, we passed some of the Staffordshires going to the front line. It was a very dark night, but we could see that they were carrying more than usual and that their equipment looked very bulky. They were wearing life belts.

The secret could now be kept no longer, and as soon as possible orders were made known to all. They were brief : " The 46th Division will on a certain date, as part of a major operation, cross the St. Quentin Canal, capture the Hindenburg Line, and advance to a position on the high ground East of Magny la Fosse and Lehaucourt (2 miles E. of the Canal)."

The St. Quentin Canal, or Canal du Nord, as it is called further North, runs for the most part North and South. At Bellicourt, opposite the Americans, 1,000 yards North of our sector, it enters a tunnel and is for a considerable distance underground. At Bellenglise, opposite the right of our Divisional sector, it takes a sharp turn to the East, and runs, past Lehaucourt and le Tronquoy, for 2½ miles before again turning South. The main Hindenburg Line followed the line of the Canal, just East of it. The Americans would attack the line above the tunnel, and North of them British Divisions would continue the advance far to the North. The 46th Division would attack with its right on Bellenglise, and a gap of 1,000 yards from its left to the Americans. South of us no attack would be necessary; for, once across the Canal, our right flank would be defended all the way to le Tronquoy by the Canal itself and this portion of the Hindenburg Line, which we should " roll up " from the flank. Tanks could not cross the Canal except over the tunnel at Bellicourt. Consequently the IXth Tank Battalion, allotted to our Division for the attack, would advance with the Americans, and, once in Bellicourt, turn south and join us to assist in the advance to the village objectives and the heights. To the Staffordshire Brigade was alloted the crossing of the Canal and the taking of the Hindenburg Line. Then, after a pause to allow the Tanks to come round, the Sherwood Foresters on the right and our Brigade on the left would sweep on, still under a barrage, to the final objective. We should have to deal with Magny village, the Right Brigade with Bellenglise and Lehaucourt. On the final objective there would be another pause, then, if all had gone well, the 32nd Division would come through to the " Red " Line of exploitation—another two miles still further East. Maps were issued with the objective of each unit shown in colour. The Staffordshires had the " Blue," which was the Hindenburg Line, and the " Brown " further E. to hold till we came up; the 4th Leicestershires had the "Yellow," which included Knobkerry Ridge, the 5th Lincolnshires the "Dotted Blue"—just beyond Magny village; we had the last of all, the "Green" line, including a sunken cross-roads, an old mill on some very high ground, and a small copse called Fosse Wood. It was argued that by this time either the attack would have failed and we should not be wanted, or, if successful, there could not be very much resistance; we were very weak after Pontruet, and this was considered the easiest task. The day chosen was September 29th— the time, dawn.

Outside le Verguier there runs a muddy lane with an old quarry beside it. In this quarry, in an evil-smelling but very deep dug-out lived Battalion Headquarters; everybody else occupied trenches in the fields round about. On the opposite side of the lane was a battery of 9.2's, firing almost continuously day and night, making it almost impossible to reach the Headquarters, and quite impossible to ride down the lane. Altogether our surroundings were unpleasant. The enemy soon made them worse, for about an hour before dawn on the 28th he suddenly put over a few small shells, apparently high explosive, round "B" Company's trenches, while one or two also fell round "C" and "A" Companies. Finally he pitched three clean into the quarry, and the sentry woke up to the fact that they were not only high explosive, but contained a very fair percentage of mustard gas. It was about an hour before the discovery was made and still longer before all troops were moved away. "C" Company wisely took no risks and were soon across the road, and "A" and "D" were practically unaffected. "B"

Company, however, were not warned, and it was nearly two hours after the first shell had come before they were finally moved grumbling to another area. Apparently no one was gassed, but we knew mustard only too well and feared very much what the enemy would bring forth. However, at 9-0 a.m it came on to pour with rain, and we got more hopeful.

At 11 o'clock Col. Griffiths, taking the Adjutant and Company Commanders with him, set off to a Conference with the Tank officers at Brigade Headquarters. The enemy were shelling le Verguier, the 9.2's were firing vigorously, it was pouring with rain, and the horses were very nervous. The ride was consequently exciting. Led as usual by "Sunloch," the party galloped past the 9.2's and halted at the entrance to the village to try and "time" the Boche shells. One came, they dashed in, turned the corner and just got clear in time; the next shell skimmed over the last groom's head and wounded a German prisoner.

Our conference with the Tank officers caused a slight alteration in Colonel Griffiths' plan of attack. He had intended to advance with two companies in front and two in support, but finding that a three company frontage was more suitable for Tank co-operation, this was adopted—"A" Company (Petch) to be on the right, "C" Company (Banwell)) to be in the centre, and "D" Company (Corah) on the left. "B" Company (Hawley) would be in support. The front line Company Commanders arranged rendezvous with their Tank Commanders, and we rode back.

By evening our worst fears had been realized, and forty-five of "B" Company had to be sent to Hospital, too blind from the mustard gas to be of any use.

CROSSING THE CANAL.

C.S.M. Wardle and about five men from each of the other Companies had also to go, while Headquarters lost Mess Corporal J. Buswell. As we had lost L/Cpl. Bourne a few days before, this left us rather helpless, and, but for our energetic Padre-Mess-President, should probably have starved. We had one consolation. Towards evening on the 28th the rain stopped, the weather brightened, and there seemed to be every prospect of a fine Sunday. Bombs, flares and extra rations were distributed at dusk, and we turned in for the night during which, except for a few aeroplane bombs, the evening left us in peace.

At 5-0 a.m., Sunday, the 29th of September, the barrage started. There was the usual thick morning mist, and even at 7-0 a.m. we were unable to see more than a few yards in any direction. Even gun flashes could not be seen, and the only intimation we had of the progress of the fight, was the continuous "chug-chug-chug," of the tanks, moving along the valley North of us, completely out of sight. As we were not due to move until 9-0 a.m. we spent the time having breakfasts and reorganizing the remains of "B" Company. Lieut. Hawley, with the aid of the recently returned C.S.M. J. B. Weir, D.C.M., formed one large platoon with as many Lewis Guns as possible. Between 7-0 and 8-0 a.m. the mist lifted once for a few seconds only, and, looking Northwards we could see the top of the next ridge. Along the skyline as far as the eye could see from West to East stretched a long column of horses, guns and wagons—moving forward. Below them, in the shadow, moved a long procession of Tanks. Then the mist closed down and we saw no more.

As soon as breakfasts were finished, picked N.C.O.'s and men were sent forward to get in touch with the rest of the Brigade and reconnoitre roads forward to the Canal. At 7-45 a.m. came a message from Brigade Headquarters, to say that, as the mist was worse further East, we had better start moving at once. Parade was accordingly ordered for 8-30 a.m., instead of 9-0 a.m., and we tried to form up in a field near the quarry. The mist was so thick one could not see from one end of a Company to the other, and it was nearly nine o'clock before Capt. Jack and his orderlies with their medical box appeared in the field, and we were ready to move off. Even so, we had to leave the mess staff behind, but the Padre promised to bring them along.

At 9-0 a.m. we moved off in single file, Col. Griffiths leading, and the Companies following in the order "A," "C," "D," Battalion Headquarters, and "B." It was terribly difficult to keep touch, as, with many oaths, we stumbled over ditches and holes until we reached the lane from le Verguier to Grand Priel. Here we picked up the Headquarter horses, and also were much cheered by some wounded soldiers, who told us the Boche was running away for all he was worth. Unfortunately our column was cut in half by some artillery coming down the line, who passed between "D" Company and Headquarters. Alongside us, moving on the same track, were the 5th Sherwood Foresters, also bound for the "Green Line"; their "all up" was passed to the head of our column, and the Colonel, thinking we were intact, moved on. At Ascension Farm, the Adjutant was sent in to report to Brigade Headquarters and the Colonel struck off into

CROSSING THE CANAL.

the mist, marching entirely by compass bearing. Periodically he and Captain Petch stopped to check their direction and then moved slowly on again; there was some barbed wire and the horses were sent back. Eventually, after crossing the old front line and going half way down the next slope the Colonel halted, and allowing the Companies to form up by platoons, waited until it was time to go on. He judged that he should be somewhere near the original starting line of the Staffordshires. " C " and " D " Companies came up but there was no Battalion Headquarters and no " B " Company—incidentally no Adjutant. The latter, coming out from Brigade Headquarters, found that the Battalion had gone and tried to ride after them. He merely succeeded in getting into a wire entanglement and having no groom had to leave his mare. With Lieut. Ashdowne, the Intelligence Officer, and Scout-Corporal Gilbert—the only ones left of Battalion Headquarters—he went on, hoping to catch up the Battalion before they reached the Canal. Fortunately at 10-45 the mist blew right away, and the sudden daylight which followed showed him where the Battalion lay; it also showed the Staffordshire's starting tape only 60 yards from where the Colonel had halted.

Until 11-20 we sat in the sun and waited in the hopes that some of the missing people might join us. We held a short Conference, and the Colonel decided that if there was any more fog or difficulty of any sort, Company Commanders should make their way at once to their places in the " dotted blue " line. Scouts were sent out to reconnoitre Canal crossings, and as soon as the barrage started for the 4th Battalion's advance, we moved forward in rear of the 5th Lincolnshires.

There was some scattered shelling, but our formation —lines of platoons in fours—was found very suitable. On reaching the Canal the two right Companies crossed by the remains of an old dam, the left by Riqerval Bridge, and all formed up in the ruins of the famous Hindenburg Line on the far side. It had been terribly battered, and here and there the remains of its occupants showed how deadly our barrage, and how fierce the assault of the Staffordshires had been. As we reached the Canal a single Tank was seen coming down from the North, another followed and then others; " our " Battalion had crossed successfully at Bellicourt, so the battle must be going well.

After a short pause, the advance up towards Knob-kerry Ridge started. As we crossed Springbok Valley we could see the 4th Battalion consolidating their newly-won positions on the top, and there was little opposition from this quarter. On our right, however, there seemed to be a stiff fight going on in Bellenglise, and several dropping shots from machine guns fell round us. We deployed into the " blob " formation, before ascending the ridge, and for the next half-mile our advance was worthy of a plate in Field Service Regulations. In front the Colonel, with his eye on Magny village, kept the direction right. Behind him the three Companies deployed, their " distance " and " interval " perfect, and working so well together that if one was checked for a time, the others saw it at once and conformed. Behind the centre a small red cross flag and the " red, white and black " marked the position of the Regimental Aid Post and Battalion Headquarters. The latter's flag was already becoming famous; it was the one with which " A " Company had

CROSSING THE CANAL.

tried to signal from Pontruet. A few yards short of the summit of the Ridge we halted and lay down again while the 5th Lincolnshires did their advance. While we were here, the Tanks came up, and so excellent had been the liaison, that from the Tank which stopped behind "A" and "C" Companies stepped the officer with whom they had arranged details the day before.

At about 1 o'clock we moved on again—our centre through Magny la Fosse and our Flank Companies on each side of it. The fight in Bellenglise seemed to be over, and for the moment things were very quiet. Swarms of prisoners, waving their arms, were seen coming from various trenches and the village; no one was looking after them, we were all much too keen on getting forward. Here and there, when a few Boches showed signs of getting into a trench instead of keeping to the open, some soldier would administer a friendly jab with the bayonet to show them what was expected of them. The Tanks came along behind us, meaning to form up in Magny woods, and wait there till we went on. As the Lincolnshires got their objective without trouble, we moved close up to them and once more lay down to wait for 1-40 p.m., the time for our own barrage and advance.

Unfortunately, though screened from the East, the corner of Magny Woods, was visible from the South. Across the Canal on the high ground, some German gunner must have seen the Tanks assembling, and, finding no attack was coming his way, started to shoot at point blank range at our right flank. The right and centre became very unpleasant, and there was a veritable barrage round "A" Company. Through it, very hot and very angry at being shelled, suddenly appeared Padre Buck, a heavy pack of food on his back, and behind him the Regimental Serjeant-Major and the missing Headquarters. He had found them near Ascension Farm and knowing enough of the plan of attack, had "sweated" them along as hard as he could. It is impossible to imagine what we should have done without runners, signallers or batmen, to say nothing of the food. As we were now only 600 yards from our final objective the Padre and Captain Jack went off to find a Regimental Aid Post and finally settled in a small dug-out in a sunken road just outside the village.

At 1-40 p.m. our barrage started and our advance began; our shelling was slightly ragged in one or two places, but for the most part it was very accurate— wonderfully so, as guns were firing at extreme range. On the right "A" Company working along, and on both sides of an old trench, reached their objective without difficulty except for the shelling which, aimed at the Tanks, was falling all round the Company. Captain Petch, after L/Cpl. Downs and others had removed some twenty-one Boches from a hole under the road, made his Headquarters there, went round his outposts, and sent patrols out to his right flank, where the Sherwood Foresters, delayed in Bellenglise, had not yet reached Lehaucourt. They soon came up, however, and our right flank was secured. In the centre "C" Company had even more shells and did not have the satisfaction of evicting any Boches. They reached their objective and put outposts round the Mill and along a sunken road to connect with "A" Company. The protective barrage was still in front of them, and through it, in the direction of Levergies, could be seen several German batteries limbering up. One was quite close. This was too much for C.S.M. Angrave and Serjeant Tunks, who collected some twenty men and, regardless of the barrage, took advantage of the cover of a sunken road running East, and pushed forward. They could not cross the open, but, using their rifles, drove off the gunners and killed the horses, so that the battery remained in our hands. This very enterprising party then went on under Serjeant Tunks and had a look at Levergies, finally returning after it was dark.

Behind "C" Company, the Colonel and Adjutant after lying for some time in a small hole, and wondering whether they would be rolled on by one of our Tanks, or hit by the shells aimed at it, finally planted their flag outside a little dug-out on the N.E. corner of Magny Woods. However, the Colonel would not rest here, but was off again at once to see how we had fared. He first met Captain Banwell looking for a "success rocket"; this sounded satisfactory, and, as about the same time, Lieut. Hawley appeared with "B" Company, and we once more had a "reserve," all looked well. On the left—"D" Company (Corah), after chalking their names on a battery of deserted whizz-bangs, collected a Boche officer and some 50 men from a 4.2 gun battery without any trouble; hurrying on, they found some 20 others trying to blow up a 5.9 Howitzer in Fosse Wood, demonstrated that this could not be allowed and took them all prisoners; then, without further opposition, they dug in round the E. side of the wood and continued the line Northwards to the Divisional boundary. After visiting these, the Colonel went off to look at the left flank, and here, except for an Australian Machine Gun Section under a

Serjeant there was no one. The Americans were not up to their objective, they had not even taken Etricourt, and for nearly a mile back our left was "in the air." Worse still, the Australian Serjeant had just been ordered to withdraw; the Colonel pointed out the situation, and the Serjeant, dying for an excuse to stay where he could see enemy to shoot at, called back his men and said "he'd stay as long as we wanted him." It was not very satisfactory, but we could do nothing else except pray hard for the arrival of the 32nd Division. When the Colonel arrived back at Battalion Headquarters we thought at first that our casualties had been very light indeed, but it was not long before we got some bad news. On our right flank the Tanks had suffered heavily at the hands of the German gunners on the Le Tronquoy high ground, and one of them, disabled and on fire, was a mark for several German batteries. Some of the crew managed to escape, but others, too badly wounded, were left inside; one crawled to our Aid Post. Padre Buck heard of this and at once went off to the rescue. The shelling was very heavy, and he was hit almost at once and wounded in many places. He was carried back to the Aid Post, but died soon afterwards, conscious to the last, but not in great pain. The Padre had been with us two years, and during all that time, there was never a trench or outpost that he had not visited, no matter how dangerous or exposed. In addition to his Chaplain's duties, he had been O.C. Games, Recreation Room and often Mess President—a thorough sportsman and a brave soldier, we felt his loss keenly.

Meanwhile every effort was being made to tell Brigade of our success, and, while one aeroplane with

British markings bombed us (in spite of numerous red flares), another took down a message from the " Popham " sheet, which Serjeant Signaller Wilbur was operating. Soon after 4.0 p.m. Captain D. Hill, the Brigade Major, appeared and told us that the 32nd Division would soon arrive, and at 5-15 p.m. their leading Battalions came through us. However, they found it was now too late to go forward, so put out Outposts just in front of our line. Their appearance provoked the Boche to further shelling, and an unlucky hit killed Serjeant Taylor, an experienced and valuable platoon Serjeant of " C " Company. Serjeants Marshall of " C " Company and Clarke of " D " Company, were also wounded, but our total casualties for the day were under 25. We had reached our objective at all points and captured 8 guns and about 100 prisoners. The Division altogether had taken 4,000 prisoners and 80 guns and had smashed the Hindenburg Line.

Though the machine-gun fire from low flying aeroplanes was somewhat troublesome at dusk, we had a quiet night after the battle, and were able to distribute rations and ammunition to the companies soon after midnight. At the time, we hardly gave a thought to this last, but it was a feat deserving of the highest praise. We had advanced some four miles into the enemy's country across a canal, and by dusk bridges and roads had been built sufficient to enable horse transport to carry rations and ammunition to the most advanced units. Ours were delivered just outside Battalion Headquarters, and the Companies fetched them from there. The admirable organization of the Staff, and the skill and pluck of our Transport Drivers, had enabled us to go into action carrying only our rations for the one day—very different from the Germans in their March offensive, when each man was loaded up with food for five days.

The following morning, the 32nd Division continued the advance, with a small barrage, against Sequehart, Joncourt and, in the near centre, Levergies. The enemy had found it impossible to remain in their positions at Pontruet and South of the Canal, and hustled by the 1st and French Divisions, had evacuated them. The French were now therefore continuing our line Southwards from Lehaucourt. The attack started at dawn and soon afterwards the valley past Fosse Wood was thronged with Whippet tanks and cavalry, waiting in case of a possible "break-through." It was the first time most of us had seen Cavalry in action, and they made an imposing sight as they filed along the valley in the morning mist. At the same time several batteries of Horse Artillery trotted up and taking up positions near our "D" Company, opened fire to assist the attack. Levergies, overlooked from two sides, was soon taken and several prisoners were captured on the left, but elsewhere the enemy had been strongly reinforced, and the attacks on Sequehart, Preselles and Joncourt broke down under heavy machine gun fire. Apparently a stand was to be made along the "Fonsomme" trench line—running N. and S. along the next ridge. After waiting all day, the Cavalry and "whippets" slowly withdrew again in the evening.

That night and the following day, as the 32nd Division had now definitely taken over the outpost line, the Companies were brought into more comfortable quarters near Magny la Fosse and Headquarters moved into an old German Artillery dug-out on the hill. In these positions "A" Company had the misfortune to lose Serjeant Toon, a most energetic and cheerful Platoon Serjeant, who was wounded by a chance machine-gun bullet, but otherwise we had a quiet time. Reorganization and refitting once more occupied our minds, and, as "B" Company's gas casualties had made them so weak, all "battle details" were ordered to join us. The following day they arrived under C.S.M. Cooper, who resumed his duties with "D" Company. 2nd Lieuts. Todd and Argyle also rejoined us from leave, and the Stores and Transport moved up to Magny village. The same afternoon there was a Battalion parade and General Rowley complimented us on our work during our two battles. He had visited Pontruet since the attack and was unable to find words to express his admiration for our fight in the village. The arrival of the "Daily Mail," and the discovery that at last the name "North Midland" figured in the head lines cheered us all immensely, and the fall of St. Quentin to the French gave a practical proof of the value of our efforts. We were all very happy and said "Now we shall have a good rest to re-fit."

Nothing, however, appeared to be further from the intentions of the Higher Command, and on October 2nd the other two Brigades came through us to take over the line from the 32nd, and again attempt to break the "Fonsomme" Line—on the 3rd. The French would attack on the right, the 32nd Division would be responsible for Sequehart, and the 46th, with Stafford-shires on the right and Sherwood Foresters on the left, would sweep over Preselles, Ramicourt and Mont-brehain, and make a break for the cavalry and

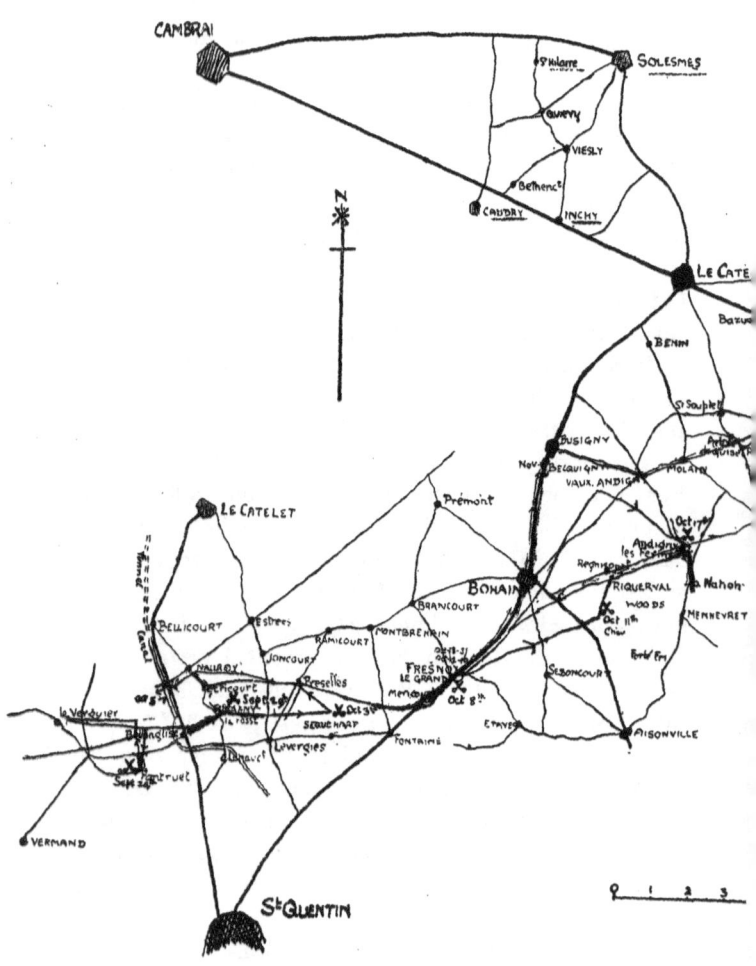

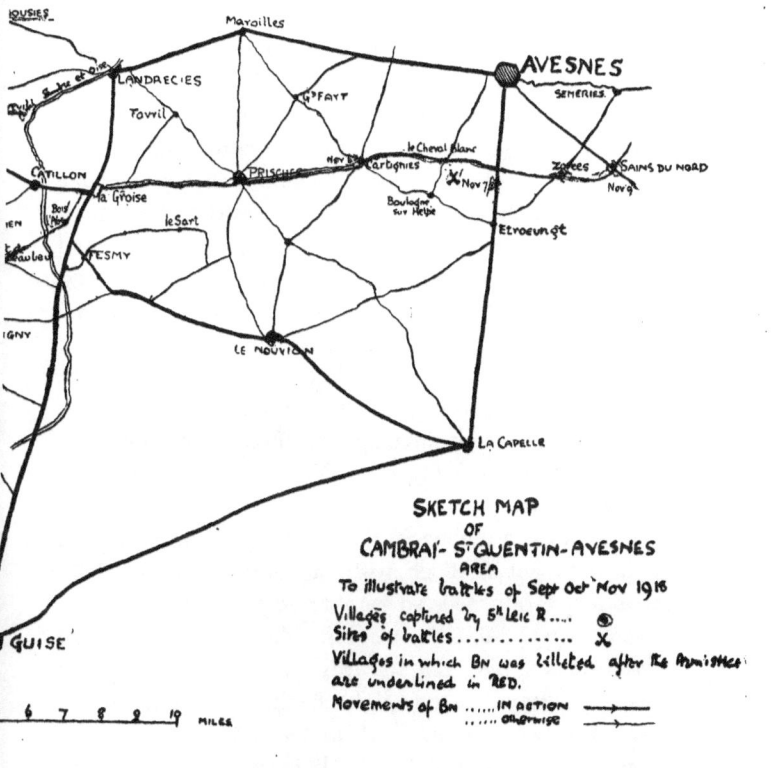

"whippets." Joncourt had already been captured and the left flank was therefore secure. Our Brigade was in support, and would not be wanted to move until 8-0 a.m. There was not much time for making preparations, and the Artillery, who had particularly short notice, spent the night before the battle getting into position near our Headquarters.

Once more a thick morning mist covered our attack and the first waves, advancing with the barrage at dawn, quickly got possession of Preselles and the Fonsomme Line, killing many Germans and taking large numbers of prisoners. There was considerable resistance in the centre, but the Sherwood Foresters, led by such men as Colonel Vann, disposed of it, and by 10.0 a.m. all objectives were gained and everything ready for the Cavalry. Meanwhile, soon after 8-0 a.m., the Battalion was ordered to move up at once and support the Staffordshires. We were to be under the orders of General Campbell, but would not be used for any purpose except holding the Fonsomme Line, to which we were now to go. We had been warned the previous evening that, if used at all, it would be on the right flank, and reconnoitering parties had already gone forward to get in touch with the Staffordshires; these had not yet returned, so we started without them.

Soon after 9-0 a.m. we left Magny la Fosse and moved down the hill towards Levergies, which we decided to leave on our right flank, as it was full of gas. We were in lines of platoons in fours—" D " Company (Corah) and " C " (Banwell) leading, bound for the Fonsomme Line, " A " Company (Petch) and " B " (Hawley) following with orders to find support positions to the other two. The Headquarters moved by the railway line N.E. of Levergies to take up a position as near as possible to the Support Battalion Headquarters of the Staffordshires. All went well until the leading Companies were beginning to climb the hill E. of Levergies, when a runner from Brigade Headquarters caught us up with a message to say that the 32nd Division had not taken Sequehart in the first attack, and that it was uncertain in whose hands the village now was. Every effort was made to warn the Companies, but we could not reach " D " and " A " in time, and we could only hope that if Sequehart was still in the enemy's hands, they would be warned of it in time to deploy their right platoons, which would otherwise march in fours close to the edge of the village.

Sequehart, however, if not at this time actually in our hands, was at all events clear of the enemy, and our right flank had no trouble. The mist and smoke made communication between the Companies very difficult, and so each moved, more or less independently, to its allotted station. " C " was the first to reach the " Fonsomme Line," only to find that the line was nowhere more than six inches deep, and, except for its concrete machine gun posts, was only a " big work " when photographed from the air. Captain Banwell accordingly took up his position in a sunken lane running between Sequehart and Preselles. Meanwhile, the other leading Company, " D," had moved too far to the left, a very fortunate circumstance, because Colonel Griffiths was able to change their direction and dispose them facing right, to form a defensive right flank opposite Sequehart. " B " Company was also ordered to face right in support to " D " Company. " A " Company, however, had not made the same error as "D," and Captain Petch, keeping his direction, found, as "C" Company had, that the "Fonsomme Line" gave him no cover. He, therefore, occupied the same sunken lane, about 300 yards south of "C" Company. Soon afterwards an intercepted message told Captain Petch of our changed dispositions, and, to protect his right, he too moved his Company to conform with "D." Battalion Headquarters had by this time occupied a large bank at the bottom of the hill, where Colonel White, of the 5th South Staffordshires, had already planted his flag.

From our new positions we had an extensive view to the East. Mannequin Ridge was on the right flank with Doon Hill at the end of it, held by the enemy, though we could see the Staffordshires holding the ridge. In the foreground was a valley, and on our left another ridge stretching from Preselles to Ramicourt. The Staffordshires did not appear very numerous for their large frontage, and it was clear that unless the Cavalry appeared soon, there was danger that they would be counter-attacked. But at 10-0 a.m. the leading Cavalry were only just beginning to appear over the Magny heights. The enemy was fairly quiet, except for one field gun, 2,000 yards away on our extreme right, beyond Sequehart. C.S.M. Angrave kept sniping at the gunners, who replied to each of his shots with a whizz-bang.

It soon became obvious that so long as the enemy remained on Doon Hill, the Cavalry could not advance, and shortly after midday we received orders to place two Companies at the disposal of the 137th Brigade, to assist in an attack on the Hill. Colonel Griffiths decided to use "A" and "D"

CROSSING THE CANAL.

Companies, and Captain Petch and Lieut. Corah were at once summoned to Headquarters, when we were told the attack was to be made by the North Staffordshires, Colonel Evans, and that our Companies would be in support. Accordingly Colonel Griffiths and the Company Commanders set off for Colonel Evans' headquarters while the two Companies moved over the open to " C " Company's sunken lane, where they formed up for the attack. A few of "A" Company under 2nd Lieut. Whetton crossed the lane and reached the Staffordshires' front line. There was no fixed time for the assault, but the hill was to be shelled by our Artillery until 2.30 p.m. This shelling ceased as our Companies reached the lane, nearly a mile from the objective, and Colonel Evans tried in vain to have it renewed.

Meanwhile the enemy had been assembling out of sight behind Mannequin Ridge, and now suddenly attacked the Staffordshires heavily, driving them from their positions on the crest. At the same time the valley was swept from end to end by bursts of machine gun fire, and it was obvious that an advance across the open could only be made with very heavy loss. Colonel Griffiths wished to stop the attack at least until Mannequin Ridge was retaken, but, before anything could be done, the enemy opened a heavy artillery barrage on the lane, and the Colonel was badly wounded. Some of " A " Company had pushed forward a little, and Captain Petch and 2nd Lieut. Dennis managed to find some cover for No. 4 Platoon about 200 yards East of the Lane. It was now about 3-0 p.m. and Colonel Evans, probably intending to alter his plans, sent for the Company Commanders.

As they arrived a shell fell on the party, killing the Colonel, Lieut. Corah and 2nd Lieut. Christy, wounding Captain Petch. A few minutes later 2nd Lieut. Mace was hit in the leg with a bullet, and both he and Captain Petch were sent down. " D " Company was officerless, " A " had three isolated groups, two forward and unapproachable, the third under 2nd Lieut. Edwardes in the Sunken Lane. There were no orders and no one knew what to do, so C.S.M. Cooper collected " D " and 2nd Lieut. Edwardes and C.S.M. Smith collected all they could find of " A," and both prolonged " C " Company's line to the left. The lane here was less sunken than on the right, and the cover was very poor, affording little protection against the enemy's shells, which came from front and flank.

We were now very short of officers. The Adjutant, Captain J. D. Hills, was in command, with Lieut. Ashdowne as Adjutant; 2nd Lieut. Argyle was acting Liaison Officer with the Staffordshires, so there was no one else except the M.O. at Headquarters. Captain Jack, it is true, was a host in himself, for, when not tying up the wounded, he was always ready with some merry remark to cheer us up; we needed it, for our railway line was as heavily shelled as the sunken lane. In addition to the killed and wounded the Companies had also lost two new subaltern officers who had joined the previous day and gone away slightly gassed, while 2nd Lieut. Griffiths, who had gone forward with the reconnoitering parties, had not been seen since. Captain Banwell was therefore alone with " C " Company. Lieut. Steel was at once sent to command " D," and, on arrival at the sunken lane, at once received a shell splinter in the leg; fortunately, however, this was not serious, and he and C.S.M. Cooper were soon hard at work straightening out the Company. This Warrant Officer and C.S.M. Smith of " A " Company were admirable; it was largely due to them that both Companies, badly shaken after their gruelling, were within a few hours once more fit for anything. Our shortage of officers was likely to continue, for our only " battle detail," Major Burnett, had just gone to England, to the Senior Officers' School at Aldershot. Our casualties during the afternoon included one who could ill be spared. A direct hit with a shell on " C " Company Headquarters wounded C.S.M. Angrave in the back. He died a few days later. One of the original Territorials, he had served with us the whole time, and even four years of France had failed to lessen his devotion to " C " Company.

Soon after 3-0 p.m. General Campbell himself rode up to Battalion Headquarters and after explaining the situation, pointed out the importance of holding a little group of trenches on some high ground three-quarters of a mile E. of Preselles. Accordingly " B " Company (Hawley), now only 25 strong, were sent there with two Lewis Guns; at the same time some of the Monmouthshires were sent to help him. Meanwhile, all the afternoon and evening, the enemy kept making small attacks on Mannequin Ridge and towards Sequehart; several of these were broken up by Artillery fire, and after his first efforts he had no further successes. Our Cavalry, having arrived too late in the morning to pass through when the enemy was really disorganized, waited all day in the valley behind Preselles, and after losing several men and horses in the shelling, had once more to withdraw at dusk. Their horses were sent back, but as many men as could be spared were sent up dismounted, with rifles and bayonets, to help hold the "Fonsomme Line" in case of strong enemy counter attacks. They did not move up until dark and, of course, could not find the "Fonsomme Line," any more than we could in the morning, so started to dig where they could. Fortunately the Commanding Officer, going round the line, found them, and, sending one party up to help "B" Company, who were now alone, he and Captain Banwell guided the rest across the valley, where they could find some cover on the hill side. Had they been allowed to remain where they had started to dig, they would probably have suffered very heavily in the morning from the Ridge opposite, whence the enemy would have had a beautiful view of them.

Rations arrived soon after dark. During the afternoon 2nd Lieut. Todd had reconnoitred a route for his limbers, and, after a narrow escape from some heavy shells, had managed to find a passable road. With the limbers came also 2nd Lieut. Griffiths, who had been wandering all over the countryside in his efforts to find us. By midnight the companies had their rations and their mail, and, even in the sunken lane, a smile could be seen here and there. The night was quiet, and we were able to collect all scattered parties and see what our casualties had been. Fortunately the loss of other ranks was not in the same proportion as of officers, but we had started so weak that we could ill afford to lose the seven killed and 30 wounded which were our total casualties for the day. "A" and "D" Companies had been hardest hit and Lance-Corporal

Company Headquarters, Loisne, 1918.

The Bathing Pool, Gorre Brewery, 1918.

Pontruet.

Meakin was amongst the killed; Serjeant Ward had been wounded, Serjeant Peach of " B " Company had also been killed, while " C " Company, in addition to their C.S.M., lost Serjt. Bond gassed and Cpl. Foulds wounded.

At dawn on the 4th, as there was no sign of any attempted counter-attack on the part of the enemy, most of the dismounted cavalry were withdrawn, and we remained in our positions of the previous day. The morning was slightly misty and Battalion Headquarters had one bad scare. The Commanding Officer and Adjutant were out looking for new quarters, when they suddenly saw coming over the hill W. of Sequhart—behind their right flank—a number of Germans in open order. A battery of 60 pounders in Levergies saw them at the same time and opened fire at point blank range. It was fully five minutes before a few leisurely French soldiers appearing over the same crest, showed that the Germans were merely a large batch of prisoners collected by the French at dawn. Throughout the day the enemy shelled various parts of the back area, and in this respect Headquarters came off worst, being more bombarded than even the sunken road. The bank under which they sat did not give them much cover, and the Boche managed to drop his shells with great accuracy on the Railway line and even hit the R.A.P. By the afternoon they were so tired of being chased backwards and forwards along the bank that they followed the example of the M.O., who with a wonderful display of calmness, which he did not in the least feel, sat reading a book of poems and refused to move. He admitted afterwards that he had not read a line, but it looked very well, and as usual he kept us all cheerful.

Late in the afternoon the long expected orders for relief came and we learnt that we were to come out that night with the Staffordshires. " B " Company on the left were actually relieved, but the other Companies had merely to wait until the front line Battalions were clear and then march out. The Boche shelled Headquarters once more just as they were going and fired a considerable amount of gas shells all over the countryside, but no one was hurt, and eventually, some by Magny, some by Joncourt, all arrived at the little village of Etricourt. Some of us rolled into dug-outs, some into ruined houses, some in the road; all of us murmured " Now we shall have our real rest at last," and went to sleep—tired out.

CHAPTER XVIII.

FRESNOY AND RIQUERVAL WOODS.

5th Oct., 1918.   11th Oct., 1918.

ONE night was all we spent in Etricourt, bitterly cold but quiet and unmolested by the enemy. The following day, the 5th of September, was bright and warm, so we at once set about improving our surroundings, started to bring some of our stores from Magny La Fosse, and were just beginning to think we might make the place fairly comfortable, when orders came for another move. There was going to be another battle, and, though we were not taking part, our area was wanted for a Support Division, so we were to go back across the Canal, and take over some shelters in the old front line trench on the Ridge. This sounded rather cold, but at all events we were going backwards to that long expected rest; not too soon, for at midday an observation balloon made its appearance, and its section chose Etricourt for their home, with the result of course of annoying the Boche to such an extent that he fired some shells over the village. At 5-0 p.m. we fell in and marched by Riquerval Bridge over the Canal and up to the Ridge, passing the Brigadier on the main road by the Canal, and found the Brigade we were to relieve, sitting very comfortably in their shelters and huts. Unfortunately they had no intention of moving until the following morning. It was now 6-30 p.m. and would soon be dark, so we were faced with two alternatives—one to sit on the road, send for the Staff, and wail loudly, the other to help ourselves.

The other two Battalions chose the former; we, being now very old soldiers, chose the latter. An open patch of ground with some good large shell holes was before us, we had a tool cart with us, and here and there might be seen a sheet or two of corrugated iron. Long before it was dark a thin curl of smoke coming out of the ground, a snatch of song, or someone grousing in a loud voice, were the only indications that there were four Companies of Infantry living there. The officers were a little less fortunate; knowing that there were bell tents coming on the limbers, they waited for them. At last they came, and very good tents, too, but someone had forgotten to bring the poles. In spite of this, we were soon all under cover, and in Headquarter Mess were actually having a hot dinner when the Staff arrived and informed the other two Battalions that they would now (in the dark) have to make the best of whatever cover they could find.

The following morning our tent poles arrived, and, having planted the red, white and black flag outside the C.O.'s, tent and mounted guard, we felt quite respectable again. By the afternoon we had so far increased in pride that the Drums not only blew "Retreat," but gave us an excellent concert while the guards were changed. We expected every hour or so to get orders to go back to some place of greater comfort for our rest, but thought it best to take no risks, and, on the morning of the 7th, gave everybody a hot bath. Two wagon covers and a cooker on the Canal worked wonders in this way. This day we lost two more officers—2nd Lieut. Whetton went on leave, and Lieut. Steel had to go to Hospital as the wound in his leg would not heal. " B " Company, being little larger than an ordinary Platoon, Lieut. Hawley was transferred to " D," and 2nd Lieut. Cosgrove commanded " B." Captain Banwell had 2nd Lieut. Griffiths in " C " Company, and 2nd Lieuts. Edwards and Dennis were still with " A." There were no other Company officers, as 2nd Lieut. Argyle was kept at Headquarters for Intelligence work. Fortunately 2nd Lieut. Todd still remained to look after the Transport, which throughout the fighting had been excellent, and Capt. Nicholson, though suffering from " flu," stuck nobly to his work and looked after our comfort at the Stores.

Just after 10 o'clock on the 7th, orders came from Brigade for a move on the following day—forward, not further back, and once more our hopes of the promised rest were dashed. This time the attack was going to be made by the other Divisions, and the 46th was to move at Zero to some assembly areas round Magny La Fosse, and wait there in case the enemy were sufficiently " broken " to allow of a general advance. Zero was five minutes past five—a most uncomfortable hour for a move, especially as breakfasts had to be eaten beforehand. Almost everybody was in bed before orders came, but there were some who had no sleep that night: the Orderly Room producing operation orders, the Quartermaster's department (whose wagons arrived at 3-0 a.m. !), and the cooks getting breakfasts ready, were the most unlucky, but so well did all ranks and all departments do their work, that at 5-0 a.m. the Battalion fell in ready to move. Packs had been stacked, ammunition and bombs distributed, most important of all, we had had a good breakfast. There is no doubt that our discipline and spirit were never better than during those strenuous weeks.

Seldom has more bad language been heard than on that early morning march down to the Canal again. It was half dark and there were Units assembling and marching in every direction. Eventually, finding we should be late at the starting point if we waited for the Regiment which should have been ahead of us, we decided to go on at once, and set off down the rough and slippery track to Riquerval Bridge. All went modertately well until a " C " Company limber stuck. Before it could be drawn clear, a Company of another Regiment marched up and round it, entirely preventing our efforts to free it. Curses were loud on both sides, but nothing could equal the flow of language that the two Company Commanders flung at each other over the heads of their perspiring Companies.

Eventually the limber was on the road again, and we reached the Bridge, near which the Boche every few minutes dropped a shell. This fact, coupled with a long line of Artillery horses going to "water," and the Brigadier trying to get his Brigade across the Canal, produced an effect which completely eclipsed the limber scene. However, as we crossed, the Boche stopped shelling, daylight came and we found the road good, though traffic made the rate of march very slow. The blaspheming consequently subsided, and, finding a field track going in the right direction, we continued our march at a fine pace until we reached our assembly position—an open stretch of ground on the South side of the Magny-Joncourt Road. Along this road were batteries of heavy guns, standing almost wheel to wheel and firing rapidly, so, in view of possible retaliation, the Companies were scattered over various little groups of trenches in the neighbourhood. The cookers came up and we prepared to make ourselves as comfortable as possible, while we once more had the pleasure of watching the Cavalry waiting to be used, and once more saw them go slowly back.

In the afternoon we moved into the next valley Eastwards, so as to be nearer the " line " if wanted; there was also better and less scattered accommodation. Gun pits, dug-outs and the inevitable grassy bank provided all we wanted, and when, an hour later, some few gas shells fell in the valley, we were all snugly under cover. All that is to say except the cookers and with them Serjeant Thomson and his cooks; these were in a shallow sunken road, and had a shell within a few yards of them, fortunately doing no damage. Thinking it best to take all the rest we could, we had the evening meal early, and long before it was dark most of the Battalion were asleep. The Commanding Officer himself retired before 9-30 p.m., and was consequently fast asleep when, soon after 10-0 p.m., a runner appeared with the usual " B.G.C. will see all Commanding Officers at once." The rendezvous this time was Preselles, some two miles away across country. It was a dark night, but with the aid of a compass he found his way there all right and received orders from General Rowley for an immediate move. The Brigade was to relieve a Brigade of the 6th

Division in the right British sector next the French; the Battalion would relieve the West Yorks R. in the right sub-sector. The following morning the Brigade would move forward into Mericourt which was supposed to have been evacuated by the enemy; we were to be "squeezed out" by the 5th Linc. R. and French joining hands across our front, and would come into support. Guides would meet us for the relief at Preselles at midnight, October 8th/9th.

The Commanding Officer at once hurried back to the Battalion and verbally issued relief orders while the Companies were falling in. In a little more than half an hour all were ready to move, and Companies marched independently to Preselles, where, under cover of the hill side, the Battalion assembled soon after midnight. There were no guides, so, after waiting some time in vain, the C.O. once more went to Brigade Headquarters and asked for instructions. He was given a map reference—supposed to be that of the Battalion Headquarters of the West Yorks., and once more the Battalion moved off. In single file, with no intervals between platoons for fear of losing touch, and a very uncertain knowledge of the position of the enemy, we marched slowly across country towards where we hoped to find Battalion Headquarters. Reaching the famous sunken road of the battle of the 3rd, we halted while a search was made; we had come to the place referred to on the map, there was nothing there. Fortunately, just as we were wondering what on earth to do, two W. Yorks. guides appeared, led us to their Battalion Headquarters, and soon afterwards the Companies disappeared Eastwards.

Battalion Headquarters was in a small cellar under

an isolated house just outside Sequehart on the Preselles Road. It was a most extraordinary relief in many ways, and perhaps the most extraordinary part was the scene in that Headquarters. There were four of us with the M.O., five West Yorks., a French Interpreter, a Padre, and an indescribable heap of runners and signallers, to say nothing of batmen, in a cellar which might have held four people comfortably. On one of the beds in the corner lay an officer. Noticing that he was not wearing W. Yorks badges, we asked who he was. They did not know, he had been there since they came in and had never moved; "perhaps he was gassed or dead," they remarked casually. This was typical of how we all felt, much too tired to worry over other people's troubles. As it happened he was not dead, and, though to this day we have never discovered who he was, he eventually disappeared—going out to look for his own Regiment. For some hours we sat in the most terrible atmosphere waiting for the relief to be finished, and at last, just as dawn was breaking, as three Companies had reported that they were in position, we agreed to take over the line, and the W. Yorks. marched out—to take part in some other battle further North. As soon as they had gone, the C.O., with a map in one hand and a slice of bread and jam in the other, went up to look at our front line and see whether the Boche had really left Mericourt.

The Battalion sector was astride the Sequehart-Mericourt Road which ran due East along the valley South of Mannequin Ridge. Sequehart village and the valley were both full of mist and gas which hung about in patches, and made walking very unpleasant. There were many German dead round the village and in the concrete emplacements of the Fonsomme line, and the fighting in this part must have been heavy. Keeping to the main road, the C.O. found "B" Company at a small cross-roads about one mile East of Sequehart; "A" Company, according to the West Yorkshires, should also have been here, but as this was the Company which had not yet reported "relief complete," he was not surprised when he could not find them. At the next cross-roads, half a mile short of Mericourt, were "C" and "D" Companies on the right and left respectively of the road. Small patrols had already been out towards the village and had not found any enemy, and both Companies were now engaged in finding the Units on their flanks. On the left a post of the Lincolnshires was soon found, and on the right the French were only a few yards away. The liaison here was perfect. After an exchange of courtesies by the Company Commanders, the flank posts fraternized vigorously, and the Frenchmen, by producing some "Jimmy Blink," cemented the Entente Cordiale. They were in great spirits, and since dawn had been formed up with bayonets fixed, waiting to make an attack; "Zero" hour had not been told them, but that did not worry them in the least. To improve the co-operation between us, the French sent a platoon under a Subaltern officer to work with us.

By 6-30 a.m. the mist had lifted enough for us to see Mericourt village plainly, and a strong patrol under 2nd Lieut. Griffiths was sent out to reconnoitre it. They met with no opposition. A few minutes later, a mounted Officer of the Staffordshires, without stopping at our front line to ask about the situation, rode into the village. We were all much too interested in watching to see what became of him, to think of warning him that the Boche might still be there. Soon afterwards, as there was still no sign of the enemy, " C " Company moved into and occupied the East side of the village, and " B ' 'and " D " Companies moved on to the West edge. Messages were sent back to tell Brigade that we held Mericourt, and to bring the Headquarters up there—at present they were about three miles back. From " C " Company's position on the high ground East of the village we looked across a large valley, at the North end of which could be seen Fresnoy le Grand; along the bottom ran the main Fresnoy - St. Quentin Railway, and on the other side a collection of small copses was marked on the map as Bois D'Etaves. Nowhere was there the slightest sign of the enemy. In view of the fact that we were particularly ordered to be in Support if an advance was made, the C.O. would not push on further without orders from the Brigadier. Meanwhile, he went off to look for the missing " A " Company, leaving the three Companies, " B," " C " and " D," holding the village and watching the valley.

At 7-30 the leading platoon of the 5th Linc. Regt. came up on our left, and about an hour later the French started their advance, and, passing Mericourt on the South side, deployed down the slopes towards the Railway line.

As soon as General Rowley heard that Mericourt was in our hands, he rode up to the village and reconnoitred the valley and Fresnoy himself from " C " Company's high ground. Seeing that the French were meeting nothing more than machine gun fire, and were apparently making good progress, he ordered Captain

Banwell to move at once into Fresnoy; there was no one else available at the moment, so we ceased to be in Support. The main road had been blown up in two places, but there were no other obstacles, and the Company reached the town without difficulty. The machine gun fire had been very heavy from the Bois D'Etaves on their right and from the Railway embankment, but they had had no casualties, and passed rapidly along the streets, finding no enemy, but meeting to their surprise several civilians, who, overjoyed at their "deliverance," were doing all they could with cups of coffee to welcome their rescuers.

For four years these unhappy people had lived under the heel of the German, and the rotting carcases of six-months' dead horses which littered the street showed what life they had lived during that time. They had been taught to hate the English, whom they only knew as night-bombers, and yet, when the Boche was being hunted out and offered to take all civilians back to safety in motor lorries, 300 men, women and children, headed by the Deputy Mayor, heroically refused to leave their town, preferring, as they said, to risk the bombardment and the "brutal English" than to remain one day longer in slavery.

At 9-0 o'clock, other Units made their appearance in Fresnoy, and the 5th Lincolnshires, with two Company Headquarters in the Quarry just outside the S.W. corner of the town, pushed some platoons through towards the Eastern edge—on the right of our "C" Company. Capt. Nichols of this Battalion had his Company round the large house used by the Germans as a Hospital, but, except for this, no one seemed inclined to push forward in any strength. At 11-0 a.m,

FRESNOY AND RIQUERVAL WOODS.

the Brigadier moved his Headquarters into Mericourt, and the Boche, presumably thinking the village was now as full as it was likely to be during the day, shelled it vigorously with gas and High Explosive. He paid particular attention to our ridge of observation, and, having pounded us off this, proceeded to hammer the other end of the village, whither we had moved for greater comfort. At the same time several salvoes were fired into Fresnoy. Soon afterwards a message from Captain Banwell told us that, with the exception of the Railway and Station, the whole town was in our hands. He had tried hard to reach the Railway Embankment from his side of the town, but the machine gun fire was very hot, the ground absolutely open, and after losing Gosden, a Lewis Gunner, killed, and one or two men wounded, had decided to wait for some Artillery. Meanwhile, the French had reached the Railway further South, so the C.O .sent Lieut. Hawley with half " D " Company to try and take the Station from this side. He moved off to do so at midday, leaving C.S.M. Cooper to command the other half Company. " A " Company (Edwards) now arrived, and, with " B " Company (Cosgrove), dug themselves into a bank on the South side of Mericourt village.

Lieut. Hawley and his party made their way rapidly down to the Quarry, and keeping just inside the Southern outskirts of the town, soon found the French left flank, from which they were able to reconnoitre the Railway Station. This last seemed to be the only place where the enemy was still offering any resistance, and there were apparently three machine guns somewhere near the Base of a large factory chimney in the Station yard. Lieut. Hawley divided his party into two, and while he himself gradually worked his way direct, the other party under Serjt. Marston, M.M., armed with as many bombs as they could carry, rapidly made their way round towards the enemy's rear. The Boche apparently thought he would soon be turned out, and some twenty of them, hurried along by one of our Lewis Guns, managed to escape before we arrived. However, they did not all get away, and when Serjt Marston lobbed his bombs on to them from behind and the others came up in front, they found five Germans still sitting there with their gun. These were promptly captured and sent down, and the town was now entirely in our hands.

Between 5-0 and 6-0 p.m. we received orders that the 5th Lincolnshires would take over the whole of the Railway, and that we were to come back into Mericourt and rest as much as possible. At the same time the enemy started to bombard Fresnoy with every available gun and howitzer. For an hour gas and high explosive shells fell in every corner of the town and its immediate surroundings. Capt. Banwell, who was returning to his Company from Headquarters, and the C.O., who was trying to find " D " Company, both had a very unpleasant time. One runner with the orders for the relief did manage to reach " D " Company without being hit, and soon after 8-30 p.m. they moved out from Fresnoy and dug into a bank just outside Mericourt. " C " Company, however, no one was able to find; it was a dark night and consequently very difficult to keep one's direction amongst the little streets and sunken lanes in the Northern end of the town, where they had taken up their position. The C.O. himself spent a large part of the night looking for them without success, but one of the messages, which he left at every post and Headquarters he called at, eventually found its way to Capt. Banwell, and between midnight and 1 a.m. on the 10th " C " Company at last came out and occupied a bank near " D " Company. Most of us had not had any sleep since we left our " shell-holes " Camp at dawn on the 8th—some of us none since the 7th, and when we finally lay down, tired out, we slept far into the next day.

Soon after midday on the 10th Major R. S. Dyer Bennet reported for duty and took over command of the Battalion, Capt. Hills resumed his former duties of Adjutant, and for the next few weeks we had no Second in Command. At the same time orders came that the Brigade would continue its advance on the " leap-frog " principle. Each Battalion would be given a definite objective for the whole of the Brigade frontage, the rear Battalion passing on to the next line as soon as each objective was gained. We were now rear Battalion, and moved after dinners to the Railway Cutting just outside Fresnoy on the Bohain line, where, while we waited for further orders, we had teas and distributed rations for the following day. The Lewis Gun limbers and cookers were now allotted to Companies, and the remainder of the 1st Line Transport occupied a field close to us. 2nd Lieut. Dunlop, D.C.M., and 2nd Lieut. Taylor returned from leave and went to " D " and " C " Companies respectively. Lieut. Ashdowne again became Intelligence Officer and 2nd Lieut. Argyle returned to " B " Company. Each Company had now two officers and " C " Company had three. Soon after six o'clock we had orders to move at dusk to the line of the Aisonville-Bohain road, now held by the 4th Battalion, and push forward from there to the edge of the Bois de Riqurval. At the same time a patrol of Corps Cyclists was being sent along the main road towards Regnicourt, and if they reported that the enemy had evacuated this village, our orders were to advance during the night to a line running Southwards from there, through the Bois, to gain touch with the French at Retheuil Farm. At a Company Commanders' Conference, held as soon as these orders were received, Major Dyer Bennet decided that if Regnicourt was clear of the enemy, " C " and " D " Companies should advance up the main road as far as the village, and, on reaching it, turn Southwards into the Bois, spreading out along the line of our objective. " A " Company, keeping touch with the French, were to advance up the " ride " on the Southern boundary of the Brigade, while " B " Company, followed by Headquarters, would go straight through the wood in the centre. We would all form up in the present positions of the 4th Leicestershire and start our advance without a barrage at 2-0 a.m.—the 11th of October.

As soon as it was dark we moved off with our Lewis Gun limbers and medical cart, keeping as far as possible to cross-country tracks and avoiding all main roads. There was some gas hanging round the Bois D'Etaves, but we were not worried by this, and soon reached the Seboncourt-Bohain Road, held by the 5th Lincolnshires. From here onwards the route was not so easy to find, but we managed to take our limbers to within a few hundred yards of the 4th Battalion Headquarters and here, after distributing Lewis Guns and Ammunition to Platoons, the Companies were met by guides and moved forward to their assembly positions. Meanwhile

Lieut. J. C. Barrett, V.C.

The Cadre at Loughborough, June, 1919.

FRESNOY AND RIQUERVAL WOODS.

Battalion Headquarters moved into the farm house already occupied by the 4th Battalion. In the cellar we found, in addition to the usual Headquarter Officers, a French Interpreter, and part of a French Liaison platoon, no air, very little light, but plenty of tobacco smoke. Soon after we arrived a message from Brigade told us that the Cyclists had met with no enemy as far as Regnicourt, but had found a patrol of about twenty in that village and had been fired on by them. We were discussing this, when suddenly there was a scuffling overhead and we were told that there was " something ticking somewhere," and that everyone had left the house. The cellar occupants were not slow to follow, and thinking of time-bombs and infernal machines managed to empty the cellar in a record time. We settled down uncomfortably under a hedge, and prepared to read and write orders with a concealed electric torch—the maximum of discomfort. However, we did not have to stay there long, as a runner came to tell us that the origin of the " ticking " had now been discovered, and, as it was nothing more formidable than the recently wound up dining room clock, we returned to the cellar. Major Dyer Bennet, arguing that, if the Cyclists could get as far as Regnicourt, we should reach our objective without difficulty, decided that the attack should be carried out as arranged, and, sending the Adjutant to find the 6th Division, moved up himself to the Aisonville Road, leaving only the Aid Post and some Signallers and servants at the Farm.

The Aisonville Road ran almost due N. and South along a valley; between it and the edge of the Bois de Riquerval was open ground for about 300 yards sloping gently up to the wood. A small cottage marked the start of "A" Company's "ride," and the stretch of road immediately N. of this was deeply sunken. Here "A" Company formed up and tried to find the French who were considerably further South than we expected. Incidentally they were not as far forward as we were, and the Boche enfiladed the road about midnight with a whizz-bang battery from the South. "B" Company formed up in an isolated copse about 100 yards East of the road into which the 4th Battalion had made their way during the afternoon. The left half Battalion remained along the road bank and in a dry ditch 50 yards W. of it, near to the junction with the Regnicourt Road up which they were to advance. There was one solitary house, protected by the hillside, which provided Company Headquarters with a certain amount of cover. The night was dark and the enemy, except for the whizz-bangs on "A" Company, very quiet.

Soon after midnight the Adjutant returned from the 6th Division. He had found that the 1st Leicestershires were on their right flank, and that they were going to continue their advance at 5-15 a.m. on the 11th. Major Dyer Bennet therefore decided to postpone our attack until that hour, so that we might all go forward together. In any case it seemed likely that this would be a better plan, as it would be daylight soon after the advance started; and, on so wide a frontage, it would have been almost impossible to maintain direction in the woods by night, especially without a moon. At 5 o'clock we were all formed up along the road, Battalion Headquarters close to "A" Company, and at 5-15 a.m. in absolute silence and without a barrage we started to climb the rise towards the edge of the wood.

The left half Battalion along the Regnicourt Road made most progress without meeting any opposition. "D" Company leading, they advanced by platoons on both sides of the road, keeping touch with the 1st Battalion on their left, and had gone nearly a mile before they were checked by machine-gun fire ahead of them. Half-way from their starting point to Regnicourt stood a little group of houses at the top of a small hill, and from here, as well as from the thick scrub and undergrowth which covered the country on both sides, the enemy's machine gunners had a good target. Thinking that this was probably some small post left behind by the Boche as he retired, and knowing that the cyclists had been through the previous night, Lieut. Hawley decided to attack at once, and "D" Company, making use of all the cover they could find, worked their way up the hill and soon captured the house. One German came out into the road with his machine gun and started to fire at them point blank, but the leading Platoon got their Lewis Gun into action, and, knocking out the Boche, captured the gun. The two leading Platoons of "D" Company had deployed, and, with 2nd Lieut. Dunlop on the left of the road and the others on the right, tried to continue their advance. Seen from below, the group of houses had seemed to be on the top of the hill, but beyond them the road, after a slight dip, rose again to a ridge 300 yards further East, and here the enemy were in considerable force. Several gallant attempts to advance were frustrated by very heavy machine gun fire, and having lost Serjts. Bradshaw and Dimmocks killed, and several others wounded, the Company was compelled to remain lying flat just beyond the houses. One little party had taken cover in the ditch along the roadside and were seen by the German machine gunner. The ditch became a death trap. Hodges and Longden, the runners, and Maw, the Signaller, were killed, and Hall, another runner, badly wounded; Serjt. Foster and L/Cpl. Osborne, both of whom had done particularly good work, were wounded, and the casualties were very heavy indeed. In half-an-hour this Company lost 10 killed 14 wounded and one prisoner. It was obvious that the Cyclists had never been further than these houses, which they must have mistaken for Regnicourt, and their report was consequently worthless.

Capt. Banwell now arrived with two platoons of "C" Company, and thinking it possible that the Companies on the right might not have got as far even as "D" Company, decided to protect the right flank from any possible counter-attack. He sent off Serjt. Tunks and No. 11 Platoon to prolong "D" Company's line to the right; they did this and managed to advance a few yards further before being compelled to dig in and keep very flat by the enemy's machine guns. A few minutes later 2nd Lieut. Griffiths followed with his platoon, to work Southwards into the woods to try and find the centre Company, or at least discover how they were situated. They managed to advance about 400 yards before they too met with fierce opposition, and had three men cut off and captured by a strong party of Boche concealed in the undergrowth. Eventually, unable to find any trace of "B" Company, 2nd Lieut. Griffiths decided to "dig in" where he was, and by doing so extended "C" Company's line still further to the right, bending back slightly to protect the flank. At 8-0 a.m. the 1st Battalion on the left had reached the same line and were similarly held up. Capt. Banwell therefore reported to Headquarters that further advance without artillery support was impossible, and that "C" and "D" Companies were holding a line running Southwards for 400 yards from the group of houses, into the Bois de Riquerval, and would wait there for instructions.

Meanwhile the centre and right had fared even worse. In the centre "B" Company, formed up originally in an isolated copse, moved forward at 5-15 a.m. in two parties towards the main part of the wood. The left hand party under 2nd Lieut. Argyle had plenty of cover for the first half-mile and pushed on rapidly, until, coming over a small crest into the open, they too met with heavy machine-gun fire. After several ineffectual efforts to advance, they dug themselves in and remained there for the rest of the day, replying to the Boche fire with their Lewis Guns, but with no visible effect. (It was afterwards discovered that this party were less than 100 yards behind 2nd Lieut. Griffiths' platoon, unable to see each other owing to a "fold" in the ground). The other half Company under 2nd Lieut. Cosgrove started their advance across an absolutely open patch of ground, sloping gently downwards towards the centre of the woods. They had gone a few yards when the daylight showed their position to the Boche, and for the next half-hour they suffered heavily. Lying on the forward slope, with no cover, they saw 50 yards away on their right two small but deep trenches. One man tried to run there and was hit a few yards from them; another had better luck and got there safely, through a perfect stream of bullets from three guns. 2nd Lieut. Cosgrove himself was badly wounded and had to be carried out, so also was Serjt. Muggleston. The others, some crawling and some running, gradually collected in the two trenches and remained there for the rest of the day.

On the extreme right " A " Company (Edwards) made no headway at all. Between the road and the edge of the wood was about 150 yards of open ground, across which ran a Z-shaped hedge, while, at the point where the " ride " entered the wood, stood a Chateau and a large black hut commanding all the country round. Daylight came soon after they left the road and with it a burst of heavy machine-gun fire from the Chateau at close range, which split the Company into three parts. Headquarters and one platoon found some cover round the little house on the corner where they started; near them in a bank was 2nd Lieut. Dennis with his platoon, while the remainder, under Cpls. Thompson and Shilton, were in the Z-shaped hedge, unable to show themselves without being fired at. On their right the French had captured Retheuil and Forte Farms.

At 5-20 a.m., Major Dyer Bennet, finding it impossible to see anything of " A " and " B " Companies, decided to advance his Headquarters, keeping as far as possible to the centre of the Brigade frontage. Accompanied by the Adjutant, R.S.M., a few runners, and the French Interpreter, he set off for the edge of the wood, which was reached without loss; but the enemy's machine guns at the Chateau, 200 yards away on the right, and slightly below us, plainly told us that " A " Company had not gone forward. A similar distance away on the left, concealed by a wall and the corner of the wood, another gun was firing across at " B "

Company, who could be seen on the opposite hillside trying to reach the cover of their two trenches. The Headquarter party was too small to be able to help, so while the Adjutant went back to try and find some reinforcements, the Interpreter, Henri Letu, made a most gallant reconnaissance into the woods to see if he could gather any information. The " reinforcements " consisted of a platoon of French soldiers, a Lewis Gun team of the 4th Battalion and two signallers. At the same time the M.O. and Intelligence Officer (Lieut. Ashdowne) arrived, and the latter, taking two men with him, soon drove out the enemy from the " corner wall " post on the left. The Battalion Headquarter flag was hung out in a conspicuous tree, signal communication was opened with the original Headquarter Farmhouse, and at about 8 o'clock the party was still further reinforced by the arrival of Cpl. Thompson and No. 1 Platoon of " A " Company, whom the Adjutant had discovered under the " Z " shaped hedge. All these movements had to be carried out with great care, as any visible activity at once drew fire from the Chateau.

This Chateau Major Dyer Bennet now decided to attack, and soon after 9.0 a.m. a party consisting of No. 1 Platoon and some Frenchmen set off under the Adjutant to do so. Cpl. Shilton and a few men were sent through some gardens to engage the enemy on their right flank; the Lewis gun, under Cpl. Thompson, went through the woods to try and attack the buildings from the rear; the Frenchmen advancing still further into the woods, protected the left flank. Cpl. Thompson's party were soon engaged. They had pushed forward rapidly for about 50 yards when suddenly Pte. Underwood, who was leading, jumped behind a tree and fired. Nine Boches seemed to come out of the ground almost at our feet, and for a few minutes there was some lively fighting round the trees. The Germans managed to kill Pte. Blythe, a very old soldier of the Battalion, and then made off, leaving one wounded man behind them. This little fight had given the alarm to the party in the Chateau, and though Cpl. Thompson pushed forward with great courage it was too late to catch them, and we entered the house and grounds without further opposition. The fall of the Chateau enabled the remainder of " A " Company to advance and occupy the edge of the wood, which they at once did, putting out several posts round the buildings. The Adjutant's party then returned to Battalion Headquarters which had been left very weak during the attack. Soon afterwards, as the situation now seemed fairly satisfactory the wounded prisoner was sent down under the 4th Leic. Lewis Gun Section, who were no longer required.

At 10-0 a.m. we were just considering the possibility of pushing forward still further when a sudden burst of machine gun fire, sweeping low over our positions, drove us to cover. The French had apparently been counter-attacked out of Retheuil and Forte Farms and the Boche from these new positions overlooked us completely. Under cover of this fire a strong hostile counter-attack was launched against the Chateau, and " A " Company were once more driven back to the road, leaving several men prisoners behind them. But the road too was now overlooked and, though sunken, was no protection, so that, unable to stay in it, they moved to a small bank on the W. side of it and dug in there. 2nd Lieut. Edwards was wounded and sent down, and the Company was commanded by 2nd Lieut.

Dennis. At Headquarters, L/Cpl. Exton, who had just arrived with a message from " B " Company, was killed and a stretcher-bearer badly wounded. Capt. Jack, the M.O. went off to tend the latter, and was himself badly hit in the body; another stretcher-bearer was hit trying to get to him, and for a short time he had to be left. A few minutes later the enemy's fire slackened; the M.O. was carried away, and, though he lived to reach the Ambulance, died there in the evening. Captain Jack had been with us just a year, and we felt very keenly the loss of his cheerful presence at Battalion Headquarters, for he was one of those men who were never depressed, and even in the worst of places and at the worst of times used to keep us happy.

The Adjutant now went back again to the old Farm House to see if he could find out what had happened to the other two Companies. The 4th Leicestershires had been relieved, and the 5th South Staffordshires had taken over the Farm and were now preparing to relieve us in the line if possible. Captain Salter was there from Brigade Headquarters and undertook to send relief orders to the Left half Battalion, whose position was now known.

Meanwhile the South Staffordshires moved up to the copse whence " B " Company had started, and a Company occupied the line along the bottom of the " Z " hedge to the " wall and corner " position—i.e., about 200 yards behind the line held by Battalion Headquarters and " A " Company. The relief of the Left half Battalion, though difficult, was carried out in daylight, and was complete by 11-30 a.m., largely owing to the energy of the Staffordshire Company Commanders. Crossing the crest by the group of houses was by no means an easy matter, and both relievers and relieved had to crawl through the scrub, in which 2nd Lieut. F. G. Taylor of " C " Company did particularly good work, while for " D " Company C.S.M. Cooper worked magnificently. Three Platoon Serjeants had become casualties and this Warrant Officer did all their work himself, rendering invaluable assistance to his Company Commander.

The relief of Battalion Headquarters and the Right half Battalion was impossible during daylight, and the G.O.C. 137th Infantry Brigade took over the command of the line as soon as our " C " and " D " Companies were relieved, while the rest of our Brigade moved back into billets at Fresnoy le Grand; we were to follow when relieved. Meanwhile, arrangements were being made for some Artillery and Tank support, and it was proposed to try a further advance during the afternoon. At the same time the Chateau was recaptured from us, the position on the edge of the wood had become so badly enfiladed that the Headquarters moved out and started to dig a new line in the open, where, as the Staffordshires were holding the " wall and corner " position, we were fairly safe. About mid-day, however, as the enemy had become quieter, we returned once more to the edge of the wood. It was never very comfortable in this isolated position, but Lieut. Ashdowne and R.S.M. Lovett showed the most wonderful coolness, and were continually out looking for new positions or watching the flanks. At 2-0 p.m. the Staffordshires received orders that they would have the help of two Tanks for their attack, which would start at 4-0 p.m. from the isolated copse. At about 3-0 p.m. the enemy again started to enfilade our wood position so badly, that for the last time we decided to leave it and came back to our line in the open, which we deepened as quickly as possible; it was hard work as the men had to dig with their entrenching tools as they lay flat. We had not, however, been long in this position before the Staffordshires behind us withdrew to form up for the attack, and, though the party at the "Z" hedge remained, the other party left the "wall and corner" unprotected. Meanwhile, thinking that, if not relieved soon, we should be surrounded from the right flank, Major Dyer Bennet went back to reconnoitre some deep short lengths of trenches about 100 yards in rear, deciding that if the attack did not prove successful he would bring Battalion Headquarters back into them.

At 4-0 p.m. there was no sign of the attack. Instead, a German machine gun crew returned to the now empty "wall and corner" position and started to enfilade our left flank, making the hill side almost uncrossable. The C.O. decided to withdraw at once, and at 4-30 p.m. the runner, Blindley, set off with the message. It was a hazardous journey, but he succeeded in crawling to within a few yards of the end man and passed a message along. Steadied by the R.S.M., the party started one by one to withdraw, while the enemy kept up a heavy fire at them. For a moment it looked as though it would be impossible to get back, but Pte. Caunter—Lewis Gunner of No. 1 Platoon—calmly mounted his gun and "traversed" the whole edge of the wood. The Boche were silenced for the moment, and the party, making a rush at the same time, managed to reach the trenches in safety. Last of all Caunter calmly picked up his gun and came away himself, fired at, but never hit. Half-an-hour later two tanks appeared, and keeping on the West side of the Aisonville Road, climbed the rise towards Retheuil Farm. Whether the enemy imagined a general attack was coming, or merely wanted to make the road dangerous, is not known, but at 5-0 p.m. he started to bombard the area at the foot of the " Z " shaped hedge, where a Company of Staffordshires, our Battalion Headquarters, and our " A " Company were all gathered, and for nearly an hour gas and H.E. shells of every calibre fell all round. There was little or no cover, and had the shells been all H.E. the casualties would have been tremendous. As it was we escaped lightly, but the valley became full of gas and we could see nothing. The position was bad, so Major Dyer Bennet ordered a general withdrawal to a line along high ground on both sides of the Aisonville-road—the remains of " B " Company under Lieut. Ashdowne to the left and " A " Company to the right. Here we once more dug a line of pits, and by 7-30 p.m. had our new position in fighting condition, while a succession of explosions, coming from two blazing heaps near Retheuil Farm, showed how the Tanks had fared. The whole of these operations had been most difficult and, in addition to those who had been conspicuous in the attack on the Chateau in the morning, many other N.C.O.'s and men showed the utmost courage and coolness. A/C.S.M. Smith, of " A " Company, and Serjts. Wilbur and Swift and Cpl. Hubbard of Battalion Headquarters, worked particularly well.

At 8-0 p.m. we were relieved by the 5th South Staffordshires and, after placing Lewis Guns on the limbers, which had been waiting all day for us behind the farm, went to Fresnoy. It can hardly be called a march, and few of us remember much about it. Those on horses slept, those on foot walked in their sleep and woke up whenever there was a halt, because they hit their heads against the haversacks of the men in front. Soon after 11-0 p.m., tired out, we reached Fresnoy and dropped down in the billets the Right half Battalion had found for us, murmuring as we did so—" Now we shall have our rest."

CHAPTER XIX.

THE LAST FIGHT.

12th Oct., 1918.   11th Nov., 1918.

The following day—the 12th of October—our hopes of the long expected rest were still further raised by the news that General Rowley was going to England on leave, for we all knew that he would never be absent if there were any prospect of a fight, and we accordingly began at once to make ourselves comfortable. Fuel was plentiful, and baths were soon fitted in " C " Company's factory, while in another part of the same building we found and used an excellent concert room. R.S.M. Lovett also went on leave, taking with him to Loughborough one or two small battle trophies, including our Headquarter flag, which had seen so much fighting during the past few weeks. Many of " B " Company's gassed men now returned, and these, with a large draft of N.C.O.'s and men, proved a welcome reinforcement, but we still had very few officers. The new draft was composed mostly of young soldiers who had not seen service before, but fortunately this did not matter, as we still had a number of our experienced junior N.C.O.'s left, and some " new blood " was useful.

Meanwhile the Staffordshires stayed in the line, and, as by the 13th there was no prospect of their being

THE LAST FIGHT.

relieved, we were not surprised on the 14th to receive some more battle orders, and consign our rest hopes, like their predecessors, to an early grave. It appeared that all frontal attacks on Riquerval Wood had proved disastrous, and, although the 6th Division on the left had reached the outskirts of Vaux Andigny, our Divisional front was still the same as we had left it on the 11th. The new attack, to take place on the 17th, would therefore be directed against the North West flank of the wood, and would be made by ourselves and the 139th Brigade, while the Staffordshires made a frontal display. The French, on the right, were making a similar movement, and there would be a general attack North of us. It was hoped that by the end of the day, or before if possible, the French and ourselves would meet on the East side of the woods at Mennevret, and so cut off any Germans who remained on the Staffordshires' front. The actual objective for the Brigade was the same Regnicourt road up which the Left half Battalion had advanced on the 11th; this was to be taken by the other two Battalions, while we were kept in reserve near Vaux Andigny.

The usual reconnaissances were carried out on the 15th, and the following morning the customary distribution of bombs, flares, rockets and other warlike paraphernalia took place. This was done with great regularity before every battle, and yet on reaching an objective we could never find the required rockets. The men carrying them seemed invariably to become casualties. It was the same with equipment and other necessaries—we started the day with everything and ended with nothing. A very welcome issue was the new map of Riquerval Woods, made from the most recent aeroplane photographs, and accurate; the old one, compiled from a pre-war survey, still showed as thick forest the ground where the Boche had cut down every vestige of a tree, and its inaccuracies in this respect had been one of our greatest difficulties in the previous battle. With the map came an issue of officers, five reporting during the afternoon, but as they were all new to the Battalion, they remained with the Stores.

Our march to the Assembly position was tedious, but we were not worried at all by the enemy, for, to avoid Bohain, which was at this time frequently shelled, a track had been taped out across country. As we were the first to use this, we escaped the usual slipping and ploughing through mud, which are a bad feature of most tracks in autumn. Lewis Gun limbers and Tool carts went by the road and reached the Andigny-Becquigny Railway line—our assembly position—before us, so that as each Platoon arrived it was able to collect its guns and tools and move straight to its position. We rapidly dug ourselves some excellent cover, and were able to take no notice of some four point twos which arrived during the night, though the other two Battalions, who had to assemble near the Andigny Road, suffered fairly heavily.

At 5-20 a.m. on the 17th the barrage opened and the battle began in a mist, which was thicker even than usual. Many Tanks accompanied by the Highlanders of the 1st Division, came through our position and passed down the hill towards Andigny, but of our own Brigade we could see nothing, and could only judge by the lessening of the enemy's machine gun fire, that the attack was successful. It must be admitted that our

THE LAST FIGHT.

attention was somewhat distracted by the appearance of a hare, rather frightened by a Tank, and we forgot the battle to give chase. It was a short but exciting run, and the victim was finally done to death by "D" Company and provided the Serjeants with a good dinner. It was not until 10-0 a.m. that we first learnt how the attackers had fared. On the right our Brigade had taken their Regnicourt road objective, but in the fog several posts of the German front line had been missed and were still causing trouble, preventing the complete capture of the village of Andigny les Fermes, the left of our objective. In the same way the 6th Division had missed posts in the two farms Gobelets and Bellevue on their front, and we were ordered to send two companies to clean up these places and generally assist with the left of the attack. A few minutes later, however, this order was cancelled, as the 5th Lincolnshires and 6th Division both reported that they now held all objectives. Instead, "B" Company (Pierrepont) and "C" Company (Banwell) were placed at the disposal of Colonel Wilson of the 5th Lincolnshires, to exploit his success and patrol the Mennevret road to meet the French, and at 11-30 a.m. these two Companies moved off to the old German front line and waited there for instructions. Col. Wilson decided to use one Company only, and at 2-0 p.m. Capt. Pierrepont moved his Headquarters into Andigny les Fermes and sent off a strong patrol under 2nd Lieut. Davies towards Mennevret. As the enemy was still holding the woods in considerable strength, and the first mile of the road was under direct observation, the patrol met with heavy machine-gun fire at once, and 2nd Lieut. Davies returned for the time, preparing to make another attempt when the advance of the Divisions on our left had made it impossible for the Boche to remain in his positions near the E. edge of the village. Half " A " Company had already been attached to the 4th Leicestershires for carrying work, so that we had now only " D " Company (Hawley) and the remainder of " A " Company with Battalion Headquarters. No more orders came for us, and during the afternoon, as the sounds of war had become more and more distant, Cavalry and Whippets had disappeared Eastwards and there was nothing to do, we lay and basked in the sun, which was very hot and pleasant.

At 6-0 p.m., just as the Boche started to fire gas shells into the valley up which all troops had to pass to reach Andigny les Fermes, orders came that we should take over the Brigade front. Accordingly, " A " and " D " Companies were sent to relieve the 4th Battalion on the right, " C " Company was made responsible for Andigny les Fermes, and the extreme left was held by " B " Company, whose duty it still was to find the French. The relief in the village might have been a very lengthy and difficult proceeding had not Capt. Nichols, of the Lincolnshires, taken great trouble to co-ordinate the work of all their three Companies, and so been able to hand over to Captain Banwell a single complete scheme of defence. Our Headquarters moved into the sunken road between Regnicourt and Vaux Andigny. It was a dark, foggy and bitterly cold night, and, experts as we had now become in the art of living in banks and sunken roads, still it was impossible to be comfortable, and German waterproof sheets spread over slots cut in the banks, failed most miserably to keep us warm. Transport arrived before midnight and the drivers, as usual, saved us endless carrying parties by taking the limbers right up to Company Headquarters in the village. They were unmolested by the enemy, and 2nd Lieut. Davies, seeing this, made another attempt to reach Mennevret. His patrol made much more progress, and was only held up at La Nation, a cross-roads a few hundred yards from his goal, but here he met with bombs and more machine guns and had once more to fall back.

At 1-0 a.m., the 18th, we were ordered to take over the line on the East side of the village from a Battalion of the 1st Division, who had relieved the 6th Division and were now on our left flank. For this purpose the luckless "D" Company, who had just settled down after relieving the 4th Battalion, had to move across our front and take over the new line, which consisted of four large shell holes and a shallow sunken lane. In spite of the difficulties of darkness and fog, relief was complete before dawn when the 1st Division moved forward towards Wassigny, and we were able to look round our new sector. We found a ghastly relic in the sunken lane where a German cooks' wagon had been hit by one of our shells as it tried to escape, and now, in the early morning light, the scattered remains of wagon, horses and cooks, all smashed up, were a horrible sight.

At last, at 5-30 a.m., 2nd Lieut. Davies and Serjt. Whitworth met the French near Mennevret, and after an enthusiastic exchange of greetings, accompanied by much handshaking, arrangements were made for establishing a line along the Nation road, and so cutting out the other two Brigades, who for some time past had been arguing vigorously as to whose duty it was to fill the gap between ourselves and the French. At the same time a single weak-looking Boche came out of the now completely surrounded Riqerval Wood and surrendered to " C " Company, into whose cellar Headquarters he was at once escorted. Here, while being questioned by two officers, neither of whom could speak German, he absent-mindedly picked up a German grenade which was lying on the floor, creating, of course, an immediate disturbance. Revolvers appeared on all sides, and the visitor's life was nearly ended, but as it was really absent-mindedness and not the fighting spirit which prompted him, peace was soon restored, and he explained that there were 24 others who wished to surrender. He wanted to go back and fetch them, and seemed in fact quite pained when we would not let him and sent him down instead. A few minutes later a battery of 8in. howitzers with tractors and motor lorries came along the main road as far as the end of the village, having been told that the road was clear up to Andigny les Fermes. The Colonel of R.G.A. who commanded was surprised to hear of the 24 Boche, who for all we knew might be within 100 yards of his lorries, but instead of withdrawing for the time, he set off with Capt. Banwell into the woods to look for them, happy as a schoolboy engaged in some forbidden adventure. They found no one, but probably, if there were any at all, they had by this time surrendered to the Staffordshires.

From dawn until 10-30 a.m. the enemy bombarded our village with gas and H.E., and the Brigade Major (Capt. D. Hill, M.C.) who tried to go round the front line posts at this time had an unpleasant journey, while, shortly after him, the C.O. and Adjutant were similarly treated and had to hurry in a most undignified manner through an orchard. However, no damage was done, and, when at midday we were relieved by the Staffordshires, we had had no casualties. As we marched out past the little group of houses on the Regnicourt Road, where " D " Company had fought so gallantly on the 11th, the Burial Party were just burying Serjeants Bradshaw, Dimmocks and the others in a little cemetery which had been made in one of the cottage gardens, and they lie now within a few yards of where they fell. The rest of the march was a cheerful affair, for it was a bright afternoon and we were not as tired as usual after a battle. Drums and Band came out to meet us, the people of Bohain greeted us on the way, and our old friends in Fresnoy gave us their customary warm welcome. Here we were a little more crowded than before, but still had plenty of room, and could look forward to a comfortable rest. The following day, after a full Divisional Church Parade to return thanks for our victories, we were definitely promised a fortnight's rest, and General Boyd and many others went home on leave.

For the rest of the month the Battalion remained in Fresnoy le Grand, training, refitting, and playing games. Here, Lt.-Col. A. J. Digan, D.S.O., of the Connaught Rangers came to command us, and Major R. N. Holmes, M.C., of the Lincolnshires to be 2nd in Command. As we had already Major Dyer Bennet and the Adjutant, who had " put up " crowns before going on leave, as aspirants for this position, Major Holmes was transferred to the 137th Brigade. Lieut. T. H. Ball returned from leave, and in addition to the five, nine other officers arrived, including Capt. E. G. Snaith, M.C., from the 2/4th Battalion, and the two "old hands" Lieut. C. S. Allen and 2nd Lieut. J. A. Hewson. Capt. Snaith went to "A" Company, and the other two became Signalling and Intelligence officers respectively as soon as active operations began again. Our work consisted of steady drill, musketry and, in the evenings, lectures, the best of which were Col. Jerram's on the "Royal Navy," and the Brigade Interpreter M. Dovet's on "French Army Life," the latter was particularly interesting. The Drums now under Serjt. Drummer Price performed on every possible occasion, and made an excellent display with the two new Tenor Drums which had arrived during the fighting, and now appeared in public for the first time. The weather throughout the fortnight was not perfect, but might have been far worse, and we were able to play games almost every afternoon. Our fixtures included two football matches against the French. The first, at Seboncourt, was against the 55th Infantry, whose liaison platoon had done such splendid work at Riqueval, and the game, thanks to the efforts of Start and Corporal Shirley Hubbard, ended in a victory, 5-1—a fact which merely increased the fervour of the welcome we received from our opponents. A few days later some French sappers came to play us at Fresnoy, and they, too, were defeated, 5-0, in an excellent game watched by many people. The language on both these occasions would sound as foreign in London as in Paris, but this did not in the least diminish the cordiality of the Entente. In this way the fortnight soon passed, and on November 1st we left Fresnoy.

Our first move was to Becquigny, where we arrived soon after midday, and found good billets with plenty of accommodation. In the evening, orders came that

THE LAST FIGHT.

at an early date the IXth. Corps, with 1st and 32nd Divisions in front and 46th in Reserve, would attack the German positions on the Sambre - Oise Canal, which had been holding out for the past ten days. The next day the officers rode through Molain to Ribeauville and, leaving horses there, reconnoitred an assembly position North of Mazinghien. The C.O. and Company Commanders then went foward and reconnoitred a second position near Rejet de Beaulieu, about 1,000 yards West of the Canal. On the 3rd, orders arrived for the attack to take place the following morning, and at 5-0 p.m. we moved off in pouring rain through Vaux Andigny to a bivouac position near the Railway North of Molain—a bad march, for the roads were very muddy and hopelessly congested with traffic, and the men heavily laden. It rained hard all night, but a small house for Headquarters, and the usual tents and "bivvie" sheets kept out some of the wet, and we should have been far worse in the open. Unfortunately, 2nd Lieut. J. A. Hewson, who had never really recovered from his gassing in May and had returned before he was fit, had to leave us, unable to stand the exposure in such weather. It was very bad luck, for there was never a keener officer.

At 5-45 a.m., the 4th, the battle began, and we fell in outside Headquarters, having previously had hot breakfasts and distributed large numbers of bombs and flares, also a generous supply of sickles and bill hooks, as the country was reported to be full of hedges. We marched at once to our first assembly position, Mazinghien, and at midday, as the battle reports were good, moved forward again, passing the Brigadier in the village; he seemed very cheerful, and we saw several droves of German prisoners, so concluded that everything must be satisfactory. In order to avoid the main roads, the C.O. led us round to Beaulieu by a field track which he had reconnoitred; unfortunately the night's rain had made the going very heavy, and this not only tired the men, who were heavily laden, but also proved difficult for the limbers, several of which stuck and had to be man-handled. At Beaulieu we had dinners and rested while parties reconnoitred the Canal crossings and discovered various pontoon bridges built by the Engineers soon after the attack. As no orders came, we waited here until soon after 3-0 p.m., when we were sent forward to support the 2nd Brigade on the right flank of the advance.

The C.O. with the right half Battalion crossed the Canal opposite Bois L'Abbaye, and pushed on into the village untroubled by shell fire, which was at the time mostly directed against the left half Battalion, which, with Battalion Headquarters, crossed further South. The country beyond was very thick, and by the time the left Companies reached L'Ermitage it was almost dark, and consequently communications were difficult between the two half Battalions, more particularly as the C.O. was separated from his runners and signallers. The Companies at L'Ermitage dug themselves in and were fairly comfortable, but they were not destined to remain so for long, for orders soon came that they would relieve the 2nd Brigade. These orders, however, were cancelled before being sent out, and instead the Brigade was ordered to relieve the 1st Brigade, who were on the left. The reason for this was that the 32nd Division, who were on the left of the Corps attack, had not yet reported the capture of all objectives, and it was consequently necessary to secure the 1st Division's left flank. While, therefore, the other two Battalions took over the line facing East, we found a defensive flank facing North—the Battalion being organized in depth on a single Company front. "A" Company (Snaith), with "B" Company (Pierrepont) in close support, was a few yards South of the main Catillon - La Groise Road; behind them came "C" Company (Banwell), while Battalion Headquarters and "D" Company (T. Ball) remained in Bois L'Abbaye. These positions we occupied all night.

At dawn the following day the advance was continued by the 137th and 139th Brigades who passed through us, but, as the 32nd Division had still no definite information, we maintained our defensive flank position—a ludicrous performance in view of the streams of unmolested traffic which passed along the road in front of us. Later in the morning, however, "B" and "C" Companies were sent forward to occupy the line that the Lincolnshires had held during the night, where they found no cover except one large farm house which the Boche was shelling heavily. It was raining hard, and for some time they sat in the fields hoping for the rain or the shelling to stop; the latter did eventually cease, but not until a large shell had gone through the roof of the farm house, making it uninhabitable. During the afternoon the weather became so appalling that they all moved into houses in Mezières and spent the night there, while the remainder of the Battalion concentrated in Bois L'Abbaye.

The battle still went on the next day in the pouring rain, and our Brigade moved slowly forward in Divisional support, halting for dinners at Erruart, and reaching Prisches late in the afternoon; our only excitement throughout the day was to watch a battery of 60 pounders get into difficulties in a muddy field. At Prisches we learnt that Cartignies had been cleared by the other Brigades, and we were accordingly ordered to move up at once and take over the outpost line which was now just West of the Petite Helpe river. We moved off in fours along the road, and in the same formation marched into Cartignies, a village full of civilians and blazing with lights, although a German machine gun less than 400 yards away kept sending bullets over the main street. No one seemed very certain where the outposts were, nor who was responsible, so we mounted some sentries in the best positions we could find, and soon after midnight Colonel Digan, who had been to Brigade Headquarters, held a conference and explained the next day's plan of attack. It was now obvious that the Boche was in full retreat.

The weather the next day, the 7th of November, was fortunately much better, and we moved down to the Petite Helpe soon after dawn. Patrols had been out during the night to look for crossings, but beyond reporting that the main road bridge had been blown up, which we already knew, they gathered no information of importance, so " C " Company, who were leading, had to make use of tree trunks and cross as best they could. However, the Engineers soon appeared, and the rest of the Battalion crossed by a pontoon bridge. With the French on the right and Lincolnshires on the left, " D " Company (T. Ball) and " C " Company (Banwell) now pushed forward rapidly, and in spite of a thick mist had soon gained the first two objectives and reached the road running North

THE LAST FIGHT.

and South through a group of houses called Cheval Blanc. Battalion Headquarters and the right half followed, and at midday were quartered in a group of farm houses about 600 yards West of Cheval Blanc, where they were joined by Capt. Hills, who returned from leave and resumed his duties as Adjutant. As soon as they had had dinners, " A " Company (Snaith) and " B " Company (Pierrepont) moved forward so as to be in closer support to " C " and " D " Companies respectively.

After passing the second objective, the leading Companies soon began to meet with opposition, and a machine gun cleverly concealed at the next cross-roads made further advance by " C " Company impossible. As the Lincolnshires were similarly held up on their left, the flank could not be turned. " D " Company, however, pushed forward further in the mist, and, though there was plenty of machine gun fire, it was unaimed and did no damage. The leading Platoon, under 2nd Lieut. Bettles, crossed a valley and started to climb the rise beyond, on the top of which they expected to find the main Avesnes Road. Suddenly, as they burst through a hedge almost on the road, they came upon a German four gun field battery—officers and men standing round their guns, apparently not expecting any attack, and horses tethered near by. The platoon rushed in with bayonets, captured or killed all they could find and, led by 2nd Lieut. Bettles, dashed across the road into some houses on the far side, where they saw some enemy. 2nd Lieut. Bettles was killed with a pistol bullet, but the Boche were driven out, and Lieut. Ball came up and started at once to consolidate his captured position. One officer, 29 men and eight horses were sent down as prisoners.

"D" Company's position was precarious. Right and left, German machine gunners held the main road, and shooting along it made crossing impossible, while at the same time they took care to prevent any attempt on our part to move the captured guns. This we found impossible, so set about rendering them useless, and had already removed breach block and sights from one when a counter attack was launched from the South East. This was beaten off, but Lieut. Ball, unable to find troops on either flank and already short of ammunition, sent back 2nd Lieut. S. D. Lamming on a captured horse to ask for help. Before, however, he could return, the enemy, intent on recapturing his guns, made two more counter attacks in rapid succession, in the second of which, after losing several men, including Bolton, who had never left his Platoon during four years' service, killed and L/Cpl. Thurman wounded, the little isolated party fired the last of its ammunition and had to withdraw. The Boche recaptured his battery, and, after firing one or two rounds into Cheval Blanc, took away the guns.

At 2-0 p.m., Battalion Headquarters moved up to Cheval Blanc, but the attacking Companies still reported that they were unable to advance, and, to add to our difficulties, we were not in touch with the French on our right nor could our patrols find any trace of them. On the whole of our front the enemy had probably not more than eight machine guns, but so cleverly were they placed and so well were they served that we found it impossible to dislodge them with our weapons. Artillery or better still Stokes mortars would no doubt have cleared the country very quickly, but these were not for the time obtainable, so, until they arrived, Col. Digan determined to make every effort to find the French and protect the right flank. Capt. Pierrepont was ordered to send out frequent patrols towards Etroeungt, and, as we now had no Battalion reserve, Col. Digan asked for two Companies of the 4th Battalion to help us. These soon arrived, and while one, Capt. Holden's, remained with us at Cheval Blanc, the other, Capt. Scaramowicz's, took up a defensive flank position along the Brigade Southern boundary. At last, just as it was getting dark, Capt. Pierrepont reported having found the French in Etroeungt, and so this flank was now secure, though it had cost us the loss of 2nd Lieut. Byles and Serjt. Stretton who were both wounded. In spite of this, the forward Companies were still unable to advance, and we remained in these positions all night.

In view of the fact that the Boche was now running away, our casualties during the day had been heavy, and the Staff therefore decided on a different plan for the next morning. The Cavalry were to come up at dawn and we were not to move until they had reconnoitred the country, so that if they reported the enemy still holding out, the Artillery would be ordered to cover our advance with a small barrage. There was no doubt that the German retreat was continuing and that this was only a temporary check, for all night long the sky Eastwards was lit up with enormous flashes, as dumps, railways, cross-roads and bridges were blown up. This demolition was one of the most remarkable features of the Boche retreat, for hardly a road junction in the country was left untouched, while Railways were so cunningly mined that every single line had to be relaid. The consequent delay to our communications was appalling, and though, thanks to the Engineers and Pioneers, our 1st line Transport always reached us by the evening, and field batteries advanced almost as quickly as we did, yet our heavy Artillery was days behind us, and there was always a shortage of ammunition.

As ordered, the Scots Greys' patrols rode through our lines at dawn the next day, November 8th, and found the enemy's machine guns still very active in the same positions. The barrage was therefore arranged, and, covered by these very few shells, "A" and "B" Companies pushed forward, only to find that the Boche took as little notice of the barrage as he did of our rifle fire. On the left, as before, the attack was soon held up, this time with considerable loss to us, for the Boche allowed "A" Company to come close to his guns before opening fire. When he did, 2nd Lieut. Coleman and ten men were wounded and three men killed, and though the others made a most gallant attempt to rush the enemy with the bayonet, they were held up by hedges, and compelled to dig in once more and wait. On the right, however, we had better fortune. 2nd Lieut. Davies and the leading platoon of "B" Company reached the Avesnes main road, and in spite of very heavy machine gun fire managed one by one to make their way across. Once on the far side, this Platoon Commander, ably helped by L/Cpl. Sharpe, Pte. Beaver and others, soon worked his way from house to house until at 11-0 a.m. the Boche, finding we had a firm hold on the main road, withdrew all his guns. While this took place, Colonel Jerram from Divisional Headquarters visited us, bringing the news that the German envoys asking for an Armistice had been taken through the French lines.

As soon as they found the Germans had gone, the leading Companies pushed rapidly forward, with orders to establish an outpost line along the Zorees-Semeries road as soon as possible, in which position we were told we would be relieved by the 137th Brigade. At the same time, " D " Company moved into the houses on the Avesnes road near where they had captured and lost their battery, and " C " Company occupied the farm house which had held them up so long, being welcomed with coffee and cognac by the inhabitants, who had remained in the cellar. A troop of Scots Greys was also attached to us to act as mounted orderlies, a task which up to the present had been very efficiently performed by our grooms—Huntington, Dennis, Rogers and others. At dusk, as the leading Companies were within a few hundred yards of the Zorees road, Battalion Headquarters and " C " Company moved to the cross roads on the Avesnes road, and occupied a large farm, where the two attached 4th Leicestershire Companies were also billeted. Except for distant explosions in the East, it was a quiet night, and the M.O., Capt. Aylward, to prove we were really winning the war, solemnly went to bed in pyjamas regardless of the proximity of the enemy. Soon after midnight, " B " Company reached their outpost line, and at 7-0 a.m. the following morning, " A " Company were also in position, and we sent off Lieut. Ashdowne to billet for us in the area to which we were told we should go as soon as relieved.

The country here was in a pitiable state, for the Germans as they retired carried off everything—livestock, vehicles, all food, and most of the male population. The civilians that were left behind took refuge in the cellars during the fighting, coming out as soon as the Boche had gone, and bestowing kisses and cups of coffee with great liberality on the leading platoons as they entered each farm house or hamlet. The feeding of all these people had to be undertaken by the British Army, and as our advance continued the French Mission were kept very busily employed.

The Brigade relief was already in progress when, at 10-0 a.m., November 9th, it was cancelled, and instead we were ordered to push forward at once and establish a new outpost line East of Sains du Nord—a small town through which the Cavalry had passed in the morning. The right half Battalion was ordered to concentrate in Zorees, while the rest of us with the two Companies of the 4th Battalion formed up near Battalion Headquarters, had dinners, and at 2-15 p.m. moved off. As we did so, an amusing incident occurred. A certain Company Commander, picking up his box respirator, found that he had thrown it off into a patch of filth; copious oaths followed, and he vowed that he would murder the next Boche he saw. Some half hour later, as we entered Zorees, a cyclist patrol met us, escorting one undersized little prisoner, splay footed and bespectacled. The Company was delighted, and with one accord hailed their Commander with cries of "Now's your chance, Sir." No other enemy were seen, and we marched straight into Sains by the Railway station, to receive a welcome from the civilians which rivalled even Fresnoy in cordiality. They thronged the streets with flags and great bunches of chrysanthemums which they showered upon us, so that by the time we reached the Mairie we looked like a walking flower show—every man having a flower in his

THE LAST FIGHT.

hat. The 4th Battalion Companies found the outposts, and we billeted in a large factory which had been used as a Hospital, while Battalion and Company Headquarters occupied various magnificent Chateaux.

Throughout the following day, November 10th, we remained inactive, unable to move because our supplies and rear communications could not move at our pace owing to the German demolitions. All day long reports came in from the East showing the hopeless state of confusion to which the German Army had come. Civilians told us of Artillery drawn by cows, airmen reported roads congested with traffic and columns of troops, it really looked as though at last we should have a chance of delivering a crushing blow. Late that night came the telegram ending hostilities, and the chance was gone for ever.

CHAPTER XX.

HOME AGAIN.

11th Nov., 1918.   28th June, 1919

For the first few days after the signing of the Armistice we remained in Sains, the outpost line was maintained, roads to the East were reconnoitred, and everything was made ready for a resumption of hostilities. But it was soon obvious that the Germans had no more fight in them, and our only interest was in whether or no we should form part of the Army of Occupation. It was known that the 4th Army was going to Germany, and some of us hoped to go with it, but it was not to be, and we were transferred to the 3rd Army, XIIIth. Corps. When we went, General Rawlinson, genuinely sorry to lose us from his Army, expressed his appreciation of our services during the past three months, in a farewell letter, copies of which were given to all ranks. Soon after our transfer, we moved to the Landrecies area, and went into billets in the dirty little town of Bousies.

Our duties were now threefold—to clean up France, to get demobilised, and to amuse ourselves in our spare time. Cleaning up was a gigantic and not very pleasant task, for it meant filling up shell holes, collecting empty bully-beef tins, and generally becoming scavengers. Demobilisation, though more congenial, was at first inclined to be slow, and it was with considerable annoyance that we saw among the first to go, young men who had joined us since the Armistice, because they were "pivotal." Coal-miners were soon called for, and under this heading we lost many of our oldest and best soldiers, so that by Christmas the Battalion was no longer the same. To amuse us, various sports meetings were arranged—all rather hampered by the weather, though we managed to gain much credit in football and running, while the Divisional Rugby football side won the Corps Championship. In these games we were lucky to have the assistance of a new Padre, the Rev. H. P. Walton, who came to take the place of Padre Buck. Concert parties became more numerous, and, in addition to the "Whizzbangs," who worked very hard, the Brigade had a show of their own, known as the "138's."

While at Bousies we marched one Sunday to Landrecies, where H.M. the King paid a visit. It was an informal affair, no guard of honour and no lining the road, and none of us will ever forget the scene. The King of England followed by his officers, all on foot, walking down the little street of the old French town, while both pavements were packed with soldiers and French civilians, who cheered, shouted, sang and rushed into the road to gain a nearer view of His Majesty.

In January we moved to Pommereuil, a clean little village, where Mayor and people did their utmost to make us comfortable. Here, under the new scheme, demobilisation became more rapid, and the older soldiers were sent home in consideration of their service. We also learnt for the first time that the Battalion was to be reduced to a Cadre, and all short service or retainable soldiers would be sent to the 11th Battalion on the Rhine. Before this last move could take place, we moved again—to Solesmes, where we stayed for a fortnight and then moved to St. Hilaire. A new feature was now introduced in the " amusements " department, which was much appreciated by all of us. Once or twice a week we were given one or two motor lorries to take parties to Douai, Valenciennes or the recent battlefields. We had many pleasant trips, and saw several towns in France which we should never otherwise have seen.

At St. Hilaire the C.O. left us to rejoin the Connaught Rangers, and we were reduced to a Cadre, consisting of five officers, forty-six men and the Colours. A large draft of 200 all ranks, with Lieuts. Steel, Ashdowne, Todd, Dunlop, Argyle and other officers who volunteered for further service, went to the 11th Battalion, and the rest were demobilised. The Cadre was chosen so as to include as far as possible W.O.'s, N.C.O.'s, and men of long and distinguished service, who would form a suitable guard for the Colours; at the same time we tried to have representatives of each of the larger towns in Leicestershire, and in this we were successful.

In April we moved to Inchy Beaumont, where we stayed until the Cadre finally went home in June. Wagons and all transport were sent to Caudry, and we settled down to a wearisome existence, having too little to do. Cricket succeeded football, and we beat the 4th Battalion at both, and had several other victories. Finally, on the 28th of June, leaving Capt. Nicholson, 2nd Lieut. Griffiths, R.Q.M.S. Gorse and 11 others with the stores, the remnant of the Battalion sailed for England, landed at Dover, and reached Leicester the same night. The next day the Mayor (Ald. Coltman) and people of Loughborough turned out to give us welcome, and our long months of waiting in France were soon forgotten in the fervour and enthusiasm of the greeting we received, as we marched through the old town and placed our Colours in the Hall. Six weeks later the baggage guard returned, and the Battalion was finally disembodied.

APPENDIX I.

Officers who sailed to France with the Regiment, February, 1915.

Lieut. Colonel C. H. Jones.
Major R. E. Martin.
Captain and Adjutant W. T. Bromfield.

"A" COMPANY.

Major W. S. N. Toller.
Captain P. C. J. R. Rawdon Hastings.
Lieut. A. T. Sharpe (Machine Gun Officer).
Lieut. J. D. A. Vincent.
2nd Lieut. D. B. Petch.
2nd Lieut. J. W. Tomson.

"B" COMPANY.

Captain J. L. Griffiths.
Lieut. A. P. Marsh.
Lieut. E. G. Langdale.
2nd Lieut. C. H. F. Wollaston.
2nd Lieut. C. W. Selwyn.
2nd Lieut. R. B. Farrer.

"C" COMPANY.

Captain T. C. P. Beasley.
Captain C. Bland.
Lieut. R. D. Farmer.
2nd Lieut. G. Aked.
2nd. Lieut. G. W. Allen.
2nd Lieut. R. Ward Jackson.

"D" COMPANY.

Captain H. J. F. Jeffries.
Captain J. Chapman.
Lieut. A. G. de A. Moore.
2nd Lieut. R. C. L. Mould.
2nd Lieut. C. R. Knighton.
2nd Lieut. J. D. Hills.

Transport Officer ... ... Lieut. J. Burnett.
Quartermaster ... ... Lieut. A. A. Worley.
Medical Officer ... Lieut. G. H. H. Manfield, R.A.M.C.

APPENDIX II.

Honours.

V.C.

Lieut. J. C. BARRETT.—Pontruet, Sept. 24th, 1918.

C.M.G.

C. H. Jones.   R. E. Martin.

D.S.O.

W. S. N. Toller.   J. L. Griffiths.

M.C. & BAR.

G. B. Williams.   D. B. Petch.
G. E. Banwell.   J. D. Hills.

M.C.

A. G. de A. Moore.   A. E. Brodribb.
M. H. Barton.   W. B. Jack.
C. H. F. Wollaston.   C. B. W. Buck.
A. N. Barrowcliffe.   S. G. H. Steel.
T. P. Creed.   A. E. Hawley.
J. R. Brooke.   K. Ashdowne.
R. H. Stentiford.   T. H. Ball.
C. F. Shields.   S. D. Lamming
W. M. Cole.   C. H. Davies.
         H. G. Lovett.

D.C.M. & BAR.

T. Tunks.   A. Wilbur.

D.C.M.

H. G. Starbuck.   A. Passmore.
W. H. Hallam.   J. B. Weir.
R. E. Small.   C. W. Jordan.
J. Emmerson.   F. Lane.
C. Hurley.   W. Toon.
E. M. Hewson.   J. Wardle.
J. Hill.   H. G. Lovett.
T. Needham.   J. Cooper.
A. Brooks.   W. Hubbard.

M.M. & TWO BARS.

T. Marston.

M.M. & BAR.

J. Burbidge.   W. Lilley.
R. Downs.   F. W. Gorf.
         A. Thurman.

M.M.

J. T. Knott.	R. Hollingsworth.	A. Hewerdine.
W. A. Berridge.	A. W. Martin.	W. Smith.
H. Beardmore.	J. W. Tookey.	G. W. Tomblin.
G. A. Bent.	H. W. Stone.	L. F. Crocker.
W. Braybrook.	T. Andrews.	E. Cooper.
F. Clapham.	D. Mackey.	H. Edge.
E. Diggle.	H. Whitmore.	W. Mouldsworth.
E. Foulds.	G. O. Pickles.	S. W. Taylor.
R. Goodman.	W. Raven.	W. Orton.
C. B. Love.	J. H. Bullen.	W. Powell.
M. O'Brien.	H. Cato.	A. Daniels.
W. Pickering.	A. H. Culpin.	J. Coles.
T. Slaymaker.	A. E. Palmer.	A. Holmes.
B. Staniforth.	A. Baker.	R. B. Haynes.
T. Hawkesworth.	F. P. Pymm.	G. Emmitt.
F. Eastwood.	E. R. Smith.	G. Bedford.
A. Passmore.	W. Bennett.	F. Smith.
J. Meakin.	J. Balderstone.	P. Thompson.
T. Marshall.	H. Pollard.	J. H. Caunter.
H. Dawes.	J. Ryder.	F. Bindley.
A. Carr.	T. Starbuck.	L. H. Fortnum.
J. T. Allen.	J. Hyden.	R. Redden.
E. V. Woolley.	S. G. Barber.	A. Sharpe.
E. Crow.	F. Bloodworth.	A. Beaver.
J. W. Putt.	A. Wedge.	H. Shepherd.
A. Hickling.	S. Dawson.	T. Parker.
W. E. Lester.	H. B. Garrett.	A. Randall.
	S. Satchwell.	

M.S.M.

J. Cooper.	H. Foster.	J. H. Robinson.
W. Fairbrother.	R. Gorse.	N. Yeabsley.
	C. F. Bailey.	

MENTIONED IN DESPATCHES.

C. H. Jones (2).	W. Fisher.
W. S. N. Toller.	H. Swift.
W. T. Bromfield.	A. A. Archer.
J. L. Griffiths (2).	J. A. Walton.
E. G. Langdale.	T. Foster.
C. H. F. Wollaston.	R. Gorse.
M. H. Barton.	W. Agar.
A. G. de A. Moore.	C. Brown.
J. D. Hills (2).	A. Hurst.
J. Burnett (2).	T. F. Marston.
C. F. Shields.	J. Lincoln.
G. W. Allen.	F. J. Williamson.
T. W. Tomson.	
W. R. Todd.	
F. G. Taylor.	

379

FOREIGN DECORATIONS.

FRENCH.

Légion d'Honneur (Officier)	C. H. Jones.
Croix de Guerre (with palm)	L. H. Pearson.
Croix de Guerre (with silver star)	A. D. Pierrepont J. Whitworth.
Croix de Guerre (with bronze star)	J. D. Hills W. Green.
Medaille Militaire ...	E. Angrave.

BELGIAN.

Décoration Militaire ... A. Wilbur.

APPENDIX III.

THE CADRE AND EQUIPMENT GUARD.

Major J. D. Hills, M.C.
Captain G. E. Banwell, M.C.
Captain C. S. Allen.
Captain and Quartermaster W. A. Nicholson.
2nd Lieut. G. H. Griffiths.

R.Q.M.S. Gorse, R.
Col.-Serjt. Hanson, A. W.
Corpl. Lincoln, J.
Serjt. Yeabsley, N.
Pte. Hughes, E.
 " Ribbons, F.
 " Rawlings, G.
 " Mutton, E.
 " Nichols, L.
 " Hewerdine, A.
 " Major, T. O.
 " Bradshaw, R.
Corpl. Bartram, E.
Serjt. Sills, R.
Pte. Rock, F.
 " Webbs, H.
 " Rogers, A. A.
 " Riley, S.
 " Beards, A.
 " Brampton, T. C.
Sig. Rollson, E.
C.Q.M.S. Hurst, A.
Serjt. Slaymaker, T.

L/Cpl. Underwood, A.
 " Caunter, J.
Pte. Lewis, B.
 " Clarke, G. L.
Corpl. Baker, A.
Pte. Deacon, W.
 " Morley, G.
 " Hunt, G.
L/Cpl. Tookey, J.
Pte. Wormleighton, R.
 " Sear, W. J.
 " Myers, J. T.
 " Godsmark, G.
Corpl. Mead, B.
L/Cpl. Law, A. B.
 " Harris, J.
Pte. Allen, W.
 " Moule, F. T.
Corpl. Goss, J.
Pte. Smith, E. A.
 " Neaverson, R.
 " Hayward, J. R.
 " Ratcliffe, G.